E X P L O R I N G   B R I T A I N
GREAT GARDENS

CONTRIBUTORS

MAIN TEXT BY EDWARD GREY AND DAVID WARD
GAZETTEER BY BELINDA HUNT

A NATION
OF GARDENERS

In the colourful disorder of a cottage plot and the formal grandeur of a Chatsworth – in Blenheim's suave lawns and lakes, in the exotic paradise of Tresco – the gardens of Britain contain a wealth of interest without parallel anywhere in the world.

Gardening in these islands is more than a hobby, it amounts to a national compulsion. And although a rich history, varied soils and mild climate have all contributed, some human instinct to nurture and adorn seems to underly this very British passion. Indeed, few people in Britain would consider their home complete without a garden – even if it is only a window box or a tub or two on the balcony of a city centre flat.

Shakespeare's poetry and plays express an intimate love of flowers; it was to a garden that Tennyson invited his Maud. And Kipling, that most robust of poets, evoked both the joys and the rigours known to enthusiasts when he wrote:

> *Our England is a garden, and such gardens are not made*
> *By singing: – 'Oh, how beautiful!' and sitting in the shade.*

Much toil, and much science too, lies behind the nation's heritage. It was from Britain that many of the world's greatest plant hunters set out, gathering seeds from wild valleys in the Himalayas, from Amazonian rain forests and elsewhere. Today, the fruits of their labours grace small town gardens and rolling country acres alike. Study of climate has permitted subtropical jungles to flourish on the rugged north-west coast of Scotland. And sheer energy, allied with enthusiasm, has been responsible for such transfigurations as occurred at Cragside in Northumberland. There, the industrial magnate Sir William Armstrong had over 7 million trees planted to make a vast woodland garden where only bare, windswept moorland had been before.

The great gardens of Britain exist in testament to an age-old tradition of love, labour and experiment. Tastes and styles may have changed over the centuries. But the tradition itself has survived, and flourishes today as strongly as ever.

Fortunately another tradition also continues to flourish – that of opening private gardens to the public. For generations now, the owners of Britain's greatest gardens – from the royal family down – have shared their treasures with the rest of us and given pleasure to countless millions.

ABBOTSBURY *Dorset*

Palm trees are not the first things a visitor might expect to find growing among the thatched cottages of Dorset. Yet, situated to the west of Abbotsbury village, on the road to Chesil Beach, is a 20 acre paradise of subtropical trees and shrubs. Here, rhododendrons, camellias, hydrangeas and magnolias grow in splendid profusion. Their rounded clusters are diversified not only by the upthrust of huge Chusan palms, but also by ginkgo and sword-leaved cordylines.

The gardens form part of the Fox-Strangways estate and were originally those of Abbotsbury Castle, an 18th-century summer residence built by Elizabeth, Countess of Ilchester. The building itself was destroyed by fire in 1913, and its replacement was eventually demolished in 1936. The gardens though have remained.

The climate in this corner of England is exceptionally mild and the gardens, protected in a hollow of chalk and limestone hills, are sheltered from sea gales

TROPICAL DORSET *A palm tree sets the tone for this lush corner of the subtropical gardens at Abbotsbury, where exotic plants flourish in the mild climate buttressed by the protection of high walls.*

by a windbreak of holm oaks. The soil is a heavy and acid loam. Many of the old plantings come from China and the Himalayas, specimens grown from seeds collected by such indefatigable Far Eastern plant hunters as George Forrest (1873–1932) and E. H. Wilson (1876–1930).

An old walled garden forms the centrepiece of the estate, containing such glories as the golden false acacia (*Robinia pseudoacacia* 'Frisia'), and a Caucasian wing nut (*Pterocarya fraxinifolia*), which is the largest in Britain. The West Lawn near by is dominated by a magnificent *Stranvaesia nussia*, the *Stranvaesia* genus being named after William Fox-Strangways, 4th Earl of Ilchester (1795–1861). To the east is the Woodland Garden where ponds and streams glimmer amid lush, jungle-like banks; informal ways include the Hydrangea Walk and Azalea Path.

A Victorian bog garden has recently been restored, and a Eucalyptus Walk laid out. But the character of

MORNING PARADE *A row of yew arches in a quiet corner of Alton Towers (opposite) awaits the daily rush of holidaymakers who come to visit the extraordinary combination of leisure park, sports centre, entertainment village, fairground and magnificent garden. It is all based upon a dream landscape created by Lord Shrewsbury at the beginning of the 19th century.*

the whole remains determined by venerable specimens grown to enormous size: the old camellias and magnolias especially, which are seen at their finest in late spring. Peacocks strut the lawns, exotic cousins for the graceful white birds which haunt Abbotsbury's famous swannery near by. This was established by Benedictine monks in the 14th century or earlier in the brackish waters of the Fleet, behind Chesil Beach. The colony still flourishes, feeding chiefly on eelgrass and tassel pondweed which abound in the lagoon.

ALTON TOWERS *Staffordshire*

The great garden at Alton Towers is one of the largest and most fantastic landscape creations in Europe. It was the brainchild of Charles Talbot, 15th Earl of Shrewsbury, a nobleman of immense wealth whose mania for building and landscape is said to have matched in extent that of 'mad' King Ludwig of Bavaria who decorated his kingdom with fairy-tale castles. For most of his life the earl lived in his palace at Heythrop in Oxfordshire. But he also owned some 10,000 acres of lean farmland in Staffordshire's picturesque Churnet Valley. And there, in 1812, at the age of 60, the earl decided to indulge his interest in landscape design.

Over the next 15 years while the original bailiff's house, Alveton Lodge, was being transformed into a Gothic-style palace, by a succession of no fewer than eight architects, an army of labourers and gardeners was brought in to sculpt the rugged countryside with terraces, pools, canals and winding paths. The planting of trees and shrubs was not enough to improve the vistas. There had to be architectural features too – temple, pagoda, grotto and splashing fountain – all the picturesque effects in which early 19th-century landowners delighted.

INCREDIBLE VARIETY

At Alton Towers an incredible variety of such features was introduced. Entire dead trees were even planted for dramatic effect. In the immature garden their impact must have been garish – even outrageous.

With the passing of time, however, the woods and shrubs have ripened to full-blown maturity, diminishing the shock of the architectural fantasies. Softened by the shade of foliage, the follies no longer intrude.

Especially delightful is the Pagoda Fountain, designed by Robert Abraham (1774–1850) and completed in 1826. It is situated on an island in a chain of small lakes, an airy, three-storey structure from the top of which a fountain spurts a further 70 ft into the air. Tinkling bells hang from upcurving extremities of each octagonal roof – the effect is enchanting.

Other notable structures include a fine, seven-domed conservatory, also designed by Robert Abraham, the Corkscrew Fountain and a hilltop Chinese temple. The most fanciful creations, though, remain gloriously bizarre. There is, for example, an imitation Stonehenge, bearing little resemblance to the famous circle on Salisbury Plain since it is constructed in a straight line. In addition, the garden is graced by a

FANTASY WORLD *In its heyday Alton Towers was one of the grandest houses in Europe, set in fantastically landscaped gardens. The house (above) is now a shell, but the gardens are totally unspoilt, and the pagoda (below), which is really a fountain, still jets water 70ft into the air.*

AGES IN HARMONY *Nothing at Anglesey Abbey (opposite) is quite what it seems. Parts of the apparently Tudor house are the remains of an Augustinian priory founded in 1135, and other parts date from about 1930. The gardens which look as though they were created in Georgian times, were laid out just before the Second World War.*

Swiss cottage, the size of a warehouse, in which lived a blind Welsh harper who used to play music for the benefit of the earl's strolling guests.

The 15th Earl of Shrewsbury died in 1827, but the house and garden were extended and further embellished by his nephew, John, the 16th Earl. It was he who gave the name Alton Towers to the mansion and its grounds, and he also erected the Corinthian-style memorial to his uncle, which crowns a knoll above the chain of small lakes. On its walls, the 16th Earl caused a noble inscription to be placed, in tribute to the founder: 'He made the desert smile.'

Yet there is much more to admire at Alton Towers than the unique collection of ornamental follies. The lawns are interspersed with well-planted rosebeds, and the garden is renowned for its rhododendrons which bloom in vivid masses in mid-June. From the memorial, a splendid rock garden, probably the finest in Britain, tumbles down the hillside, crowded with dwarf conifers and spiraeas.

Backing the central chain of lakes are beautiful woods where many miles of winding pathway lead among oaks, cedars, sycamores, horse chestnuts and Wellingtonias. The many ornamental specimens include the fern-leafed beech (*Fagus sylvatica* 'Laciniata') and the magnificent tulip-tree (*Liriodendron tulipifera*) whose large leaves, turning bright butter yellow, contribute to the autumn mosaic of tones.

Today, the garden is well maintained as a showpiece, secluded from the other enterprises at Alton Towers, billed today as Europe's premier leisure park with attractions that include alpine cable cars, the world's largest roller coaster and a 'haunted house'.

ANGLESEY ABBEY *Cambridgeshire*

The house is old, a Tudor mansion built from the ruins of a 12th-century priory. And the gardens, too, have an air of antiquity, laid out in the grand manner with the confidence and spacious scale of earlier eras. Their impression of age, though, is illusory, for Anglesey's broad avenues and bosky groves, its elegant statuary and urns – all were established in the present century. The grounds of the abbey are a

testament to creative ingenuity and flawless taste combined. And the wonderful diversity of scenes were all coaxed from the same uncompromising landscape – of fenland loam spread broad and level under the vast East Anglian sky.

Anglesey Abbey in Cambridgeshire, which takes its name from the nearby hamlet of Angerhale, was founded in 1135, probably by Henry I. Its inhabitants were Augustinian canons who carried out their offices at the house for four centuries before the abbey was closed during the Dissolution of the Monasteries in the 1530s. Thereafter, the abbey was rebuilt as a secular residence which passed through the hands of many different owners. And in 1926 it was bought in partially ruined state by Huttleston Broughton, the son of an industrial magnate, who in 1929 became Lord Fairhaven.

The grounds were enormous, comprising well over 100 acres of rough parkland and farming country. There were a few fine old trees; close to the house, for example, was a splendid copper beech, and a weeping silver lime (*Tilia petiolaris*) which was to remain Lord Fairhaven's favourite in the garden. These and a few other mature plantings he kept – otherwise, the canvas was bare.

DRAMATIC FOCUS

Lord Fairhaven had space in abundance to work with. The problem was the lack of natural drama in the terrain. And this he resolved through subtly contrasted plantings, balancing formal beds and clipped hedges with generous profusions of natural foliage. Above all, he achieved interest through the thoughtful disposition of fine statues and urns. Executed in stone, marble or metal, they remain a focus for the eye in practically every vista.

The most spacious symmetries are found to the south and west of the house, and the prelude is quite delightful. From the front drive a beautiful expanse of grassland, known as the South Glade, curves round the sunny southern face of the house. It is a mass of cowslips in spring.

The glade narrows at its end, hemmed by trees and with a romantic Daffodil Walk running off to left and right. Though the yellow trumpets were lost to a virus infection some years ago, the walk remains immensely seductive, especially in May when its wild banks are snow-drifted with cow parsley. The focus for the eye is a great stone urn, set up by Lord Fairhaven to mark the 800th anniversary of the priory's founding.

A little further along, the glade issues into a walk with a very different aura. This is the great Coronation Avenue, an immense green way which runs ruler straight for half a mile into the distance, flanked to each side by horse chestnuts ranked four trees deep. The avenue was laid out in 1937 to commemorate the

FENLAND SPRING *Creating landscape surprises in the Cambridge fens is not easy, but it has been achieved at Anglesey Abbey by the clever blending of several features including trees of contrasting foliage and dramatic patches of spring bulbs.*

coronation of King George VI and Queen Elizabeth. The perspectives are huge. At one point, cross vistas lead the eye south to a statue of Apollo Belvedere; and north to a circular temple.

The grand effects are only part of Anglesey's attraction. Returning towards the house you come to the secluded Narcissus Garden, where a statue of the mythical youth may be seen mirrored in a pool. Beyond it is the Hyacinth Garden, Anglesey's great springtime showpiece, where 4,000 bulbs are planted out in formal beds every year to create a scented paradise of blue and white.

A short walk brings you back to the front drive where you may begin to explore the eastern grounds. A winding path leads through a wooded dell to the Dahlia Garden, cunningly conceived as a curved corridor of beech hedges which enclose a multicoloured crescent of flowers. Statues of Pan and Apollo embellish the walk, and in spring, before the dahlias appear, it floods blue with forget-me-nots.

Situated beside the Dahlia Garden is one of Anglesey's most imaginative features. This is the Herbaceous Garden, devised by Major Vernon Daniell in 1937 as

CROWNING INSPIRATION *It has long been a tradition at Anglesey Abbey to celebrate national occasions by establishing some new, grand feature in the gardens. This group of pillars was erected in the middle of a vast lawn in 1953 to commemorate the coronation of Queen Elizabeth II; they contain a copy of the statue of the Boy David by the 17th-century Italian sculptor Bernini.*

one grand semicircle framed by a towering beech hedge. The long sweeping curve of flowers is broken only by recessed seats and clipped box trees in leaded tubs. The borders, seen at their best in June and July, are massed with lupins, scented paeonies, salvias and huge delphiniums. Less familiar species include the white-flowering sea kale (*Crambe cordifolia*) and the aromatically leaved burning bush (*Dictamnus albus*) with its white or pink flowers borne on upthrusting spikes. A statue of Father Time provides a stabilising element in the seasonal riot of colour.

From the masterpieces of formal plantsmanship, a beguiling path strikes out to the north where the setting is more rural. It reaches the millstream of the Lode, lined with poplars on its far bank, and winds on through natural woodlands past the willow-fringed Quarry Pool.

Another of Anglesey's grand formal walks – Emperor's Walk – leads you back south from the north-

eastern boundary wall. Conceived in 1953, it takes its name from 12 marble busts of Roman emperors which line one side of the green way.

Halfway down you come to a circular bay, adorned with statuary, and if you turn right you arrive at a curious temple. With classical pillars and a Chinese-style roof, it was built to enclose a huge porphyry urn. The bowl is 6 ft 4 in. wide, making it the largest single piece of the crystalline rock which exists in England.

Beyond it the path cuts through the Warrior's Walk, a narrow way lined with spruce trees which runs parallel to the broader Emperor's Walk. The path returns to the front drive of the house by way of a magnificent arboretum. The specimen trees are informally planted on a swathe of greensward, merging to the north with regularly spaced lime avenues.

The collection is fittingly varied for a garden as diverse in character as Anglesey. A circuit recommended by the National Trust takes in all of the features mentioned. Yet even this does not do full justice to the range of scenes and moods. There is, for example, a pinetum to the east, containing a collection of young conifers; and Pilgrim's Lawn south of Coronation Avenue, where trees and shrubs are grown chiefly for their foliage tones. Within the private area of the house are the Monk's Garden, the Wrestler's Lawn and the Rose Garden – each a delight in itself.

ARLEY HALL *Cheshire*

A Saracen's head has been the crest on the Warburton coat of arms since 1218, when Geoffrey Warburton lopped one off as a gory trophy of the Crusades. The 'mighty Warburton' is one of Cheshire's great families and their first hall at Arley was built in 1469. The gardens, then, have an impressive lineage – they have been in the hands of one family for over 500 years.

Arley's soil is an acid Cheshire clay which requires good drainage and aeration if it is not to revert to the swampy condition noted by an early 19th-century visitor. And the estate found its saviour in 1831 when it passed to Rowland Egerton-Warburton, who nurtured the property over the next 60 years until his death.

Rowland Egerton-Warburton rebuilt Arley Hall as a romantic Jacobean-style mansion. He closely supervised the work of his architect, George Latham, and devoted equal personal attention to the creation of his 'garden fair'. Though relics of earlier eras were incorporated in the design – existing walled kitchen gardens, for example, and a fine old 15th-century tithe barn – much that is seen today is the work of Rowland and his wife, Mary.

In the surrounding parkland they cleared views, planted new woodlands and laid out new drives. To separate the 8 acre garden from the park they made a ha-ha with a 220 yd terrace known as the Furlong Walk. This became a much-trodden way, and towards the end of his life when Rowland became blind he used to walk it guided by a wire with bells to warn when he approached either end.

One of the most important innovations was the

ESTABLISHED BORDERS
Herbaceous borders of carefully planned associations of colour and form are very much a 20th-century concept, yet many such borders at Arley Hall were planted as long ago as 1846. Those in front of the pavilion (above) must be among the earliest of their kind, and the original associations are maintained to this day. The great walled garden (left) was originally the kitchen garden, but is now laid out with walks and massed flower beds.

planting of the double Herbaceous Borders, laid out in 1846 and among the first ever established in England. A central grassy path some 90 yds long leads to a classically styled pavilion, flanked by massive buttresses of clipped yew.

Many of the plants growing in the Herbaceous Borders can be seen in a painting of 1889, made by George Elgood. Viscountess Ashbrook, who has cared for the gardens since 1939, has been careful to preserve the old flowers as well as introduce some new varieties. Though splendid in high summer and lit with the orange and yellow warmth of heleniums, dahlias and solidagos in autumn, the borders are perhaps at their loveliest earlier in the year. As the viscountess wrote in *The Englishwoman's Garden*: 'In early June the border has its "blue period" and I prefer this to any other season. The varied blues of *Delphinium, Campanula*, and "Johnson's Blue" *Geranium* are magical against the velvety green of the young growth on the yew hedges.'

GREEN PILLARS

The most striking and unusual feature of the gardens at Arley also dates from the time of Rowland Egerton-Warburton. This is an avenue of the evergreen or holm oak (*Quercus ilex*), planted in about 1840. The tree is Mediterranean in origin and normally spreads wide to about 60 ft. The 14 specimens at Arley, however, have been clipped in cylindrical shape and stand ranked like the huge green pillars of some great, unroofed temple.

The Furlong Walk, Herbaceous Borders and Ilex Avenue form a rough triangle to the south-west of the hall. In the middle is a half-timbered tea cottage used in Victorian times for tea parties in the garden. Round about are irregular plantings of shrub roses which form exuberant displays in the summer. The June-flowering 'Sancta' is a particular enchantress, petalled a delicate pink and thought to be among the most ancient garden roses known.

Lady Ashbrook made several important modifications to the 19th-century design. A garden is, after all, a living organism whose needs change with the years. The terrace, for example, originally ended at a winding pool and alpine rock garden designed by Mrs Rowland Egerton-Warburton. This has been replanted with azaleas, rhododendrons and other flowering shrubs. Fern-edged, the pool has become a place of seclusion where, at dusk, the blue neon flash of a kingfisher may sometimes be seen.

Though necessity has determined some of the changes at Arley, others have been effected for sheer pleasure. In 1969, for example, Lady Ashbrook established a herb garden where, among thymes, bergamots, marjorams and a host of other delights, the eau de Cologne mint was to prove one of her special favourites: 'far superior to the bottled stuff'. There is fragrance in the air at any time of year at Arley, for Lady Ashbrook also planted a scented garden stocked with shrubs and flowers selected specifically for their aromas: lilies, heliotropes, mignonettes, dwarf lavenders and pink floribunda roses, for example.

BARNSLEY HOUSE *Gloucestershire*

Approach the garden by the village of Barnsley and you bring one impression with you. It is of the warm Cotswold stone which abounds in this corner of Gloucestershire, lining cottage fronts and drystone walls with shades of soft grey and honeyed yellow. Barnsley House partakes of the mellow aura. Coming up the drive you encounter a creeper-clad building so clustered with mounds of 150-year-old clipped box around one ground-floor window that the very walls seem rooted in the soil.

The house was built in 1697, and there were many well-established trees when the present owners – Mr and Mrs David Verey – took up residence in 1951. But Mrs Rosemary Verey, now a distinguished writer on gardening, began as an enthusiastic amateur. An existing path of Cotswold stone flanked by Irish yews provided a straight vista from the house. In crevices between the worn stones Mrs Verey planted rock roses (*Helianthemum*).

An avid reading of 16th and 17th-century gardening manuals has produced many inspired touches. By the kitchen door, for example, is a geometrical herb garden rich in time-honoured aromas: of camphor, rue, lovage, thyme, sage, teucrium and filipendula – even woad. Facing the main lawn a delightful knot garden has been laid out. At the four corners, clipped variegated hollies stand sentinel.

Though the whole garden covers no more than 4 acres, thoughtful use has been made of its longest perspectives. The yew walk, for example, meets a long grassed allée at right-angles. Look left and the eye travels to an 18th-century 'temple' (brought from Fairford Park in 1962) with a lily pool to catch its reflections. Look right and a specially commissioned fountain provides focus for the eye. Explore the allée and a more secret vista opens up, leading through a narrow gap in a hedge to a statue of a veiled huntswoman. This is cunningly contrived – blink as you walk and you miss it.

An avenue of pleached limes runs parallel to the grassed allée and issues into a laburnum tunnel. This becomes bewitchingly beautiful during the first two weeks in June as the golden cataracts of laburnum fall towards upthrust mauve heads of *Allium aflatunense*.

Barnsley's garden is for all seasons. In winter, scented shrubs flower near the house. Spring colour arrives as early as February, when golden winter aconites spread in sheets under the tall trees bordering the drive. After the vivid displays of summer, foliage and form come into their own. Mixed beds around the yew walk are mosaics in autumn, picked out with silver-leaved plants and variegated ivies. Among them subtle touches catch the eye: here a creamy swathe of *Nicotiana affinis*, there the twinkling of a late viola or dianthus. In October, among the last blooms of the roses, one incident of vehement colour arrests every passer-by. It is a planting of sensational pink asters (Elma Potschkii) grouped by luminous blue *Salvia patens*, and 6 ft tall *Nicotiana sylvestris*.

'DELIGHT IN SIMPLE THINGS'
Rudyard Kipling lived at Bateman's (opposite) from 1902 until his death in 1936. His children grew up there – the boy and girl who figure in Puck of Pook's Hill, *a story set in the surrounding countryside – and he loved the place dearly. When he first saw the 17th-century house, he wrote: 'We went through every room and found no shadow of ancient regrets, stifled miseries, nor any menace, though the "new" end of her was 300 years old …'*

BATEMAN'S *East Sussex*

Rudyard Kipling was 36 when he discovered Bateman's. The author of *Kim* and *The Jungle Books* was already prospering in his career and had spent some three years searching with his wife for a new home. And when they came upon the fine old Jacobean house at Burwash in Sussex they knew that they had found it, declaring, by Kipling's own account: 'That's her! The Only She! Make an honest woman of her – quick!' The year was 1902, and Bateman's was to be Kipling's home until his death in 1936.

Kipling and his wife created a 10 acre domain designed to blend in with the low Sussex hills around. They had acquired some existing features which lent a mature charm to the garden. There was, for example, an old 'Maiden's Blush' rose by the front door, a flower which has bloomed in English gardens since the time of the Wars of the Roses (it is in fact a coloured form of the white rose of York). South of the house was the bole of a huge 300-year-old white willow and, near by, well-established rows of pleached lime trees.

But the Kiplings gave the garden its present shape. To suit the character of the house, they divided their acres up into compartments with formal yew hedges and paths flagged with local stone. The main area extends to the south of the house, where Kipling designed a rectangular pool for the children to bathe in. It was not merely a utilitarian feature though. At one end he placed a seat backed by low stone walls

'A PROPER GARDENER'S WORK' *Kipling felt that this was best accomplished on the knees, and he should have known, since he designed or planted much of Bateman's garden himself, including the yew hedges and several beds of old-fashioned roses.*

and a curved hedge of clipped yew; at the other a paved rose garden.

At Bateman's you never stray far from associations with the writer's life and work. From the south garden, for example, you can see Pook's Hill, famed through Kipling's Puck tales. By the yew hedge which bounds the garden is a sundial on which the writer inscribed 'It is later than you think'. Beyond, is a natural garden which stretches down to the trout stream of the Dudwell, and secluded among trees is a pets' cemetery where several much-loved cats and dogs are buried.

The bridges crossing the stream lead to an old watermill which features in several of Kipling's Sussex stories. It is intimately connected with the history of the house, for in 1903 the writer had it equipped with turbine and generator, which provided the electricity at Bateman's for 25 years.

A pleasing riverside path follows the stream's course among banks which are radiant in spring. Daffodils, narcissi and anemones grow in profusion, with the yellow blooms of skunk cabbage (*Lysichiton americanus*) and the huge overhanging umbrellas of *Gunnera manicata*. The many unusual trees include one startlingly gnarled and twisted hazelnut tree (*Corylus avellana* 'Contorta') and the balsam poplar (*Populus balsamifera*).

To the north of the house, the chief attraction is a walled flower garden. Its wrought-iron gates (bearing the initials RK) lead to an enchanting pleached pear walk laid out by Kipling. Clematis intermingles with the trees while lily of the valley carpets the beds in which they are planted. And to the north-west is an extensive herb garden.

MUTED HARMONY *The trees at Bedgebury National Pinetum have been imported from all over the world and planted there in order to study their potential usefulness in afforestation schemes, for timber, or for some other practical purpose. Decoration is a secondary consideration, but no one would realise it from a stroll through the magnificent planned rides and family groupings of conifers. When the light falls true, the soft greens, greys and golds of the trees combine in a symphony of pastel hues.*

BEDGEBURY NATIONAL PINETUM *Kent*

The Weald of Kent is known more for the fragrance of its orchards than for the resinous scent of pines. Yet at Bedgebury, in the Garden of England, is the most comprehensive collection of conifers in Europe.

The National Pinetum covers 100 acres of rolling country near the red-tiled Kentish village of Goudhurst. The great woodland garden was created in 1924 as an extension of the Royal Botanic Gardens at Kew. The purpose of the pinetum is chiefly scientific. The 200 species, and a further 200 varieties of conifer, were planted for botanical study. But the presentation of sheer visual delights has also played its part in the pinetum's planning.

The pinetum was established jointly by the authorities at Kew and the Forestry Commission. What they had acquired was a tract of pleasantly undulating country, dipped by two small valleys with a ridge of higher land between. The ground varies in elevation between 200–300 ft, and each of the valleys is threaded by a stream. Marshall's Lake, a sizeable sheet of water where wild ducks abound, is situated at their confluence.

The entrance to the pinetum leads to several Japanese dogwoods (*Cornus kousa*), katsuras (*Cer-cidiphyllum japonicum*) and sweet gums (*Liquidambar styraciflua*), large trees native to North America whose leaves blaze with scarlet in autumn. Immediately, you are made aware of Bedgebury's varied attractions. The sweet gum is not a conifer, and around the pinetum are a number of other broad-leaved trees and shrubs included for pictorial effect.

SPRUCE VALLEY

A bridge leads across the western stream to Dallimore Avenue. The broad way runs as far as Marshall's Lake. This is Spruce Valley, with notable specimens including fine Brewer's weeping spruces (*Picea brewerana*), recognisable by their horizontal branches from which hang long pendulous branchlets.

At the end of the walk, at the lake's edge, is an impressive plantation of swamp cypresses (*Taxodium distichum*), their rusty autumn tones mingling with the deeper reds of Chinese dawn redwoods (*Metasequoia glyptostroboides*). The swamp cypress, a native of North America, is unique among conifers in that it grows readily standing in the water itself.

Back from the lake, on the summit of the ridge separating Bedgebury's two valleys, is one of the pinetum's finest effects. This is the spacious Cypress Avenue, planted in 1935 with the hybrid Leyland cypress (× *Cupressocyparis leylandii*). In less than 50 years the trees have grown to heights of 90 ft or more. For the sheer drama of lofty elevation, however, they are surpassed by a nearby group of silver firs from North-West America. The largest of these were planted in 1925 and have reached well over 100 ft. Tallest of all is a Grand fir (*Abies grandis*) over 10 ft in girth and more than 110 ft high.

THE GRAND STYLE *Belton House was built in the days when Sir Christopher Wren held sway, and though he does not seem to have had anything to do with the actual design, his influence is clear in the clean, classical lines, the ornamented pediment and the cupola. The first stone was laid by Sir John Brownlow in 1685, and the Brownlows have lived there ever since, maintaining the gardens in the serene formality that complements the house.*

The cone-bearers represented at Bedgebury have been garnered from temperate regions the world over. There are cedars, larches, hemlocks, sequoias and monkey puzzles. The rarities include examples of the American white cedar (*Chamaecyparis thyoides*) and the Chinese golden larch (*Pseudolarix amabilis*) which turns orange in late autumn.

Bedgebury is open to visitors every day of the year. You may come in spring and summer to admire the flowering species, in autumn for the foliage tones. And even in winter Bedgebury remains a marvel. When snow hangs from the great firs and Marshall's Lake is a leaden sheet, the woods have an aura of magnificent austerity; you can fancy yourself in a piece of Siberia, grafted into the Garden of England.

BELTON HOUSE *Lincolnshire*

Formal gardens, an elegant orangery and a fine Restoration home – everything at Belton House in Lincolnshire speaks of ancestral wealth and style. Standing proud in its 600 acres of rolling parkland, the building has been the home of the Brownlow family for 300 years.

The gardens north of the house are Italianate in style. From the stepped terrace you look down an immaculate gravel path flanked by columnar yews and symmetrically patterned parterres planted with roses and edged with clipped box. To the left, beyond a frame of trees grown more naturally, are shaved green lawns with a central round pond and fountain.

Behind rises the tall and finely proportioned orangery, designed in 1819 by Sir Jeffry Wyatville and

standing on the site of Belton's early manor house (mentioned in the Domesday Book). In reality, it was not built for orange cultivation; it is a camellia house, erected to shelter the delicate Far Eastern plants in an age when their nurture was still fairly new to Europe.

To the right, set somewhat back from the orangery, is the little church of St Peter and St Paul which predates the great house by many centuries but forms an indissoluble feature of the garden's views.

Urns and statuary complete the serene composition of the formal gardens. Away to the east are more naturally landscaped acres of parkland, where lakeside and woodland trails have been laid out.

BERKELEY CASTLE *Gloucestershire*

'How far is it, my lord, to Berkeley now?' asks Bolingbroke in Shakespeare's *Richard II*. Steeped in history and romance, the 12th-century battlements of Berkeley Castle loom in high drama above the Severn Vale. Edward II was foully murdered there, and the walls were breached by Cromwell. But apart from one great void in the ramparts which testifies to the Roundhead siege, the fortress has survived as one of the best preserved in the country.

The 8 acre terraced garden faces south and east, overlooking the lovely water meadows of the Doverte Brook. Today the castle's mighty buttresses shelter not armoured soldiery but a wide range of interesting plants. They thrive in the reflected warmth of the old stonework, some even seeding themselves in the ancient mortar.

The terraces were skilfully planted in this century

WYATVILLE – ARCHITECT ROYAL

In 1777, James Wyatt was employed to give a face-lift to Belton, and in 1819 his nephew Jeffry received a similar commission. He remodelled several interiors and built the camellia house, now the orangery, a stately building which occupies the site of the former manor house. Later, Wyatt was knighted for his renovations at Windsor Castle and changed his name to Wyatville, since it suited his knighthood better.

by Major Robert Berkeley. The shrubs and flowers which surge from the borders include yuccas, fuchsias, acanthus and red-hot pokers, while sheltered in one particularly warm corner is an especially fine, tender *Cestrum*. Mature climbers cluster the castle walls. There are roses, clematis, hydrangeas and wisterias, for example, and two magnificent *Magnolia delavayi* which are smothered with creamy-white flowers in June.

BICTON GARDENS *Devon*

Avenues of chestnut or lime are common enough features of Britain's great gardens. But at Bicton in Devon you find something more unusual – an avenue of monkey-puzzle trees (*Araucaria araucana*), laid out in 1840 and still flourishing. Trees grow to great heights in this 50 acre garden, and among its gigantic conifers is the tallest monkey puzzle in Britain (over 90 ft high). And the trees are only one feature of the estate. In reality, Bicton holds five gardens in one – the Italian Garden, Pinetum, American and Hermitage gardens and the Conservatories.

The old manor of Bicton, near East Budleigh, dates back to the reign of Henry I. The estate passed in time to the Rolle family, who held it for over 300 years before the Clinton family, the present owners, acquired it through inheritance. Today the great house serves as an agricultural institute, but the remarkable gardens are still held by the Clinton estate and are open to the public.

The Italian Garden is the formal centrepiece. It seems to have been laid out about 1735 from designs by André Le Nôtre, gardener to Louis XIV. In particular, it bears strong similarities to his work at Château Pomponne near Paris. Certainly the layout is fine and stylish. A handsome Neoclassical temple, flanked by an orangery and the Conservatories, looks down over a terraced lawn to a sunken garden with an ornamental pool and fountain, surrounded on three sides by a canal. Bronze figures are grouped around, and from the central fountain the eye travels on up a broad avenue cut through trees to a stone obelisk on a distant hilltop.

But the refined symmetries of the Italian Garden are modified by the strong growth of trees. Many were planted during Victorian times; a great deodar cedar on the upper terrace is especially prominent. And adjoining the garden is the Pinetum, renowned for its lofty conifers. There are rare specimens too: Mexican juniper (*Juniperus flaccida*) and Tasmanian cedar (*Athrotaxis* spp.) among them. The Pinetum was established in 1840, and extended in 1910 when many new trees were added following the discoveries of the great Far Eastern plant collector E. H. Wilson (1876–1930).

SUN KING'S GARDENER *André Le Nôtre, garden designer to Louis XIV, exerted a tremendous influence on 17th-century garden planning. Bicton is said to be laid out to his designs, but he could have made little personal contribution, since he died in 1700, 35 years before the gardens were built.*

GRANDEUR AND SIMPLICITY *The formal gardens at Bicton were laid out in the French grand manner in 1735, at a time when most English gardens were yielding to landscaping. The centrepiece consists of canals, pools and a fountain, surrounded by charming lead figures.*

Beyond the deep shade of the woodland garden is a charming 19th-century garden with a summerhouse known as the Hermitage, set among rhododendrons and overlooking a small lake. It is a remarkable structure, covered with wooden shingles and with a floor inlaid with deer bones.

The Victorians, of course, delighted in such unusual effects and the Hermitage is not the only curiosity at Bicton. There is also a little building constructed of flints and overlooking a picturesque rock garden. Known as the Shell House, after a collection of shells which it contains, it is situated at the northern end of the American Garden, an area laid out in the last century to display trees and shrubs from North America. The specimens include a particularly good Monterey cypress (*Cupressus macrocarpa*).

The mild Devonshire climate has assisted the growth of plants at Bicton. And, in the conservatories beside the temple, the natural advantages are augmented to permit the growth of real exotica. There are five hothouses and greenhouses. One is devoted to cacti, and another to tropical species – here the bird of paradise plant burgeons among ginger, pineapple, lemon and banana. The most arresting structure is the isolated early 19th-century Palm House, half-domed and elegantly contoured with glass panes on a cast-iron framework. Within it grow the heavenly bamboo, the dense New Zealand manuka (*Leptospermum scoparium*) and a large Mimosa (*Acacia dealbata*) whose fern-like leaves are entwined with passion flowers.

BLENHEIM PALACE *Oxfordshire*

It is like driving into a much-publicised masterpiece: the grouping of palace, lake and bridge is familiar through countless reproductions. And yet their reality is more impressive than a printed image could hope to express. Blenheim's grandeur is out of scale with the present century. In visiting the park you seem to trespass against the laws of time.

Queen Anne gave the royal domain of Woodstock to her victorious general, John the 1st Duke of Marlborough, in 1705. And she promised to build for him there a palace worthy of his glorious achievements. It was to be called Blenheim after a German village where the duke had won a famous victory over the French and Bavarians in 1704. The brilliant young Sir John Vanbrugh was commissioned as architect, and the sums donated by the Treasury amounted to close on a quarter of a million pounds. Yet even this fortune proved insufficient to the needs of Vanbrugh's vision.

Some 9 miles of drystone walling enclose the park today. And if you approach by the Triumphal Gate in Woodstock, its classic vista bursts immediately on the eye. There in the foreground is Vanbrugh's Grand Bridge, balancing with its mighty proportions the more distant mass of the palace itself.

The bridge was designed at huge expense to span the valley of the little River Glyme, which flows across the park. The main arch alone is 101 ft in width, and

MAN OF PARTS *Sir John Vanbrugh (1664–1726), soldier, actor and playwright, seems to have turned to architecture and garden design more or less for the fun of it. Yet he had a tremendous effect on both in his day, and made the baroque style his own, his two greatest works being Castle Howard and Blenheim Palace. His bridge at Blenheim (opposite) contains 30-odd rooms within the structure, but most of them are flooded since Capability Brown dammed the stream some 40 years after Vanbrugh's death to create the lake that is now the glory of the park.*

Sarah, Duchess of Marlborough told a friend that she had counted 33 rooms within the stonework.

What made the project so fantastic was the trifling nature of the river that it crossed. In 1708, when work on the bridge started, the Glyme was no more than a marshy stream. It was Lancelot 'Capability' Brown who justified its proportions by creating the great sweep of water seen today.

Brown was commissioned in 1764, long after duke, duchess and architect were dead. And he transformed Blenheim's appearance by damming the Glyme near Bladon to engulf the whole valley with water. He left only one small strip of rising ground marooned in the flooded basin. It was an inspired act. The moated knoll is known as Queen Elizabeth's Island, and survives as one of the park's most enchanting effects.

As for the lake, it is widely considered Brown's supreme achievement. Sir Sacheverell Sitwell, for example, called it 'the one great argument of the landscape gardener. There is nothing finer in Europe'. At the western end, Brown created a Grand Cascade which still roars with some fury today. But it is the great curved sheet, backed by hanging woodlands of beech, which gives Blenheim its spacious harmonies.

Blenheim's perspectives change constantly with the sinuous course of the water. But one landmark which constantly recurs is the Column of Victory, topped by its lead statue of the 1st Duke. Standing 134 ft in height, it was completed in 1730 and holds the eye as firmly as the palace and bridge.

ALCHEMY OF AUTUMN

The central vista of the park runs dead straight from the palace, across Vanbrugh's bridge and up to the Column of Victory. Beyond, there was once a fine avenue of elms which were lost in the 1970s. Otherwise, the woods remain hauntingly beautiful. Autumn, of course, brings its natural alchemy to their foliage. And there is a moment in September, before the leaves turn, when you look back from the column and see nothing but muted greens until the eye meets a blood-red mass of Virginia creeper growing at the North Front.

Back from the main park, however, entirely different effects have been achieved. At the East Front is a sheltered Italian garden carpeted with scrolls and arabesques in dwarf box, with pink roses and topiary grouped around a mermaid fountain. The garden was laid out in the early years of the 20th century by the 9th Duke of Marlborough.

There is so much at Blenheim to delight the eye. The oldest feature is a never-failing spring known as Rosamond's Well which was frequented by Rosamond Clifford, the lover of Henry II. An 8 acre kitchen garden holds considerable fascination, laid out for the 1st Duke in military style with walls bastioned like those of a fort.

And yet that first heart-stopping vision from the Triumphal Gate may survive as the most powerful memory. To describe it as fit for a king does it scant justice; it caused George III to exclaim: 'We have nothing to equal this!'

BLICKLING HALL *Norfolk*

A certain mystery surrounds the beautiful crescent lake at Blickling in Norfolk. The mile-long curve of water which lies to the north of the hall is backed by woodlands of beech and oak. It is landscaped in the manner of Humphry Repton, who may in fact have been responsible for it. No records, though, confirm this theory. The lake is just one of the enigmas of Blickling, whose 46 acre gardens were laid out over many centuries and remain imprinted with the tastes of several epochs.

The house itself is Jacobean, a red-brick building rising with pinnacled symmetry from a foreground of green lawn and flanking yew hedge. It was reconstructed from a 14th-century fortified house between 1619 and 1625 for Sir Henry Hobart, Lord Chief Justice to James I. The moat, which guarded the original medieval building, has been dry for three centuries; an account book of 1676–7 refers to it as a haven for summer bedding plants. And today it is maintained as a sheltered garden where fine old roses, camellias, hydrangeas and fuchsias are grown.

CENTREPIECE *The 16th-century fountain was set up at Blickling Hall as an eyecatcher in the midst of a formal garden created by Lady Lothian in 1872. It commands the view down a long vista of flower beds and clipped yew, and up flights of steps to the woodland garden beyond.*

FRUITS OF VICTORY *Blenheim Palace (opposite) was Queen Anne's gift to her most successful general, the Duke of Marlborough. The original formal gardens were swept away by 18th-century landscaping, and the present water terraces were built in the 1920s.*

The park in which Repton's hand has been detected extends to the north and west of the hall. It was clearly laid out in the early 18th century, for an estate map dated 1729, which hangs in the house, shows the splendid artificial lake marked as the 'New Pond'.

Some features of the grounds can be dated with confidence. Not far from the water, for example, is a massive pyramidal mausoleum, rising to 40 ft and built in 1794 by the Neoclassical architect Joseph Bonomi. Inside, contained in three marble sarcophagi, lie the remains of the 2nd Earl of Buckinghamshire (died 1793) and his two wives. But other features are as uncertain in origin as the lake. To the south of the hall, for example, is an elegant orangery known to have been in existence in 1793 and sometimes attributed to William Ivory. A statue of Hercules, sculpted in 1632 by Nicholas Stone, stands inside, among tubs in which grow such exotica as *Cupressus cashmeriana* and the plantain lily (*Hosta sieboldiana* 'Elegans').

The garden's main vista looks east from the hall to a fine Doric temple of the early 18th century. A parterre and raised terrace extend between the two, and this is probably the oldest part of the garden. Certainly it is the most complex in its history. It is thought that a great Jacobean parterre originally occupied the area. What is seen today is an array of beds first laid out in 1872 for Constance, Marchioness of Lothian. She had it planted in the somewhat fussy mid-Victorian manner, however, and it was again rearranged in the 1930s by Mrs Norah Lindsay, a well-known garden designer.

SENTINEL YEWS

In place of the elaborate beds which had to be stocked with flowers in season, Mrs Lindsay simplified the design, retaining only four large rectangles in the parterre adjacent to the house. The corners of each are marked by sentinel yews. The two beds near the house are pastel-toned with pink, blue and white flowers which include phloxes, campanulas and delphiniums. The two further beds are more boldly massed with yellows and oranges: orange sunflowers, golden rods and creamy Nankeen lilies (*Lilium* × *testaceum*) among them. The spiky *Yucca filamentosa* grows in all the beds, providing a unifying factor.

Beyond the parterre, a raised terrace leads to the large woodland garden in which the temple stands. The groves of oaks, beeches, sycamores and yews are intersected by long, straight rides which may date back to the 1620s. Avenues of Turkey oaks, limes and beeches were added in the 19th century, and rhododendrons planted along the rides. In addition, several small specimen trees may be found flanking the central walk to the temple, leading the eye up from the broad way to the taller trees behind. Among them a group of Far Eastern maples.

MELLOW WALLS *Rose-red, Jacobean Blickling Hall and its lovely gardens look as though they have existed since time's beginning. But their positions were determined by the moat of a house, owned by Anne Boleyn's father. Father and daughter still haunt the drive.*

BODNANT *Gwynedd*

No garden in Britain commands finer long views. Looking south-west from the terraces at Bodnant, the eye ranges across the Conwy Valley to the mountains of Snowdonia beyond: Carnedd Llewelyn, Foel Fras, the Drum and Tal-y-fan are clearly discernible. And the foreground frame is exceptional. Level green lawns and formal rose gardens, the glimmer of lily pools and the deep shade of great trees – all drop away to paradisaical woodlands.

Bodnant has often been called the greatest garden created in Britain during the last 100 years. The claim is a bold one, but amply justified by the splendour of Bodnant's effects.

Come to the garden in June and you are greeted almost immediately by the shock of sheer colour, for situated near the entrance is the astonishing Laburnum Arch overhung by shimmering cascades of bright yellow. The long, curved walk extends for 180 ft, between trees pleached over an arched framework. A bedazzling tunnel, the arch assaults not only the eyes but the nostrils too with its fragrance.

FAMILY CREATION

Bodnant is the creation of the Aberconway family, who have held the house and its grounds since 1875. The Laburnum Arch was established by Henry Pochin, great-grandfather to the present Lord Aberconway. Though some of the large native trees date back to the 18th century, the tremendous old conifers rising from the lower garden were planted in the late 19th century by Henry Pochin who, with the help of a landscape architect named Milner, laid out several of the first formal beds and shrubberies.

Bodnant, at the time of Pochin and Milner, lacked the impressive set-piece of today. This is a series of grand Italianate terraces which lead down from the West Front of the house to the course of the Hiraethlyn, a tributary of the Conwy. The great stepped garden is the work of Henry Duncan, the 2nd Lord Aberconway, who from the turn of the century until his death in 1953, shaped the development of the whole. Skilfully assisted by his head gardener, F. C. Puddle, and after, the son C. E. Puddle, the 2nd Baron worked on the garden for more than half a century.

Originally, a vast grassy slope had descended from the house, and establishing the terraces was a major undertaking. The work began in 1905 and took nine years to complete.

In creating the great tiered apron for Bodnant, the 2nd Baron achieved more than formal discipline; he also brought the mountains of Snowdonia into the garden.

In all, five terraces run down from the West Front, each with its own distinct character. The highest is the

GREEN LAWNS, BLUE DISTANCE *The great terrace at Bodnant, with its formal pool aswim with water lilies, reaches out to embrace the Conwy Valley and the far-off peaks of Snowdonia. This majestic platform was part of a gardening concept that took 50 years to realise.*

stone-flagged Rose Garden, and from it there are glorious views down the four other steps, flanked by trees so that they channel the eye to the skyline of mountains beyond. Steps lead down to a lower level where there is a French baroque fountain and pool overgrown with two white wisterias (*W. venusta* and *W. floribunda* 'Alba'). Below, you come to the wide Croquet Terrace backed by fine shrubs which shelter against the terrace wall: eucryphias, magnolias and dwarf lilacs among them.

The third level is the beautiful Lily Terrace, its rectangular design broken by a semicircular bay to the west. The pond is kept stocked with a wonderful diversity of water lilies, flowering from June to September in tones from snow white to wine red.

The fourth terrace is the Lower Rose Garden. It is reached by a pergola clustered with climbing roses and the blue-flowering, climbing *Solanum crispum* 'Glasnevin', a delight throughout spring and summer. Planted against the curved walls of the steps are *Magnolia grandiflora* 'Goliath', valued for its giant blooms, and the Chilean lantern tree (*Crinodendron hookerianum*), distinguished by its crimson flowers which hang like lanterns from long pedicels.

At the lowest level is the Canal Terrace, named after a long and narrow rectangle of water which is the centrepiece. Though planted with water lilies at either end, the central stretch is kept mirror-clear for reflections. A fine green lawn surrounds the water.

Looking down the canal from the north you can see a charming 18th-century garden house at the other end, with its reflection caught in the water.

When you leave the terraces, the mountain vistas are lost. But there is rich compensation in the profusion of exotic trees and shrubs. The North Garden, for example, may be reached by either of the two upper terraces and is more secluded in mood. A sloping lawn here is enclosed by beeches, cedars and yews, and banked with magnolias, azaleas and eucryphias. Above all there are the rhododendrons: the bright blue *R. augustinii*, and the 'Penjerrick Cream', a hybrid, often considered the loveliest rhododendron.

REMARKABLE RHODODENDRONS

Stripped of all other features, Bodnant would remain remarkable for its rhododendron collection, which is among the finest in the country. The plants root readily in the garden's lime-free soil, and many were grown from seeds sent back to England by such intrepid collectors as E. H. Wilson, George Forrest, Frank Kingdon-Ward and Dr J. F. Lock.

The rhododendrons flower from December to the height of summer: white, yellow, orange, red, pink and purple. Plant breeding has flourished for years at Bodnant, and the hybrid rhododendrons raised in the garden include the cherry-pink 'Winsome' and scarlet 'Elizabeth'.

In 1949, the 2nd Lord Aberconway gave the garden to the National Trust, and it is now looked after on their behalf by the present Lord Aberconway, with the help of Martin Puddle, the third generation of his family to tend the garden.

BORDE HILL GARDEN *West Sussex*

When Colonel Stephenson Clarke bought the stone-built Sussex mansion of Borde Hill in 1893 he acquired an unremarkable garden. The property stood on a saddle of ground rising from the valley of the upper River Ouse, and the garden had been landscaped in conventional style. There were a few good trees and, to the south of the house, a large lawn extending to a ha-ha, which gave fine views towards the South Downs. There were equally pleasant vistas to the north, over wooded farmland towards the High Weald.

Yet this unexceptional domain was to provide the framework for one of the most luxuriant gardens in England. Within the half century before his death in 1948, the colonel had filled every dull space with a vivid mass of colour: the blooms of rhododendrons, azaleas, camellias and magnolias.

The great transformation did not begin immediately. The colonel started by levelling the large south lawn to open up views beyond. But his plantings at first were fairly orthodox. In 1895, for example, he had a venerable *Magnolia × soulangiana* brought to Borde Hill by horse and cart from its original site near London. It may be seen today, growing near the Old House, a cottage in the garden.

What revolutionised Borde Hill – and other gardens across the face of the nation – was the great era of Far Eastern plant collecting. It began with E. H. Wilson's first expedition to China in 1899, and brought an especially rich harvest in the years 1912–30. The colonel, himself a keen naturalist and big-game hunter, helped to finance expeditions to the Himalayas, Tasmania and the Andes.

COLLECTOR'S PIECE *The astonishing array of exotic trees and shrubs at Borde Hill was the work of Colonel Stephenson Clarke, a well-known amateur plant collector. He began his plantings of rare rhododendrons, camellias, viburnums and others with seeds obtained from China, the Andes and outposts still further outflung. The greeny-yellow* Euphorbia characias *shown here, however, is of less romantic, native European origin.*

UNDER THE TERRACE *Dropping down from Bodnant's terraces, the grand views across half of Wales are lost, but the compensation is the half-secret dells, among rocks and rushing water. There, the garden's famed collections of exotic trees and shrubs have been established. Supreme among them is the wonderful gathering of rare rhododendrons which have been sent from many parts of the world to flourish in Bodnant's lime-free soil (opposite).*

JOY OF SPRING *Colour grouping was and is another major preoccupation at Borde Hill. Here, a flowering cherry – the hybrid* Prunus *'Accolade' – presides over a brilliant spring assembly of camellias.*

Borde Hill burgeoned as a result. From the Buddhists' sacred mountain of Omei-shan in Western China, for example, E. H. Wilson brought the seed of the fine *Viburnum cinnamomifolium* which grows just outside the South Walled Garden; it has become one of the largest specimens in the British Isles. The garden boasts an award-winning *Rhododendron vellereum*, an early flowering plant from the Tibetan Himalayas; this was an introduction of the collector Frank Kingdon-Ward. And the great tradition of specimen hunting did not end with the pioneers. One of Borde Hill's most remarkable climbers is a red-flowering *Mitraria coccinea* from the remote forest slopes of the Andes; it was raised from a cutting brought to Kew by air, sealed in a polythene bag.

The gardens at Borde Hill are laid out in largely informal style, with paths that meander through woods and glades. The open vistas to north and south are edged with trees, and there are two large dells which have been incorporated into the design.

The rhododendrons, especially, are everywhere, lining paths and crowding beds with profuse displays which last through spring and summer. You could almost complete an alphabet of exotica from the collection, beginning with the mauve *Rhododendron adenophorum*, a leathery-leaved species from Yunnan, to the dainty Chinese *R. zaleucum*, a real enchantress this with her funnel-shaped flowers and pleasing leaves, which are white on the reverse.

Come to Borde Hill in late May and you are greeted by an exceptional display of deciduous azaleas which extend in vivid drifts to the east of the house. The area, known as the Azalea Ring, is planted chiefly with the Knap Hill strain, selected for colour and scent.

Not far away, near the walled garden, are several examples of the free-flowering *Camellia* 'Donation'. This greatly valued plant, noted for its large, deeply veined pink flowers, was raised at Borde Hill by Colonel Stephenson Clarke from a cross between *C. japonica* 'Donckelarii' and *C. saluensis*.

There are few formal features at Borde Hill. The Old House has a little garden of its own which is home to a collection of cistus and allied plants. Not far away, you come upon a statue of a veiled lady, known as The Bride. She has a vacant air, as if overcome by the beauty of her surroundings – or perhaps by the vapours of the large nearby Californian laurel (*Umbellularia californica*). Known as the Headache Tree, its leaves exude a volatile oil when crushed and are said to cause headaches if deeply inhaled.

Even without such disquieting effects, you are always aware of the trees at Borde Hill. Their upward growth provides a stabilising element in the profusion of exotic shrubs. One eye-catching specimen is a 95 ft Turkey oak (*Quercus cerris*) which spreads its boughs broad and wide over lawns west of the Azalea Ring. To the north, beyond the garden proper, are woods which abound in rare conifers.

BOWOOD HOUSE *Wiltshire*

They called it the Picturesque Style. In the late 18th century, English gentlemen of taste were familiar with the natural landscape pioneered by Capability Brown. But they wanted to take the informal look further – introduce such 'awful' elements as crags and caverns and raging torrents into their private domains.

Bowood House, home of the Earl of Shelburne, beautifully illustrates those mixed aspirations towards serenity and dramatic interest. Here, in one of

WILDERNESS TO TASTE *Bowood House is in Wiltshire, a county not often remarked upon for its waterfalls. This one, at Bowood, is the offshoot of a landscape created in the mid-18th century by Capability Brown who, as was his custom, dammed a stream to make a lake as a major feature of the park. The cascade is the lake's outfall, though the picturesque arrangement of the rocks was added some years later. Still, a lot of water has tumbled over them since, and the whole thing looks satisfyingly natural now, with the tangled woods above, and nodding narcissi below.*

ECONOMICAL PRUNING
Impressive though it is, Bowood House is not so grand as it was in its 18th-century heyday. The larger wing, known as Big House, was demolished in 1955 for reasons of economy. What remains is Little House attached to the palatial Orangery, designed by Robert Adam, and now a picture gallery. In the 18th century, too, Capability Brown's landscape swept up to the windows; but during Victoria's reign, in the area adjacent to the house, this was replaced by the present formality of rose beds, gravel paths and clipped yew.

Brown's noblest landscapes, you also discover a rocky Cascade and mysterious Hermit's Cave. Both were entirely artificial creations included, like gargoyles in a cathedral, to tease little thrills of terror out of the complacent observer.

The great park at Bowood in Wiltshire was designed by Brown between 1762 and 1768 for the 1st Marquess of Lansdowne. The landscapist brought all his skills to bear in creating suave perspectives across fields and beechwoods to the Wiltshire downland beyond. There had to be a lake, of course. At Bowood, Brown dammed two streams across the north end of a valley running to the east of the house to create a long, serpentine water.

Brown required that the sweep should appear continuous. But his commission did not extend to flooding the neighbouring landowner's property. So he fitted the dam in at the northern boundary of the estate and concealed it in a clump of trees; there is a considerable drop beyond.

A small Doric temple, situated on a promontory by the dam, looks out across the water. Though fitting exquisitely into the setting, it was not in fact placed there by Brown but moved to its present position in 1864 from elsewhere in the grounds.

Nor is the Cascade Brown's creation. It was designed in 1785 by the Hon. Charles Hamilton, an inventive amateur known for his work at Painshill in Surrey.

Situated in a shaded valley just beyond the dam, the

Cascade roars splendidly amid the trees, the water falling in misty skeins over successive ledges of rock.

The Bowood House seen today is a building of warm golden stonework erected by Henry Keene in 1755. On the sunny South Front is a fine orangery, designed by Robert Adam in 1769 and now serving as a picture gallery. It looks down over formal terraces boldly massed with colour, among which the main level dates from the Victorian era. Ranks of clipped yews stand sentinel here amid rose beds whose dominant reds vie for brightness with the geraniums disposed in urns around.

The whole 82 acre area north and east of the house is known as the Pleasure Grounds, and though Brown provided the frame for the picture seen today, it has been filled since his time with a magnificent collection of trees and shrubs. A few of Brown's original trees survive. There is, in particular, one tremendous cedar of Lebanon rising to 140 ft and with a trunk 22 ft in girth. It is the tallest cedar in the country bar one – a fractionally larger specimen at Petworth – and is thought to have been a Brown planting.

Quite separate from the Pleasure Grounds is a woodland garden of 50 acres, which formed part of Brown's original outer belt of trees. Here some 2 miles of walks wind today amid oak, beech, chestnut and pine. The garden is only open from mid-May to the end of June, but this is the rhododendron season and the plants – grown here from 1854 – form tumultuous displays in the half shade of the trees.

CAPABILITY DENIED *Perhaps it was Yorkshire independence that kept the Picturesque Movement, led by Capability Brown, out of Bramham Park. At any rate, it remains as one of the very few great English gardens to have retained the French-style formality popularised by such gardens as Versailles towards the end of the 17th century. This is not a place in which to brood upon the glories of wild nature. Rather, its ruler-straight grassy rides were intended to be conducive to elegant strolling and civilised conversation. The only, and mild, diversions are the handsome objects closing the long vistas, such as the Four Faces urn.*

BRAMHAM PARK *West Yorkshire*

Here is a garden *not* landscaped by Capability Brown. The boast may seem a curious one, but it remains a key to the garden's fascination. Bramham Park is 'One That Got Away'.

Throughout Britain from the late 17th century many important gardens were laid out in the French style pioneered by Louis XIV's gardener, André le Nôtre. They were characterised by formal symmetries: long vistas cut ruler-straight through woodland; hedged walks and geometrically aligned statuary, fountains and pools. When Brown and his followers introduced the natural look, a host of such gardens were swept from the face of the nation. Bramham Park is a rare survival – a little Versailles in West Yorkshire.

Robert Benson, 1st Lord Bingley and Lord Chamberlain to Queen Anne, built the house between 1698 and 1710. The 66 acre garden dates from the first decades of the 18th century, and miraculously came through the landscaping vogue with its formal features intact. Later owners also resisted the blandishments of the Victorian improvers. In fact, the only serious damage was done to the original as recently as 1962, when fierce gales brought down over 400 trees in the garden. The woodlands, though, were replanted as before and 20 years on are returning to maturity. The official handbook's claim is a fair one: John Wood's plan of 1725 would serve as a guide today.

'Curious gardens laid out with great judgment' was how one early visitor described them. The main vista in the whole design is a mile-long way, known as the Broadwalk, which separates the house from the garden. At one extremity is a Neoclassical temple, built by James Paine as an orangery and later consecrated as a chapel. The walk leads to a series of elaborate pools, water basins and stepped cascades.

The whole garden is a network of similar vistas, intersecting at focal points. Here ranks of tree trunks conduct the eye; there it travels through corridors of clipped beech. One series of ways converges on a pond and canal; another on an Ionic temple. At yet another intersection, five ways come together at a magnificent decorated urn known as the Four Faces.

The effect is not drily austere. Daffodils have been widely underplanted in the woodlands and make spring a delight at Bramham. In summer there is a formal rose garden to enjoy, situated in a walled parterre in front of the house. And in the Black Fen Pleasure Grounds, where the obelisk is sited, the plant growth is more luxuriant. Thickets of wild rhododendrons abound among the trunks of venerable beeches, cedars, chestnuts and limes.

But the Black Fen, too, is patterned with intersecting rides and vistas. The eye rarely roams freely for long, being tugged back incessantly to the designer's straight lines. Bramham's is an attraction unfamiliar in English gardens. It is of nature entirely disciplined by intellect.

BRANKLYN *Tayside*

Small, they say, is beautiful – and in the case of Branklyn this is certainly true. Situated on a rocky west-facing slope above the River Tay, the garden today covers barely 2 acres. And when John and Dorothy Renton built the house in 1922, the area was more limited still. To achieve the present acreage they had to colonise part of a neighbouring orchard.

Later, Branklyn was to be called the 'finest 2 acres of private garden in the country', and to the amateur the story of its evolution is particularly pleasing. Branklyn was from the outset a very personal creation shaped by a husband-and-wife team who started with little or no knowledge of gardening science. They made mistakes: rose beds, for example, were laid out and had to be abandoned. It was only with time that the Rentons discovered what would prosper in Branklyn's good but rather acid loam, and survive its damaging late spring frosts.

One plant which 'took' readily to the garden was the peat-loving, poppy-like meconopsis. It was an early speciality of Branklyn and, towards the end of her life, Dorothy Renton was to receive a first-class certificate from the Royal Horticultural Society for her azure-blue cultivar *Meconopsis grandis* 'Branklyn'.

But there is very much more to admire. The informal design grew around a wealth of rare and unusual plants garnered from all over the world. Branklyn was to be, in Dorothy Renton's words, a 'home from home' for any plant which the Rentons enjoyed growing and which itself favoured the habitat. Among the trees planted for shade, for example, is a

beautiful specimen of the orange-barked birch *Betula albo-sinensis septentionalis* of China; this was grown from seed planted in 1926. The many fine conifers include a notable umbrella pine from Japan, and there is a fine array of choice maples for autumn colour. A wide variety of small-leaved rhododendrons profit by the shelter of the trees, while viburnums, magnolias and hydrangeas contribute their own displays.

From the beginning, alpines and rock plants were a particular interest of the Rentons, and to accommodate them two large scree beds were laid out with advice from the great rock gardener Reginald Farrer. The screes are spangled with exquisites: starry-petalled pulsatillas, pink-and-white oxalis and daisy-like celmisias from New Zealand are just a few of the conspicuous items. There are dwarf rhododendrons in abundance, while the green plumes of dwarf conifers provide stabilising verticals. Here, as elsewhere at Branklyn, the maximum use has been made of a limited area, and every corner is embroidered with interest.

BRIGHTON – PRESTON PARK
East Sussex

The beach is the magnet at Brighton, as at coastal resorts throughout the country. Yet back from the seafront, Brighton retains a dignified aura, with much fine Regency architecture and over 3,000 acres of parks and gardens. Come in by the main London road and you pass the largest of the town's open spaces. This is Preston Park, covering some 40 acres and a delight entirely in its own right.

It caters, certainly, for the athletic: there is a cycle track, cricket and football pitches, bowling greens and tennis courts. But from spring to autumn the park is also a blaze of colour. The formal Rose Garden, for example, contains over 15,000 roses. No less emphatic in their exuberance are the Gardens of Greeting competition beds which line the verges of the park. Here, in autumn, other boroughs and local horticultural societies submit designs for their own displays. The plants are grown at Brighton to be ready for the following year.

Quite different in mood is the walled garden of Preston Manor, half hidden among the trees in the north-west corner of the park. The Queen Anne house was bequeathed to the borough in the 1930s, and its plot has the intimacy of a cottage garden, with crowded box-edged beds and an arch of trained laburnums. Adjoining the enclosed garden is a scented garden for the blind, equipped with guide rails and notices in Braille.

But Preston Park's most notable feature is its huge rock and water garden, known as the Rookery. Situated across the road from the main park, it was laid out in the 1930s on sloping ground with a rushing stream which tumbles down to a lily pool. The rocks are massed with aubrietas, dwarf pinks and candelabra primulas, while flowering cherries and many dwarf trees and shrubs vary the forms, textures and tones.

GIFT OF THE GULF STREAM *On the Isle of Arran, between Brodick Castle and the sea, there is an opulent southern garden totally at odds with the wild Highland hills that surround it. The variety of its planting is the result of the labours of the late Duchess of Montrose, but its existence is due to the warm Gulf Stream, or rather to a quirky offshoot called the Atlantic Drift that sweeps up to these northerly latitudes. The main theme is rhododendrons, but there are also fine formal gardens like these running down to the shore.*

BRODICK CASTLE *Arran*

The landscape is stern. Above Brodick Castle the ridge of the Arran mountains soars to 2,866 ft at Goat Fell. The castellated mansion itself is situated 150 ft up, and commands sweeping vistas back across the Firth of Clyde to the Ayrshire coast beyond. The Vikings first fortified the site, and there is much in the setting that evokes Wagnerian images of the wild north.

And yet the gardens of Brodick are lush. Occupying a wooded valley under the massif, their 65 acres are sheltered from Arran's howling south-westerlies by the very ridge which confers its drama on them. The climate, moreover, is moderated by the warm Atlantic Drift and the loamy soil is enriched by quantities of leaf-mould shed by the enfolding forests.

The red-brick mansion, built at different stages from the 14th to 19th centuries, was a seat of the Dukes of Hamilton until 1895. It subsequently became the home of Mary Louise, Duchess of Montrose, daughter of the 12th Duke of Hamilton, and it was she who shaped the garden seen today. Rhododendrons were her passion, and her plantings still form the heart of the collection.

The rhododendrons were planted in the 1920s, that fertile period of Far Eastern plant collecting which transformed so many British gardens. The Duchess of Montrose financed several expeditions, and Frank Kingdon-Ward, one noted collector, was to name his discovery of *Rhododendron mollyanum* after her. But Brodick is particularly associated with the intrepid George Forrest, himself a Scotsman, who contributed many of the large-leaved species of rhododendron for which the garden is especially known.

MONSTER BLOOMS

The magnificent showpieces are grouped chiefly in the Lower Rhododendron Walk, an area which is largely free from frost. It is here that you come upon the huge *R. sinogrande*, largest-leaved of all, and the crimson *R. giganteum*. Both were Forrest discoveries and have grown tree-tall at Brodick – beautiful monsters which bear blooms the size of men's heads amid leaves half a yard long.

Forrest also contributed the immaculate white *R. taggianum*, one of the loveliest and most tender rhododendrons, which is often grown under glass elsewhere. At Brodick it thrives in the open in a wonderful collection of the sweet-scented *Maddenii* varieties growing closer to the house. The woodland garden though has more than its rhododendrons; it is known too for its lilies and primulas and its many rare trees and shrubs introduced by the duchess from South America, Australasia and elsewhere.

East of the house, a walled garden of 18th-century origin offers something of a change in mood. Its formal flower beds are planted with rambler roses, carnations, fuchsias and begonias, and provides moments of old world charm in a garden of exotics.

After the death of the Duchess of Montrose, the house and garden – and 7,300 acres – were given to the National Trust for Scotland.

RAGGED REFLECTIONS *Great clumps of sorrel rhubarb cast palm-leaved reflections among the pools of Burford House Gardens. The nearby River Teme feeds the garden streams, where moisture-loving plants crowd together in lavish variety of form. Well-groomed lawns curve past island beds, stemming the exuberant tide of plants and shrubs.*

VISTA FOR AN EARL *Castle Howard's acres unfold in elegant symmetry – a grand parterre of lawns and yew hedges with lakes to north and south.*

BURFORD HOUSE
Hereford and Worcester

There is a spare symmetry at the heart of this 4 acre garden, which surrounds a red-brick Georgian house whose austere form is mirrored in a rectangular canal pool to the north. But elsewhere the eye meets few dominant straight lines. For the garden is modern and laid out with curving vistas and irregular beds by its designer, Mr John Treasure, who bought the house in 1954 at a time when there was no garden worth speaking of. Apart from a few good trees and an elegant 18th-century summerhouse, the main asset was the fertile alluvial loam of the River Teme which bounds the garden to the west.

Mr Treasure's design by no means evokes lack of formal discipline. The extensive green lawns which meander between the curving beds are crisply edged and exceptionally well-groomed. This is a plantsman's garden, laid out to display its copious delights within an ordered framework. And for the home owner with a garden of small or moderate size it is fascinating to study in detail.

Harmonising combinations of colour have been brilliantly achieved throughout the garden, and especially imaginative use has been made of clematis – a speciality of the owner. It grows not only in conventionally trained fashion, but is encouraged to bloom through beds of heather, spill among brooms and yuccas, and entwine junipers and climbing roses.

Similarly pleasing associations of colour have been created among shrubs and perennials, and as much thought has been lavished on foliage and form. You find it, for example, among the moisture-loving plants; the River Teme provides an endless source of water, which is pump-fed to stream gardens. Their banks have been massed with aquatics, the broad-spreading clumps of gunnera and sorrel rhubarb (*Rheum palmatum*) diversified with the upthrust wands and pokers of *Primula vialii*, astilbes and exotic irises – all grouped with a discerning eye.

BURNBY HALL *Humberside*

Looking across the lakes of Burnby Hall, at Pocklington, you could be forgiven for thinking them entirely natural creations. Reed-edged and informally contoured, they are famed for their water lilies which form multicoloured drifts in high summer. But the two lakes are in fact artificial, extending where there was once nothing more than bare fields. Major P. H. Stewart, who bought the property in 1904, had their 2 acre extent excavated and lined with concrete.

The lakes were originally laid out for trout fishing, a passion of the much-travelled owner. His collection of hunting and angling trophies from around the world may be seen in a small museum in the gardens. But during the 1930s, Major Stewart's interests turned more and more to gardening, and brick-walled soil beds were built on the lake floors to hold the now celebrated water-lily collection.

Lilacs and laburnums flourish in the 6 acres of garden around the lakes and there are rare specimens among the trees: some 20 varieties of holly, for example, Japanese maples and other delights. The two lakes are on different levels and linked by a stream flowing down through a well-established rock garden. More recent additions include a new rose garden and – a particularly thoughtful inclusion – a scented garden for the blind. It consists of two large raised beds, stocked with fragrant plants and flowers.

The water lilies, though, remain the chief attraction. Over 50 varieties are represented, and comprise one of the best collections in Europe. They are at their best from June to September and beneath the glimmering pads you may glimpse the flash of ornamental fish, companions of the exotics.

CASTLE HOWARD *North Yorkshire*

When Granada Television chose Castle Howard as the chief location for their much acclaimed filming of *Brideshead Revisited*, they brought a sublime private palace into living rooms throughout the nation. Yorkshire's finest historic house, set in more than 1,000 acres of parkland, astonishes today through its

POETIC VISION *Level lawns spread out before the palatial grandeur of Castle Howard. The 18th-century soldier and playwright John Vanbrugh turned his creative talents to architecture, and conjured up this vision of formal harmony. Such elegant restraint gives way to natural woodland east of the house, where rhododendrons spread their glowing colours among the trees.*

grandiose conception. And it was scarcely less impressive to 18th-century visitors. Horace Walpole, for example, likened Castle Howard to a fortified city, with outlying hilltop temples, woodlands and 'the noblest lawn in the world fenced by half the horizon'.

The building was designed in 1699 as a private residence for Charles Howard, 3rd Earl of Carlisle. His architect was the soldier-playwright Sir John Vanbrugh who, remarkably, had never designed a building before. Yet, assisted by the experienced Nicholas Hawksmoor, Vanbrugh plunged with gusto into the world of bricks, mortar and measuring rods – and created a masterpiece at his first attempt.

You enter the estate today by a 5 mile avenue of beeches, and of limes which have survived from the original plantings. Two superb archways embellished with mock fortifications give notice that this is no ordinary estate, while immense perspectives across the rolling parkland unfold. A cross avenue marks the turning to the house, at an intersection graced by a 100 ft high obelisk.

There are lakes at both the north and south fronts of the house, but the really grand vista looks south. Here the eye travels from watery sheet and noble bridge to two of the finest garden buildings in Europe: Vanbrugh's Temple of the Four Winds, and Hawksmoor's Mausoleum beyond. The former is a splendid domed

building with Ionic porticoes, while the hilltop Mausoleum has been likened to a small cathedral. Walpole, a connoisseur, wrote that the rotunda would 'tempt one to be buried alive'.

Closer to the house is a grassed parterre, designed by W. A. Nesfield in the 1850s. It beautifully matches the character and proportions of the house, having as its centrepiece a baroque-style fountain showing Atlas supporting a globe from which glittering waters cascade. Formal hedges of clipped yew lend distinction to the level baize-like lawns; the symmetries are both restful and dignified.

Although the wide views and architectural features set the tone of Castle Howard, colour is not lacking. There are fine rose gardens, including one recently laid out in 18th-century style and filled with old shrub varieties: moss, damask and musk among them. It lies within an original walled garden of 11 acres which is famed for its Satyr Gate, flanked by colossal grinning heads. And 30 acres of informal woodland east of the house have been recently underplanted with rhododendrons, rare trees, shrubs and ground-cover.

Above all, honest daffodils confer a special radiance on Castle Howard. In spring they are everywhere, trumpeting stately fanfares of exuberance which recall the outrageous confidence of Vanbrugh himself, creator of this Yorkshire paradise.

HAVEN OF PEACE *The strains of political life were eased among the gentle terraced gardens of Chartwell (left), the home of Sir Winston Churchill. Here the great statesman spent his leisure hours painting, building pools, rockeries and walls. The fish pond, full of golden orfes, was his special delight, and here the fish still glide through untroubled waters.*

CHARTWELL *Kent*

Its name is inseparable from that of Sir Winston Churchill. The great statesman bought Chartwell and its 80 acres in 1922, moving in with his family two years later. And through the decades of triumph and disappointment which followed, it remained a haven of tranquillity. 'You could rest comfortably here', he once wrote to an ailing friend, inviting him to the house. 'Just vegetate as I do.'

In reality, Churchill scarcely idled in his retreat. When not preoccupied with affairs of state he wrote, he painted and besides spending £18,000 on improving the gabled Victorian house, he threw himself into garden-making with gusto. Bricklaying was a particular passion; Churchill was such an enthusiastic amateur that in 1928 he took out a card as an adult apprentice of the Amalgamated Union of Building Trade Workers.

Early on, three railway truckloads of Westmorland stone were brought to Chartwell to furnish his projects for the garden. During ten years out of office, from 1929 to 1939, Churchill 'built with my own hands a large part of the cottages and the extensive kitchen-garden walls, and made all kinds of rockeries and waterworks and a large swimming pool which was filtered to limpidity and could be heated to sup-

plement the fickle sunshine of an English summer'.

The house lies some 650 ft above sea level, near the head of a wooded valley sloping steeply to the south. Its green, terraced lawns command lovely views across to the Weald of Kent, while a clear spring – the Chart Well – feeds the pools and lakes. The fish pond was a particularly favoured spot, where the statesman loved to watch the gliding of his golden orfes. It has been said that the lakes below are a little obtrusive if measured against the highest standards of landscaping. Certainly, during the war, they made Chartwell so easy to identify from the air that they had to be covered with brushwood as protection against enemy pilots.

Some of the plantings were Sir Winston's choice. He ordered the trees for the orchard, for example, where the quinces, damsons and Kent cobnuts were among his favourites. But Lady Churchill contributed as much to the garden as her husband. Her taste was essentially for country simplicities; she created a rose garden and widely planted such 'cottage' shrubs as lavenders, fuchsias and potentillas. Buddleias were also established to attract butterflies, which her husband adored.

In addition, it was Lady Churchill who had the Marlborough Pavilion commissioned. This is a summerhouse, approached by a vine-covered loggia,

ENGINEERING MAGIC
Chatsworth found in Joseph Paxton (below) its own grand master of special effects. His illuminations kept Queen Victoria spellbound, and his conservatories were forerunners of his masterpiece – the Crystal Palace.

which is one of Chartwell's most attractive features. Plaques and friezes commemorate the achievements of the 1st Duke of Marlborough – Sir Winston's illustrious ancestor whose great estate at Blenheim presents such a marked contrast to Churchill's unobtrusive country retreat.

There is no Column of Victory at Chartwell. On the contrary, its associations are intimate, recalling above all the hobbies and pastimes of Britain's wartime leader. A white-flowering *Magnolia grandiflora*, for example, still grows by Sir Winston's bedroom window; he used to delight in its blooms, which featured in his canvasses. At Chartwell you come upon the gravestones of two favourite brown poodles and, near by, a croquet lawn where Churchill used to play with a casual single-handed style.

The most striking formal feature at Chartwell is the Golden Rose Garden, created not to commemorate a battle but a marriage. The garden was a present to Sir Winston and Lady Churchill from their children, and laid out in 1958 to celebrate their golden wedding anniversary. It lies in the original walled kitchen garden where much of the statesman's bricklaying can be seen. Yellow and gold rose varieties line a sloping walk with a sundial at its centre. 'Peace', 'Allgold' and 'Arthur Bell' are among the plantings, while the long beds are edged with drifts of blue catmint.

It was a gift appropriate to Chartwell. For the house was always a home, and the garden a union of tastes. Churchill himself once sketched his life story in the briefest of terms: 'I married and lived happily ever afterwards.'

CHATSWORTH *Derbyshire*

When Queen Victoria and Prince Albert visited Chatsworth House in 1843 they were treated to a fantastic display of illuminations. At night the garden's fountains and waterfalls, its great conservatories, and the River Derwent itself sparkled with multicoloured lights, so that the whole domain appeared a fairyland. The Duke of Wellington, accompanying the royal couple, was so dazzled by the display that he determined to find out how it had been achieved. Rising at dawn he scoured the garden to find the abandoned lanterns, charred grass where the fires had been, the debris left by the hundreds who had come to attend the entertainment.

He found nothing. The garden was as immaculate as if the display had never been. Joseph Paxton, head gardener and engineer of the entertainment, was ahead of him. He had arranged for gangs of workmen to toil all night to remove every trace of his efforts. Wellington was amazed: 'I should have liked that man of yours,' he told his host, the Duke of Devonshire, 'for one of my generals.'

The names of Chatsworth and Joseph Paxton are intimately associated. Remembered today chiefly for his design of the Crystal Palace, built in London to house the Great Exhibition of 1851, Paxton learned his architectural skills at Chatsworth. He was head gardener there from the age of 23, and it was from his work on the conservatories – more particularly his construction of a Lily House in 1850 – that he conceived his revolutionary plan for the Crystal Palace. An airy structure of wrought iron and glass, the great building housed the finest Victorian products.

The Lily House and Great Conservatory (so spacious that a horse and carriage could be driven through) were sadly demolished after the First World War. But there is much else at Chatsworth that recalls Paxton's hand. Charged with one of England's noblest country seats, he contributed a whole chapter in its history.

WELL-GROOMED PARKLAND

Chatsworth House lies on the banks of the River Derwent, in an area of well-groomed parkland once backed by what Daniel Defoe called the 'houling wilderness' of Derbyshire moorland. The dark moors have retreated from the vistas today, forced back by two centuries of landscaping. But they still formed a sombre frame for the estate when the first house was built in 1552, by Sir William Cavendish and his wife Elizabeth Hardwick.

Little remains of the Elizabethan gardens. A high, balustraded stone wall retaining the South Lawn is a vestige, and there is a Bower house and hilltop Hunting Tower. The 1st Duke of Devonshire (1641–1707) built the main block of the great house seen today, and it is from his time that the garden's main features date. There is, for example, a lovely fountain on the South Lawn, with sea-horses carved by Caius Cibber. A more sensational survival though is the great Cascade executed by the Frenchman M. Grillet.

The Cascade forms a glittering display against the hillside to the east of the house. Water streams over the domed roof of a temple at the top, gushing from ornate fountains to flow down a long, stepped ladder of falls. Daniel Defoe, who visited Chatsworth in 1724, provided a description which holds good today: 'out of the mouths of beasts, pipes, urns etc, a whole river descends the slope of a hill a quarter of a mile in length, over steps, with a terrible noise, and broken in appearance, till it is lost underground'.

Water – spouting, tumbling or flowing in the serene sweep of the river – supplies Chatsworth with many of its finest effects. The 4th Duke of Devonshire (1720–64) brought in Capability Brown to landscape the park in natural style. Several fountains installed by M. Grillet were obliterated, and the landscapist wrought his own tricks with water. Brown altered the bends on the river to improve the views, and selected a new site for a bridge to span its course (this was to be executed in fine style by the architect James Paine).

Many of the trees seen today on the south-west slopes of the park are original plantings by Brown. He brought the grassy parkland right up to the walls of the house, so that many formal features were lost. The Chatsworth gardens of today are chiefly the creation of the 6th Duke of Devonshire (1790–1858). It was he who discovered Paxton while the young man was working in the gardens of the Horticultural Society at Chiswick. Impressed by the youth's intelligence, the duke brought him back to Chatsworth to take charge of his Derbyshire seat, then in a state of neglect.

Paxton's ingenuity is everywhere evident. Though the Great Conservatory and Lily House have vanished, a range of glass cases positioned against the so-called Conservative Wall survive in testament to his architectural skill. Built by Paxton in 1848, they ride up the sloping ground as if on an elegant escalator. The large central case contains two rare *Camellia reticulata*, planted by Paxton, which have grown to a great size and provide a beautiful display in March and April.

At Chatsworth, Paxton had vast boulders moved to create romantic arrangements of rockwork; they include the Wellington Rock with its waterfall leading down to the Strid (an imitation of the famous narrows of Wharfedale). He established the fine pinetum and arboretum, sending expeditions to India and America to seek out new seeds and specimens. The seedling of an early Douglas pine came to Chatsworth in his hat; a weeping ash came from Derby fully grown and with so much soil round its roots that, it is said, turnpikes had to be removed along the route. It was in Paxton's Great Conservatory that the giant water lily of the Amazon (*Victoria regia*) first flowered in Britain and its size caused him to build the Lily House for it.

But among all Paxton's works, one sensational feature surpasses all. This is the Emperor Fountain, capable of playing its jet 260 ft from the long Canal Pool in the South Lawn. It was installed by Paxton in honour of a planned visit by Tsar Nicholas of Russia in 1844; a visit which ironically never took place. To provide the necessary water pressure, Paxton had to dig a lake 8 acres in area on the hills above. The miles of conduits, pipes and valves are Paxton's design and are still in excellent working order.

The Victoria lily still blooms at Chatsworth – in a new greenhouse completed in 1970. The estate is a living tradition whose recent features include a yew maze planted on the site of the Great Conservatory, a serpentine beech walk, and a living ground-plan of Chiswick Villa (the Devonshires' London residence) planted in low, clipped box at the West Front of the house. Chatsworth's splendours stretch back over four centuries, and the garden is not the creation of a single individual. Yet it remains the case, as the 7th Duke noted in his diary on Paxton's death in 1865, that 'there is no one whose name will be so permanently associated with Chatsworth as Paxton'.

LANDSCAPED MOORS *The River Derwent wends its way through verdant parkland – those Derbyshire moors now tamed by two centuries of landscaping. Even the bends in the river were redefined, by Capability Brown in the 18th century. The manmade waters of Chatsworth's Canal Pool stand out in rigid contrast, and Joseph Paxton's Emperor Fountain sends its pillar of white spray soaring 260 ft into the air. To the right, glimpsed through the trees, are the bronze-leaved curves of the serpentine beech walk, and the maze established on the site of Paxton's former conservatory.*

MELLOWED GRANDEUR *Steps of age-worn brick link the formal terraces of Chilham Castle, dropping away in level plateaus of green to the woodland beyond. The house was completed in 1616 by Sir Dudley Digges (below), Master of the Rolls to James I. Royal connections extended to the gardens, designed by John Tradescant – Royal Gardener to Charles I. The gentle formality of the Stuarts blends into parkland landscaped by Capability Brown in the 18th century.*

the ones that had the greatest attraction for our ancestors. There is angelica, for example, that was 'contrarie to all poysons', including the bite of mad dogs and serpents. Bluebells whose glue was used to set flighting feathers upon arrows and to make starch. Borage to dispel melancholy, comfrey to aid 'such as are bursten and that have broken the bone of the legge', and larkspur that could paralyse a snake in mid-strike.

CHILHAM CASTLE *Kent*

The lovely climbing *Wisteria sinensis* with its pendulous mauve racemes was first introduced to Britain from China in 1816. The examples at Chilham are among the oldest in the country, and grow against the red-brick walls of the Jacobean house with a magnificent Banks's rose (*Rosa banksiae*) which is 170 years old. Chilham's history is a long one, and the veteran trees, shrubs and climbers in the 36 acre garden are the key to its great attraction.

John Tradescant (d. 1637), Charles I's Royal Gardener, was responsible for the formal south terraces with their flights of brick steps dropping away from the house. And although the grounds were later landscaped with lake and ha-ha by Capability Brown, the 17th-century terraces survived.

A splendid holm oak rising from the west lawn holds pride of place among Chilham's aged trees. It is said to have been planted on the day of the house's completion, and its 350-year-old boughs are supported by chains around which the bark has grown. Black mulberry trees growing near the Rose Garden may be older still, having been estimated at as much as 500 years of age. They were certainly well established in the 17th century when a member of the Digges family was appointed governor of Virginia. He took cuttings of them to the New World, and it is from these that Mulberry Island, Virginia, takes its name.

Yews grown as topiaries frame the terrace vistas, lending a formal solemnity to the views. But they look down towards the lake across a Quiet Garden, informally planted as a little wood of beeches and limes. Although the trees make up much of Chilham's appeal, colour is not lacking. In spring, the Quiet Garden – like much of the woodland – becomes radiant with underplanted bulbs. And the terraces are lined with long flower borders where, in summer, old roses bask in the sunshine.

CHENIES MANOR *Buckinghamshire*

Just beyond the edge of hearing there is the tinkling of virginals or the pleasing sound of a lute. Or, if not, there should be. Elizabeth I stayed at the manor, sat beneath one of its oaks to watch the hunt go by and walked in its gardens. Sometimes, on early summer mornings, it would not seem impossible to see the short turf spring back from her step.

Neither Capability Brown nor any other improver ever laid hands upon the gardens at Chenies, which are purely Tudor and quite charming. The lawns have taken 400 years to achieve their velvet quality, and the stone flags that form most of the paths are worn by generations of pensive strollers. Here are yew walks and pleasaunces, a sundial, an ancient well and a sunken garden bordered by beds of old-fashioned flowers with sweet perfumes. It is approached by wide, shallow steps and its stone paths are guarded by low drums and mounds of box, with reinforcements of yew pompoms in the background. In the first days of the year there are snowdrops in the grass, in the spring fruit blossom and daffodils, and in the summer beds of roses edged with lobelia.

Chenies' most famous feature, however, is its Physic Garden, which embraces one of the most comprehensive collections of herbs in the country. There are plants from which perfumes are made, plants that yield dyes, herbs for cooking and herbs medicinal, many of which are still used in modern drugs.

But perhaps the most appealing plants – and certainly the ones best fitted to their background – are

CLAREMONT LANDSCAPE GARDEN *Surrey*

It is amazing what neglect can do to a garden. The 50 acre landscaped estate at Claremont in Surrey was described in 1727 as 'the noblest of any in Europe'. Four great names in English gardening history – Vanbrugh, Bridgeman, Kent and Brown – contributed to its evolution. Claremont's illustrious owners included Lord Clive of India, and its visitors the young Princess Victoria.

ARCHAEOLOGICAL FIND *The turf amphitheatre at Claremont – a strange conceit of early 18th-century garden design – is the sole survivor of its kind in Europe. Shrouded in trees as part of a later landscaping scheme, it lay hidden for over 200 years, only to be unearthed again during recent restoration work. Its curving lines followed those of a circular pool below, transformed years later into a lake by the great landscapist, William Kent.*

But from the 1920s the estate suffered decades of inattention. Garden architecture fell to ruin, and the landscaped lake silted up. Some trees succumbed to disease while others, unchecked, grew rampant. Even in 1949, when the National Trust took on the property, no funds were available to meet the scale of Claremont's needs. It was not until 1975, when the Slater Foundation presented a grant of £70,000, that thorough restoration could begin. Further grants and donations provided the sum in excess of £120,000 needed for the task.

Claremont was first laid out in 1715–26 for Thomas Pelham-Holles, Duke of Newcastle and twice prime minister. He commissioned Sir John Vanbrugh and his collaborator Charles Bridgeman to shape the estate, and their works are the oldest relics in the garden. Topping a knoll close to the house, for example, is Vanbrugh's fine Belvedere Tower. It stands proud at the head of an avenue leading from a bowling green – an area of dense overgrowth in 1975.

A much more surprising discovery was a 3 acre turf amphitheatre, designed by Bridgeman and situated above the lake. Stripped of its vegetation, it has survived as the sole example in Europe of this curious 18th-century fad. The amphitheatre was never intended to stage plays, but was gouged from the hillside entirely for visual effect.

The curved amphitheatre was originally designed to echo the shape of a formal round pond below. But the lake seen today is an informal water, naturalised by the pioneer landscapist William Kent. He was commissioned in the 1730s when neat symmetries were going out of fashion. In the lake he made a little island on which a flint-work pavilion was set up for picnics and fishing. By 1975 it was no more than an unroofed shell, and it proved the single most costly item to restore. It has since been fully refurbished, however, while the lake has been dredged and its margin strengthened with elm planking.

Winding woodland groves of beech, chestnut and yew survive from Kent's day, with a ha-ha which the landscapist created as a sunken barrier between the garden and the countryside beyond. Kent's Cascade, shaped as a stone bridge, has vanished however – it was replaced in the late 18th century with a naturalistic grotto. This was included, as in so many gardens of the period, to inspire a sense of mystery in the viewer.

Vanbrugh, Bridgeman and Kent all worked for the Duke of Newcastle. When he died in 1768, Claremont was bought by Lord Clive of India. The great soldier and administrator commissioned Capability Brown to demolish Vanbrugh's original house and replace it with the Palladian building seen today, which is now a school. Brown did not much change the garden, though, for Kent was his respected mentor. His chief alteration was to move the route of the old Portsmouth Road so that coaches and wagons no longer rumbled along the lake's edge.

In essence, Claremont remains a testament to 18th-century taste in garden making. A few new features, including the Camellia Terrace, were introduced from 1816, however, when the house served as a country residence for Prince Leopold of Saxe-Coburg, the uncle of the future Queen Victoria. As a young princess she would often visit Claremont and after her accession she returned frequently with Prince Albert and her family. 'It brings back recollections of the happiest days of my otherwise dull childhood', she once wrote.

CLIVEDEN *Buckinghamshire*

There are gardens which delight through diversity, and others in which one feature surpasses all. Cliveden belongs to the second category. Though its Buckinghamshire acres contain many attractions – temples, statuary and a fine water garden, for example – the famous view down to the Cliveden Reach of the Thames is a breathtaking centrepiece. It is, quite simply, one of the finest prospects in England. The diarist John Evelyn, who visited Cliveden in 1679, paid tribute to the terrace vistas, noting that they extended 'to the utmost verge of the horizon, which with the serpentining of the Thames is admirably surprising'.

The great terrace was the work of William Winde, who built the first house at Cliveden in 1666. His patron was George Villiers, 2nd Duke of Buckingham. The house itself underwent many later changes; it was twice destroyed by fire, and the present building dates only from 1850.

Cliveden today is associated chiefly with the Astor family, who acquired the property in 1893. William Waldorf, the 1st Lord Astor, did much to develop the gardens and had a particular fondness for the Italian manner. He disposed much classically styled statuary around the grounds and one colossal item greets you at the outset of a visit, as the entrance drive winds through a rhododendron valley. It is a Fountain of Love, executed in gleaming marble, with white life-size female figures attended by cupids all grouped around a vast scallop shell of Verona marble. From the monumental sculpture, a wide avenue of limes

PATTERNED PERSPECTIVES *Like some vast ceremonial carpet spread out to greet the Thames, the great terrace at Cliveden stretches in lawns and patterns of box through woodland to the river. Created in the 17th century, it has survived changes in fortune and taste.*

ROSE-FRAMED ANTIQUITIES *In a woodland clearing, Cliveden's rose garden drowns in the colour and fragrance of summer. Roses are gathered among the arches in island beds, and graceful statuary adorns the scented glade. William Waldorf, the 1st Lord Astor, looked to antiquity for his inspiration – he filled the gardens with monuments in the classical style.*

choice shrubs which enlivens the plot with colour. In spring, for example, the tender *Azara microphylla* of Chile scents the air with its clusters of yellow flowers; *Ribes speciosum*, the flowering currant of California, contributes bright scarlet, fuchsia-like blooms.

There are many pockets of colour at Cliveden, including a rose garden laid out in 1956 with unusual, irregular island beds. Perhaps the most surprising feature is a complex water garden complete with a pagoda. Primulas and irises edge the winding lakeside with azaleas, rhododendrons, magnolias, bamboos and weeping birches massed around. Tucked away in the north-east corner of the grounds, the watery area offers a delicate complement to the majesty of the Thames, flowing serene to the south.

COMPTON ACRES *Dorset*

This is a wilderness transfigured. Heather, bracken, gorse and pines – the rough mantle of Dorset heathland – clothed Compton Acres in Edwardian times. The house was built in 1914 to exploit the clifftop views over Poole Harbour. But it was not until after the First World War, when the late Thomas William Simpson bought the property, that a garden was made from the rugged bluff.

When the conversion came, though, it came on a grand scale. Heather slopes were gouged and terraced, vast tonnages of stone and soil imported. As the planning proceeded, fine bronzes, marbles and lead figures were brought in to adorn the garden; fountains began to spurt and subtropical plants to take root where the bracken and briars had been. The cost amounted to £220,000 (more than £2 million by present-day reckoning).

Mr Simpson's gardens are in essence those seen today. But there has been an irony in their evolution. No sooner did the extravagant estate start to take on an air of maturity than the Second World War intruded. The head gardener died, and his assistants were called up for service. Soon after the war the owner himself died. Compton Acres deteriorated to the condition of a shadowy jungle. It was left to Mr J. S. Beard, who bought the property in 1950, to reclaim the wilderness again.

Compton Acres was conceived as a living museum of garden styles. There are no fewer than nine separate gardens, each planned as a self-contained unit: Roman Garden, Italian Garden, Palm Court, Rock and Water Garden, Woodland and Subtropical Glen, English Garden, Heather Dell, Garden of Memory and Japanese Garden. They are separated by high banks and sunken paths, so that the transitions come suddenly upon you.

Following (as is wisest) the prescribed circuit, you first enter the Roman Garden. This is laid out as a shady, circular retreat with a miniature pool, old Italian carved stone seats and delightful lead statuettes. It is only a prelude, though, to a more spacious elegance. Fine wrought-iron gates and herbaceous borders backed by Purbeck stone give access to the Italian Garden, a grand formal set piece of colour and

extends to the yew-hedged forecourt; the approach is from the north and the Thames views come as a wonderful surprise when you reach the south front of the house.

Aged climbing plants bask in the sunshine of the terrace's retaining wall and immediately below is a second balustrade, equally handsome, which was brought by Lord Astor from the Villa Borghese in Rome. Beyond, spreads the great parterre lawn with its geometry of wedge-shaped beds delineated with box and santolina; it ends at a statue of Pluto and Proserpine, also brought from the Villa Borghese.

Down below there are woodland walks leading to the river, and paths which rise and fall among the tree-clad cliffs. One of these is of special interest. It leads by an Octagon Temple and War Memorial Garden to the celebrated Canning Oak. The tree is said to have been planted long before the Duke of Buckingham's time, and takes its name from the great statesman George Canning (1770–1827). He loved to loiter in the shade of the old oak, delighting in the views of the Thames framed by its boughs. And he was not alone in admiring them. Garibaldi, the Italian patriot, a guest at Cliveden in 1864, compared the views to 'some of the mightiest river prospects of South America'.

The path leads on to a grass-tiered open-air theatre where in 1740 the aria *Rule Britannia* was first performed. You pass by an 18th-century temple in Palladian style to another creation by Lord Astor. This is the Long Garden, whose central mown walk is flanked by statuary, box hedging and topiary. The mood is set by the pale stonework against green foliage, but a south-facing wall shelters a host of ornament combined. It bursts in full glory on the eye as you come through the stone entrance archway: a central lake in the shape of a cross, with carved stone fountains and water lilies.

At one end of the water is a Temple of Bacchus, at the other bronze figures of the famous Wrestlers of Herculaneum. Beds lining the edge are massed with colour according to the season. Spring tulips and forget-me-nots give way later to the blooms of summer annuals and roses. The 32 flanking columns of weathered Bath stone echo the seasonal transitions, being garlanded in spring with *Clematis montana*, and in summer with *C. × jackmanii*.

Terraces at the head of the pool lead to a long and narrow Palm Court, where more fine statuary may be seen. The centrepiece here is a magnificent Venetian wishing well carved four-square from a solid block of stone. The palm fronds in the paved setting confer a hot Mediterranean aura on the court, and you come at the end to a bronze, the Dying Spartan Soldier.

From the Palm Court a sloping path leads you into an entirely different habitat. Romantic views open up of a distant fern-edged waterfall, and as you approach the Rock and Water Garden the sound of running water is everywhere, gurgling and splashing from cascades to still pools. King carp of purplish hue glide beneath rustic bridges and among water lilies.

CHAIN OF LAKES

The waters eventually descend to a chain of lakes in the Woodland and Subtropical Glen. This narrow ravine (or 'chine' as it is called in Dorset) once offered a secret pathway for stocking-capped smugglers from Poole. Today, instead of contraband, it shelters a host of subtropical plants: bamboos, palms, mimosas, jacarandas, eucalyptuses and rhododendrons.

For really breathtaking vistas, however, the English Garden holds pride of place. Situated at the south-west front of the house, it looks out across the glittering sheet of Poole Harbour, flecked with the bobbing sails of yachts. Brownsea Island and its castle are beautifully delineated and, beyond, the eye travels to the ridge of the Purbeck Hills. It is a huge and exhilarating prospect, and the garden makes no attempt to compete. The well-groomed lawns extend, as it were, a green carpet of welcome to this one feature which no garden maker could import.

From the sweeping panorama of the English Garden you come to a charming Heather Dell where the harbour is seen only in tantalising glimpses. Near by is a small, circular Garden of Memory, laid out in 1956–7 to commemorate Mr Beard's son, killed in action during the Second World War, and his two daughters, both tragic victims of polio. From there, a winding path leads to the gate of Compton Acres' last great surprise: a complete Japanese Garden.

It is reputed to be unique in Europe for its authenticity. Designed by a Japanese architect, it was also assembled stone by stone entirely from articles brought from Japan. Granite pagodas, dragon gates, a stepped temple and imperial tea house framed by wisterias are among the most eye-catching garden

ornaments. The plants include Japanese varieties of azaleas, hydrangeas, lilies and aralias.

The centrepiece of the whole fantasy is a sunken lake with cascades, stepping-stones and bridges. Here and there, little carved animals peer out amid the surrounding flowers and shrubs. Each has its own mythological significance. There is, for example, a 'broken bridge' designed to trap evil spirits; a carved toad laughs at the deception. And if the perils of the water crossings were not evident enough, a signpost in English reads:

SINCE THE GARDENS WERE
OPENED IN 1952, 207 PEOPLE HAVE
FALLEN INTO THE POND
You have been warned

Important words of caution; but considering the attraction of exploring the limpid setting, it is scarcely surprising that they sometimes go unheeded. The figures are subject to constant revision.

ITALIAN BIAS *Of the nine distinct garden styles explored at Compton Acres, the Italian Garden demonstrates the most formal elegance of them all. Bold geometric shapes are defined in colour – the blue of the cruciform pond, the green of the grass, and the ever-changing hues of the bedding plants. In the foreground, the famous Wrestlers of Herculaneum are frozen in bronze, and in the distance the Temple of Bacchus completes this interpretation of Italian sophistication.*

COTEHELE *Cornwall*

The house at Cotehele, which is approached through a maze of high-banked Cornish lanes, is a beautiful example of a late medieval knightly dwelling. Though built in the reign of Henry VIII, its grey, granite walls and lancet windows recall the Gothic era. Cornwall under the Tudors was a backward region whose ruffian gentry kept alive the building styles – and the feuding ways – of the earlier years of the sword.

The house stands above the River Tamar, and its 10 acre gardens slope deep into the wooded valley. You enter by ancient sycamores grown to great height in the sea-cleansed air, while the spruces and larches rising from the valley slopes are so tall that their tops reach the same level as the house. These trees provide protection against that great scourge of West Country gardens – the Atlantic's sledgehammer gales.

Screened from the wind, Cotehele is favoured with a warm climate, high rainfall and a good, lime-free soil. The garden's most attractive area extends from the front of the house, where a series of terraces descend towards the valley below. They were laid out in the 19th century in simple strips of lawn and flower beds; two splendid magnolias (*M. × soulangiana* and *M. × s.* 'Rustica Rubra') are the real eye-catchers, blooming in springtime tumults of pinkish-white.

Below them the ground drops sharply to provide beautiful views across the valley. A spring-fed stream threads its way down a steep-sided glen in a series of pools and cascades edged with primulas, irises, hostas

INVASION FORCES *In the steep-sided glen below Cotehele a medieval dovecote (above) takes a beleagured stand among exotic shrubs, and the manor house of grey granite (opposite) braces itself against the advancing waves of daffodils.*

and lady ferns. To either side the glen is banked with exotics. There are azaleas and rhododendrons, for example, hydrangeas and enkianthuses. A particularly fine handkerchief tree (*Davidia involucrata*) is conspicuous in late spring, while autumn's colours are enriched by Japanese maples.

COTON MANOR *Northamptonshire*

Colour plays tricks in this 10 acre garden. You may glance at a planting of shell-pink azaleas, for example, and see a blur of the same hue detach itself from the mass to strut on delicate stilts across the lawn. Coton Manor's flamingoes seem to enjoy the deception, often lingering by the pink shrubs. And they are only a few of the feathered exquisites which roam freely around the lake and lawns.

The present house, near Ravensthorpe, was built in 1926 by Mr and Mrs Harold Bryant, incorporating a 17th-century farmhouse. For all the mellow Northamptonshire stonework, this was a real working farm at the time, and Mrs Bryant had a job on her hands to shape a garden from it. Haystacks, for example, had to be removed from the old kitchen garden to make the rose garden seen today. An existing farm pond was reshaped to make the formal rectangular lake, and trees were established both for shelter and ornament. A large, flowering cherry (*Prunus* 'Kanzan') by the lake is one springtime eyecatcher which dates from the initial planting. There is also an especially fine tulip tree (*Liriodendron tulipifera*) and an unusual black walnut (*Juglans nigra*), planted in 1926.

Like so many gardens in Britain, Coton Manor suffered inevitable deterioration during the Second World War, and needed much restoration afterwards. Commander and Mrs Pasley-Tyler (daughter of the garden's creators) took up residence in 1950. And, almost immediately, the manor acquired the first of its winged ornaments.

Birds were originally introduced for purely practical reasons. In summer, the main pond used to become choked with algae, and a brace of black East Indies ducks was brought in as a remedy. It worked: the waters cleared and the feeders proved attractive features in themselves. Thereafter the owners introduced more unusual fowl: grey West African cranes, for example, and Caribbean and Chilean flamingoes. Today, black swans, blue macaws and emerald-green parrots are among other exotics on display.

The birds, however, are only one feature of a garden which delights entirely for itself. The overall design includes the rose garden, terraces, herbaceous borders, conservatory and wild garden. All are maintained at a high standard, which bears tribute to the energy of the owners.

Particular attention has been devoted to offering interest in late summer and autumn. Grey and silver-leaved plants abound, while brighter splashes are provided by late-flowering varieties: mauve-coloured asters and the scarlet Cape figwort (*Phygelius capensis*), Chinese monkshood (*Aconitum wilsonii*) and the oriental saxifrage (*Saxifraga fortunei*). Among the

CLIMATE CONTROL *A colossal screen, made up of 7 million trees, was erected at Cragside against the searing destruction of the east winds. Lord Armstrong (above), arms manufacturer and inventor, devised this protected micro-climate for his Northumberland retreat in the 19th century. Now rhododendrons and azaleas run wild over land reclaimed from the moors. Foxgloves make the most of the sheltered woods, clinging to rocky slopes below the many-gabled house (opposite).*

rarer plantings are yellow Korean waxbells (*Kirengeshoma koreana*), which grow here with their better-known Japanese cousins (*K. palmata*).

CRAGSIDE *Northumberland*

You can create a micro-climate with trees, planting them for shelter against cold winds or as shade against burning summer sunshine. The trick is worked in countless modest gardens throughout the country. And Lord Armstrong, the 19th-century industrial magnate, achieved the same effect when he planted out his estate at Cragside in Northumberland. The scale, though, was hardly modest: in a property of 1,700 acres he had over 7 million trees planted to make woods where bare moorlands had been.

Lord Armstrong was a giant in his day: inventor, engineer and the leading arms manufacturer in England. Yet he was also a lover of nature who had walked the rugged hills and loitered by the clear brooks of Upper Coquetdale as a boy. Untamed, the landscape has a sullen beauty, wooded only sparsely in the dips in the moorland and whipped by winds which seem to blow in straight from the Russian steppes. Armstrong bought the land at Cragside in 1863, to make himself a retreat; the architect Richard Norman Shaw designed the vast gabled house which presents such a striking silhouette today, perched on its craggy slope above the Debdon Burn.

Nine-hundred acres of the original estate have survived as a country park today. It is not a garden in the conventional sense, but more of a wilderness clothed. Amid its dramatic natural assets of cliffs, gorges and fern-edged falls, Lord Armstrong planted his trees, dammed streams to make lakes, and laid out 40 miles of carriageways and walks.

The trees, of course, are of special interest. Chiefly conifers, they are grown now to great height and include many titans of 150 ft or more. Among them, the great firs of western North America are well represented: the giant fir, noble fir, Douglas fir and Californian red fir. There are many other conifers to admire – hemlocks, pines, spruces and sequoias – as well as native oaks, beeches and yews. And in the cool, acid soil of Cragside, rhododendrons and azaleas have run riot, making June the high period for colour.

CRANBORNE MANOR *Dorset*

A firm rule is observed in the wilder garden areas of Cranborne Manor: no mowing before the last week of July. Beneath the old beeches and fruit trees, wild flowers are allowed to multiply in their thousands: narcissi, cowslips, primroses, anemones, fritillaries and orchids. All contribute a springtime exuberance in this 12 acre chalkland garden.

The original stone manor at Cranborne was built in 1207 as a hunting lodge for King John. Renovated in Tudor times, the house passed in 1612 to Robert Cecil, 1st Earl of Salisbury. The Cecil family have held the manor ever since. And though it suffered damage during the Civil War and neglect in the 18th century,

the house and its garden were restored in Victorian times, when a road was even rerouted so as to avoid the brick-built gatehouses at the entrance.

You enter today into a cobbled court overlooked by Jacobean towers. Though the flower beds and cobbling are recent introductions, this and other formal courts around the house derive from designs made by John Tradescant the elder in the early 17th century. Some ancient beeches and limes also survive from his original avenues, while there is a particularly interesting relic in the Jacobean Mount Garden to the west. Such points of elevation were common features of 17th-century gardens, and included to provide views over the owner's estate. At Cranborne, the mount looks out to an encircling ridge of wooded chalk hills.

The garden is watered by the little River Crane, from which Cranborne takes its name. Carving its course to the north of the house, it is a winterbourne, and dries out in summer. For about seven months of the year it runs through a stone channel broken with pools and cascades. The present Marquis and Marchioness of Salisbury were responsible for this and many other improvements. In the flower beds, for example, they had the hard chalk foundation broken to a depth of some 3 ft so that plants can root more easily. The result has been seen in more luxuriant growth; a walled White Garden in the North Court, for instance, has flourished particularly well. Conspicuous among its pale delights are large examples of *Daphne blagayana*, a spring-flowering evergreen bearing fragrant blooms in great creamy clusters.

Other new attractions include a colourful Elizabethan knot garden and a herb garden enclosed by high yew hedges. In this aromatic plot, roses and other scented flowers grow among the herbs to provide delicate miscellanies of fragrance. In the East Garden, apple trees grow in all shapes and sizes.

A rose pergola and avenues of beeches and pleached limes are among the other attractions of this very English garden. Until recently, Cranborne also contained an avenue of Cornish elms which featured in the film *Tom Jones*. They were lost, sadly, to the scourge of Dutch elm disease, and have been replaced with stripling London planes. But Cranborne survives with its charm intact.

CRATHES CASTLE *Grampian*

It would be difficult to find a more romantic background to a garden. The pale walls of Crathes Castle simply soar against the skyline to a miraculous crown of corbelled stonework and overhung turrets. This is one of Scotland's most beautiful fairytale castles – and it is authentic, too. Alexander Burnett, 9th Laird of Leys, began the building in 1553 and it was completed by 1594. His family occupy the castle still.

Titanic yew hedges planted in 1702 set the tone of the gardens seen today. Nine feet high and as much in width, they are kept trimmed with surgical precision. Though little is known of the 18th-century garden, the yews alone indicate that it was formally laid out. And it seems to have been well tended.

The north-east is known as Scotland's 'cold shoulder', and is exposed to cruel easterlies and vicious frosts. They can make gardening as much an act of defiance as of creation. But if Crathes' climate is not favourable, the soil is a good loam and a screen of great trees offers a degree of protection. Some potential for gardening was there when Major-General Sir James and Lady Burnett of Leys took up residence in 1926.

Each had a special interest: he was an enthusiast for rare trees and shrubs, while she had an artist's instinct for design and colour associations. Though their mixed aspirations sometimes led to friendly skirmishing, an extraordinary harmony resulted.

The garden at Crathes extends down a broad southeast slope beginning right under the castle walls. The Burnetts laid it out as a series of rectangular plots, which incorporate the great yew hedges as dividers.

Undoubtedly Lady Burnett's most famous conception is the White Border situated in the Lower Garden below the yews, which you come upon after entering along an avenue of limes. The backdrop is a clipped hedge of purple plum (*Prunus cerasifera* 'Atropurpurea'), and grouped in the long mixed border you find a host of showy exquisites including: white roses, white phloxes, white delphiniums, the fragrant *Philadelphus microphyllus* and the feathery *Cimicifuga racemosa*. But the border is not wholly white. It includes grey-leaved hostas, silver-leaved *Salix lanata* and the blue globe thistle (*Echinops humilis*).

A fine old Portugal laurel (*Prunus lusitanica*), clipped to toadstool shape, stands at the centre of the Lower Garden and from it the borders radiate. Apart from the White Border, a June Border is particularly notable. It has a summery exuberance, gaily flecked with the colour of lupins, poppies and bearded irises.

The compartments divided by the borders and paths each have a character of their own. There is a Camel Garden, for example (named after two raised island beds in the middle), and a Trough Garden

SUMMER FAIRYTALE *Taken straight from the pages of some tale of enchantment, the pale walls of Crathes Castle (above) rise behind the flower-spangled dream world of the June Border.*

CHALKLAND IN BLOOM *King John once had a hunting lodge at Cranborne (opposite), but since 1603 the estate has belonged to the family of the 1st Earl of Salisbury. Now his descendants coax luxurious blooms from the hard chalk, in walled gardens overlooked by the Jacobean manor house.*

RURAL RIDE *Deep in his book, the Travelling Chinese Philosopher rides for ever past the south front of Dyffryn House. If he and his ox could move, it would take them more than two hours to make a full tour of the many beautiful gardens on the 50 acre estate. The philosopher is one of four fine oriental bronzes presented to Dyffryn by the Hon. Grenville Morgan.*

whose central stone trough is overhung by a shapely *Prunus serrula*. The most recent feature is a Golden Garden conceived by Lady Burnett but not begun until 1970, after her death.

Lady Burnett's themes and designs might be thought ample reason to visit Crathes. But for the connoisseur of rarities, Sir James's contribution adds an extra dimension of fascination. As a soldier he had travelled widely in the Far East and brought a taste for exotic specimens to the garden. The official guide gives pride of place to a very rare *Staphylea holocarpa* 'Rosea' which grows in the Double Shrub Border in the Lower Garden. This is an exceptionally lovely tree which blooms with deep pink flowers in May.

On the higher level is an elegant Pool Garden laid out by Lady Burnett in 1932. While the pond itself is framed by L-shaped hedges and beds, a broad border is picked out in, for example, the red *Papaver commutatum*, deep purple *Cotinus coggygria* 'Atro-purpureus' and the golden marjoram (*Origanum vulgare* 'Aureum'). Two exceptional honeysuckles lend their yellows: *Lonicera tragophylla* from Western China and *L. splendida* from Spain.

DYFFRYN *South Glamorgan*

It was once described as being among Wales's 'best kept secrets'. Barely 3 miles from the edge of Cardiff, Dyffryn House, which wears a sober, ambassadorial air, is maintained as a conference centre. It also has some 50 acres of garden in almost every style imaginable and its attractions are being extended and improved all the time.

The present house was begun in 1893 by John Cory, a prominent businessman and philanthropist. His son Reginald was chiefly responsible for the garden's design, in which he was assisted by the landscape architect Thomas Mawson. The essential features were established between 1900 and 1915, when many fine trees and shrubs were introduced. Reginald Cory was a keen horticulturalist, who not only helped to finance several plant-collecting expeditions but also took part in some of them himself. In 1937 Dyffryn was bought by Sir Cenydd Traherne, who later presented it to the Glamorgan County Council. It is now administered by the counties of Mid Glamorgan and South Glamorgan.

One of the more recent additions is seen at the start

of the prescribed tour. It is the splendid Palm House, 150 ft long by 50 ft high. Within its airy framework of red cedar and glass grow a host of tropical and temperate exotics, from agricultural crop plants such as bananas, cocoa trees and pineapples to the pure luxury of cool house orchids.

To appreciate the diversity of Dyffryn's attractions you have only to explore the West Garden area. Here you come upon a whole complex of gardens within a garden. There is, for example, a double herbaceous border 85 yds long and massed with 130 groups of perennials. To one side is a paved court with balustrade and trickle fountain; to the other a rose garden containing 2,000 plants: hybrid teas, floribundas and a galaxy of species roses. A Roman garden with colonnades and fountain pool offers restful elegance at any time of year; for autumn colour there is a rotunda massed with fuchsias. Add 250 ft of glass planthouses where orchids, cacti and gesneriads, such as gloxinias and African violets, flourish and you have a bewildering jigsaw of plots in this one area alone.

Dyffryn is currently being developed as a botanic garden, with plants arranged and labelled for ease of study. But it is a magnet, too, for effects achieved purely to delight the eye. Drawing over 40,000 visitors a year, the gardens have become a major tourist attraction; Dyffryn's 'secret' is out.

ELVASTON CASTLE *Derbyshire*

South Derbyshire does not possess the rugged skylines for which the Peak District to the north is renowned. Watered by the rivers Dove, Trent and Derwent in their lazier moods, the terrain is remarkably level in places – and Elvaston is one of them. The grounds of Elvaston Castle quite defeated Capability Brown when he was asked to landscape them; he refused the commission because 'the place is so flat, and there is such a want of capability in it'.

The neo-Gothic castle was styled on an existing manor house for the 3rd Earl of Harrington. It was his invitation that Capability Brown turned down. But though the landscapist baulked at the proposition, he did present the earl with six cedars of Lebanon by way of compensation. They were planted to the east of the house where they still grow today.

It was Charles Stanhope, the 4th Earl of Harrington, who supervised the creation of a landscape. A famous dandy and eccentric, he brought in a talented young Edinburgh gardener named William Barron to shape his 200 flat acres. The work began in 1830, and the two men laboured in partnership until the earl's death in 1851. Throughout that period, the gardens were closed to visitors. The earl's instructions were, 'if the Queen comes, Barron, show her round but admit no one else'.

If the flat horizon does not intrude today it is a tribute to Barron's energy and ingenuity. To create interest in the level terrain he employed a variety of devices. North of the house, for example, he created a lake backed by masses of artificial rockwork. To the south he laid out long, formal vistas leading to the

stately Golden Gate (brought from Versailles by the 3rd Earl). Barron introduced topiaries, informal lawns and small gardens bounded by tall hedges. Above all he brought the trees which form such a feature of what is seen today.

Like so many of his Victorian contemporaries, Barron especially favoured conifers and evergreens: pines, yews, cedars and monkey puzzles abound, and there is an especially varied selection of hollies. Many of the trees were transplanted fully grown, using tree-lifting vehicles of his own devising. Some were real rarities brought from far afield. It was at Elvaston, for example, the first Caucasian fir (*Abies nordmanniana*) was planted in England.

The grounds suffered serious neglect during the present century, but they have been well managed as a country park since 1969. Careful tree surgery, for

example, has saved many an imperilled specimen, while new features include the Rhododendron Dell and an Old English Garden with herbaceous borders, rose garden and herb garden. In front of the house, a formal parterre in dwarf box was established in 1970. It is already coming into its own, spreading before the south front like a great patterned carpet with outlandish topiaries looming around. Elvaston, in short, is entering a second age of magnificence – not bad for a garden without 'capability'.

EXBURY *Hampshire*

To the general public the Rothschild name means wealth; but to connoisseurs of rhododendrons it has a more specific significance. Rothschild means Exbury – and a wealth of rhododendron hybrids and species without parallel in Britain.

In 20 years of gardening at his Hampshire estate, Lionel de Rothschild created over 1,200 rhododendron and azalea hybrids. The Exbury strain of azaleas in particular is famed the world over, and for specialists a visit to the garden is akin to an act of pilgrimage.

DWARFS AND GIANTS *Swelling topiaries, like giant mushrooms, mark the boundary of the formal parterre which spreads out before Elvaston Castle like a great patterned carpet. The design of the parterre is drawn with closely clipped dwarf box.*

GREEN TOUCH *Lionel de Rothschild (above) devoted his share of the family genius to creating a new form of wealth. On 250 acres of acid loam overlooking the Solent he fashioned one of the most sumptuous gardens in Britain (right), much of it stocked with new varieties of plants that he developed himself.*

To those with no more than a casual interest it is equally rewarding. In springtime, Exbury's 250 acres are upholstered with unimaginable beauty.

Lionel de Rothschild acquired the Hampshire estate in 1919. Situated by the Beaulieu River among woodlands of oak, beech and pine, Exbury enjoys the temperate climate of the Channel coast. Its soil is a very acid loam in which lime-loving plants perish all too easily. Even roses take some coaxing to produce a decent display. But the rhododendron and its relation the azalea root with glee, and these were Lionel de Rothschild's passion.

Over a period of ten years an army of 150 men laboured to create a woodland paradise. Some 20 miles of piping were laid down to conduct water to every nook in the garden, so that the soil remained cool and moist. A railway was even constructed to bring sandstone blocks for a rock garden in which, it is said, each stone was individually sited by the owner. The soil, meanwhile, was dug to prepare for the exotics, and rare trees were planted.

As for the rhododendrons, Lionel de Rothschild financed expeditions to the remotest Himalayas to extend the stock of known species. And at Exbury itself he had 3 acres of greenhouses built together with laboratories for hybridisation. He kept in close contact with other enthusiasts too; if a new plant were raised elsewhere in Britain, a car would be sent speeding off for an envelope of pollen. When 'Mr Lionel' died in 1942, his eldest son Edmund continued to experiment and to develop the garden.

PAGEANT OF COLOUR

The pageant of colour unfolds at Exbury between spring and early summer. And despite the vast range of specimens their arrangement is informal. A maze of paths winds among woods and glades, which divide into three general areas.

Yardwood to the north has an abundance of yews (which were even mentioned in the Domesday Book). The focus of interest here is the great rock garden, planted with dwarf rhododendrons and other rock-hugging plants. Witcher's Wood, the central area, has a long, curving path lined by the lovely 'Lady Chamberlain' rhododendron. The hybrid was raised at Exbury and blooms in late May in shades of apricot-pink.

Home Wood to the south is the third and perhaps the most fascinating area, where Exbury's hybrids are especially concentrated. It centres on a chain of ponds and a magnificent display of the deciduous azaleas for which the garden is also famed. Parented by the old Ghent azalea and the bright orange *R. calendulaceum*, the Exbury hybrids make up a gaudy clan. Often deliciously scented, they bloom in a wide range of colours: the orange 'Sunte Nectarine', white 'Oxydol', golden-yellow 'Edwina Mountbatten' and salmon-pink 'Cecile' are just a few of the exquisites.

The largest of the pools is edged with candelabra primulas and hung with the white *Wisteria venusta*, while bamboos, pieris and the feathery swamp cypress (*Taxodium distichum*) provide a diversity of foliage and form. The main crossroads of paths in

ROYAL SHELTER *No longer needed to protect the kings of Scotland, the palace wall at Falkland now shelters a fine herbaceous border. At the same time it has become a support for roses, ivy and other climbers, while the mortar between its stones provides a foothold for pinks, mints and other small perennials.*

Home Wood is marked by a planting of one of the best known Rothschild rhododendrons: the magnificent 'Crest' with its May-flowering trusses of luminous yellow.

The plant has an interesting history. Lionel de Rothschild made several crosses between its parents *R. wardii* and *R.* 'Lady Bessborough'; they are known as the Hawk Group, and shortly before the war he offered a pan of seedlings to his friends. Naturally enough, they took the largest and healthiest-looking ones. Of the few that were left over, only the very smallest was planted out at Exbury. It did not, in fact, flower until after the war, by which time its creator had died; but it caused a sensation as one of the best yellows available at the time.

Exbury also boasts magnificent examples of the ancestral species gathered from China and the Himalayas: the giant *R. sinogrande*, for example, the blue *R. augustinii*, the lucent yellow *R. campylocarpum* and *R. concatenans* of Tibet whose leaves have the fragrance of incense. Lionel de Rothschild was a fervent supporter of the pioneer collectors; he was himself in China in 1930, and arranged for the burial of George Forrest when the latter died in the field.

There is more to enjoy at Exbury than the rhododendrons alone. Camellias and magnolias – also lovers of acid soil – are represented by some beautiful specimens, and down by the river there are daffodil meadows which contribute an exuberance all of their own. Out of the main flowering season, March to June, Exbury does not entirely languish. Autumn's muted tones are enlivened by the scarlet glow of Japanese maples and the vivid pearls of many berried shrubs. But the rhododendron family, unquestionably, is sovereign in these Hampshire acres, and their dynasty is ever expanding.

FALKLAND PALACE *Fife*

Falkland Palace has always been a place of recreation – principally as a hunting lodge of the royal Stuarts. But it also offered other relaxations – its royal tennis court, built for James V in 1539, is the oldest in Britain, and it seems that there was always a garden to enjoy too. A plot was certainly established in 1456, when the records note that a gardener's wages were paid, then withdrawn as undeserved. Did the palace gardeners idle as much as their royal patrons, or were the Stuarts especially hard taskmasters? One or the other seems to have been the case, for in 1484 it was stated that no more wages would be paid unless the king's table was kept supplied with fruit.

The garden clearly underwent changes over the years. Great stone walls, for example, were built in 1513, and a note on work in progress for 1628 included 'planting and contriving the garden anew'. But what visitors see today is something contrived much more recently than that. During the Second World War – for all its pedigree – the garden was farmed for potatoes as part of the Dig for Victory campaign. Afterwards, when the noted landscape architect Percy Cane was brought in, he had the barest of canvasses to work with.

Cane achieved a harmony of new and traditional features, using an old engraving of the garden only for general guidance. A great lawn, for example, still occupies the central area as in the days when James V used to practise archery at 'the lang butts' on it. But where clumps of trees had been, Cane laid out a series of half-moon island beds. Massed with shrubs and perennials, they define a perimeter walk and offer vivid foreground frames for the East Range of the palace. Here and there, carefully placed trees lead the eye up to the dramatic stonework: columnar cypresses provide the main vertical accents, while Japanese cherries, maples and laburnums offer colour.

Around the main lawn there are in addition three particularly good herbaceous borders. One is devoted largely to lupins and irises; another to the pastel blues, pinks and whites of delphiniums, erigerons and salvias. The third or Great Border runs along the east wall for almost 200 yds.

Red and yellow are the colours of the Stuart livery. They are formally massed in the floribundas of a rose garden to the west of the main lawn area. Woods and orchards stretch away beyond, while north of the lawn is a hedged water garden. This is a fairly recent feature, laid out by the National Trust with a rectangular lily pool as its centrepiece. The royal tennis court near by is, of course, much more ancient: older still are the Lomond hills, looming overall.

FELBRIGG HALL *Norfolk*

The North Sea is little more than a mile away from this Jacobean house, but a great wood of 600 acres screens it from coastal winds. The trees were first planted in the late 17th century, and many oaks and sweet chestnuts have survived from that time. By the hall is an orangery of 1705, and the large old camellias inside still give fine displays from April to June. In short, much at Felbrigg speaks of a settled peace, recalling the hall's slow evolution over hundreds of years in the hands of the Windham family.

In 1969 the property was bequeathed to the National Trust, which has preserved its tranquil aura. An 18th-century walled garden of 2½ acres is an especially interesting feature. It has recently been restored as a 'potager', or formal kitchen garden, which once served the hall with fruit, vegetables, herbs and cut flowers. Divided by high walls into three sections, it originally required a vast garden staff

to meet its needs. There is, for example, a large octagonal dovecote of the 1750s which alone must have presented problems of maintenance.

Today, over half a mile of box hedging lines the paths in the walled garden. Many fruit trees are grown against the walls in traditional fashion: figs, peaches, plums and nectarines, for example. Grapes flourish in a greenhouse, and even a grapefruit tree crops.

But the great vegetable beds have largely disappeared. Instead, the walled garden contains a wealth of flowers and shrubs selected for colour and fragrance. In spring, for example, cool blues, mauves and whites are conspicuous: there are hyacinths, ceanothuses and a fine selection of lilacs. Two large rectangular plots contain 26 different species of hawthorn, while roses, paeonies, phloxes, buddleias, carpentarias and romneyas all flower according to season. Autumn holds a special attraction – and not only for its ripening fruits. The margins of the shrub borders are adrift with *Colchicum tenorii*, a rare autumn crocus which blooms in thousands.

CHANGED TIMES *A cluster of forcing pots beside the rhubarb patch is a reminder of the great days of the kitchen garden at Felbrigg Hall. Then, tended by a small army of gardeners, it supplied the hall with vegetables, herbs, fruit and flowers – not to mention fresh meat from the octagonal dovecote. Its warm walls still shelter fruit trees, but most of its 2½ acres is now given over to flowers and shrubs.*

NOT SO SMALL *A stepping-stone path which leads through the heather to a roof of thatch, belies the scale of the gardens at Furzey. There are 8 acres in all, including a water garden, a fernery and many fine borders of flowers and shrubs which give colour for much of the year.*

FURZEY HOUSE *Hampshire*

The name holds promise of rustic charm, enhanced by the Tudor thatched cottage in the garden. Not that the main house is old, it dates only from 1922 when three brothers Dalrymple acquired the property. But they built low and roofed their new house with thatch in keeping with the character of the cottage. And the grounds were 'furzey' indeed at the time, comprising 8 acres of rough gorse pastureland.

Today, Furzey House gardens remain pleasingly informal in layout. Grassy paths meander among trees and rough-mown glades; no pesticides are used, and wild flowers seed themselves in abundance. In spring, bluebells spread in dappled sheets under the New Forest oaks, while narcissi thrive under the pale birches.

The gorse waste has gone though. Two of the brothers were skilled gardeners: while Hew Dalrymple was chiefly responsible for Furzey itself, Bay Dalrymple founded the well-known Bartley Nurseries near by. Hybrids developed there may be seen not only at Furzey House, but also in gardens throughout the country. The lilac-flushed broom, *Cytisus* 'Minstead' is one example; another is the pink candelabra primula *P. pulverulenta* 'Bartley Strain'.

At Furzey House, tons of good soil were brought in to leaven the New Forest clay and permit a wide range of choice plants to take root. From April to June, massed banks of azaleas provide vivid drifts of colour. Come in late May and you find the gardens glowing with the scarlet of the Chilean fire bush (*Embothrium coccineum*), more widely planted here than anywhere else in the country. In late summer there are four different varieties of eucryphia to admire; two examples of the evergreen hybrid *E.* × *nymansensis* are nearly 50 ft high, fragrant white-flowering giants which bear their blooms into early autumn. Then, when the leaves turn under October skies, a host of fiery foliage plants come into their own: amelanchiers, enkianthuses, liquidambars, disanthuses and others.

Even in winter there is much to fascinate the eye. Furzey contains one of the biggest heather gardens in the country; the hybrid *Erica* 'Furzey' was developed here and is among the winter-flowering varieties on display. In the doom-days of February the little *Rhododendron moupinense* of Western China may sometimes be seen blooming among the jasmines and snowdrops, a rarity far from its Szechwan home.

A fernery and water garden are among the most recent features, and the abundance of primulas in this area renews the colour cycle from early spring. Despite its impression of informality, Furzey is a place of intense interest and captivates all the year round.

GREAT DIXTER *East Sussex*

A roofscape of tile-hung gables, tall brick chimneys and oasthouse towers overlooks these five Sussex acres. The 15th-century house and its outbuildings are famous for their restoration by the architect Sir Edwin Lutyens, who worked at Great Dixter from 1910 to 1914. He also designed the surrounding gardens, laying them out in different compartments and so helping to establish a now much emulated style.

But though Lutyens structured the spaces, he did not furnish them. The plantings were undertaken by the owner, Nathaniel Lloyd, who had his own ideas about gardening. Lutyens, for example, envisaged that the compartments should be walled with brick; the owner preferred yew hedging. In the end, a happy compromise evolved: both materials were used as dividers, while the old barns, sheds and oasthouses provided further screening and shelter.

Great Dixter today remains a tribute to the Lloyd family's talents for gardening. When the owner died, his wife continued his work and remained active with her trowel until her 91st year. She died in 1972, and it is to their son Christopher Lloyd, an eminent writer on gardening, to whom Great Dixter owes its present standard of excellence.

'Excellence' might not seem the appropriate word when you first arrive at the entrance. The house stands on the High Weald, about 180 ft above sea level, and there is no smooth baize carpet of welcome. You approach, on the contrary, by the roughest of lawns which looks frankly unkempt at first glance. Look again and you notice a haze of colours; this is a wild

meadow garden, studded in spring with fritillaries, narcissi and native orchids. Clovers and moon daisies succeed before the first mowing and, by September, autumn crocuses and cyclamens take their place.

The essay in wild gardening was begun by Mrs Lloyd and has been continued by her son. It is not to every visitor's taste, as Christopher Lloyd has readily conceded, though conservationists acclaim it. But there is nothing controversial about the garden 'rooms' you enter next – their decor is maintained to an exceptional standard.

Within the sound formal design, the plantings are informally luxuriant. No battalions of flowers assault the eye; every harmony has been thoughtfully contrived. The great showpiece is the Long Border, its main section 70 yds in length and 15 yds deep, backed by a stretch of yew hedging. It is a truly mixed border, with many shrubs and even small trees mingling with the herbaceous subjects. Here, for example, a white-flowering escallonia catches the eye amid purple salvias and glowing mats of ruby sedums. There, golden clouds of Mount Etna broom billow over a red pillar rose. Tamarisks and gleditsias, hostas, phloxes and asters, ornamental grasses, silver-leaved plants,

JOINT EFFORT *The architect Sir Edwin Lutyens (below) was responsible for the restoration of the house and most of the garden design at Great Dixter. But the sunken garden (above), with its octagonal pool, was designed by the owner of the house, Nathaniel Lloyd.*

wands of colour, spangled drifts – all surge and lap in brimming promontories down to the York stone path. Though the climax of the display comes in midsummer, choice plantings extend it from April to November. The Long Border has a long season to match.

This richness and variety is characteristic of the plantings throughout Great Dixter's compartments. There is, for example, a large sunken pool garden whose formal design is softened by a wealth of unusual plants spilling from raised borders and growing against the walls. The fuchsias, for example, are familiar enough in form, but here, too, you may notice a strange climber scrambling up the tiled roof of an overlooking barn: it is the rarely seen red-berried *Schisandra grandiflora rubriflora*.

There are 18 garden 'rooms' at Great Dixter, each with its own special character. Among the most memorable are a beautiful rose garden stocked with fragrant old Bourbons; and a topiary enclosure where 18 birds have been sculpted from yew. They make a curious flock, perched on their green cones, and have grown plump since Nathaniel Lloyd first shaped them. The old kitchen gardens are now given over largely to ornamental plants, though espaliered pears still line the paths. They are entwined now by many varieties of clematis, a favourite plant of the owner, which is grown elsewhere around wooden pillars.

Hydrangeas are another speciality of the garden: they seem to relish its fairly heavy clay. Great Dixter is remarkable, too, for the number of annuals which feature in its thickly planted borders. The business of sowing, pricking out and planting is an arduous one, but cheerfully undertaken by the owner. And the rewards are everywhere evident. Besides generous plantings of stocks, mignonettes and nasturtiums the garden is graced by such delicate subjects as pale cleomes and bright Mexican sunflowers (*Tithonias*). Biennial foxgloves and sweet williams take their place in the borders. The very impermanence of these and other delights is an advantage to the true enthusiast. Colour harmonies can be subtly altered year by year, and new tones added to the palette.

Of course, it takes effort – which is why so many modern gardens lean heavily on labour-saving shrubs and perennials. But as Christopher Lloyd has written: 'Effort is only troublesome when you are bored'.

HADDON HALL *Derbyshire*

If any garden distils the romance of the rose it must be Haddon Hall's. The house is one of the finest to survive from the Middle Ages, and in high summer England's favourite flower bursts on the eye in dreamy profusions of blooms. The garden offers more than a visual experience. Those cloudy fantasies of colour drifting against the mellow stonework tug deep at the inner emotions, as if emblematic of time and beauty combined.

'A good old house, all built of stone', was how one 17th-century visitor described the hall. It stands on a slope above a curve of the Derbyshire Wye and, dating

back to the time of the Tudors and beyond, is built of the same dove-grey limestone as its escarpment. If Haddon is wedded to the landscape, it is also wedded to romance. The Manners family have held Haddon Hall since 1567, the Vernons occupying it before them. And a fittingly picturesque legend surrounds the transference of the property. It is said that around 1563 Dorothy Vernon, heiress of Sir George Vernon, owner of the hall, eloped with John Manners, son of the Earl of Rutland. She escaped, so tradition alleges, by an old packhorse bridge which still graces the Haddon estate.

The gardens fall chiefly southwards to a loop in the Wye by a series of old stone-walled terraces. Their handsome balustrading, stairways and paving all date from the early 17th century. The overall design has changed little since that time, but Haddon acquired an abandoned aura during the 18th and 19th centuries, becoming a place of Gothic fascination. 'A gloomy and solemn silence pervades its neglected apartments, and the bat and the owl are alone the inmates of its remaining splendour', noted Rhodes's *Peak Scenery*

ROSES ALL THE WAY *Haddon Hall is the kingdom of the rose. Wherever you go in the gardens there are roses – climbers and ramblers go up the walls, round the doors and over the arches, while hybrid teas, floribundas and shrub roses fill the beds on the terraces like these on the south front.*

FREE FOR ALL *Unconfined by formality, shrubs and bedding plants, climbers and ground-cover species flourish together in luxuriant profusion at Great Dixter (opposite).*

in 1819. It was the 9th Duke of Rutland, father of the present owner, who from 1912 restored the historic property.

Masses of foliage were cleared: walls were freed from the python grip of ivy, and threatening limes and sycamores felled from the upper terrace. On the second level, ancient yews grown to giants were replaced with young specimens which have since been kept neatly trimmed.

Then came the roses. They were a special love of Kathleen, the 9th Duke's Duchess, and though the impression they create is of ancient enchantment, the varieties are mostly new. In particular, floribundas produce dazzling displays in the upper garden. These free-flowering roses, so familiar throughout the country today, were only developed in the 1920s by the Danish hybridist Svend Poulsen. At Haddon today a fantastic abundance garlands the formal beds, shading from white through the palest of pastels to tones of the richest blood-red.

For fragrance and perfection of form the hybrid teas hold pride of place, while for sheer magic nothing could compete with Haddon's climbers and ramblers. They burst among balustrades, festoon mullioned windows and overhang ancient portals. The varieties are too many to list, but mention might be made of two conspicuous pink roses: there is 'Albertine', that vigorous old favourite whose coral flush comes in June, a brief but incomparable vision; and 'The New Dawn', a more recent introduction, which blooms beautifully throughout the summer.

Rampant clematis also clothes the ancient stonework, and noble delphiniums here and there contribute the pure blues which no rose has yet learned to emulate. There is a rectangular fountain pool and, below, a steep drop to a lower garden of different character. In the creviced masonry of its mighty retaining walls, aubrieta has rooted in vivid mounds, and many choice shrubs flourish in the beds beneath. Yet it is above all for its roses that Haddon is visited; theirs is the motif of the garden as it was of the Yorkists and Lancastrians whose wars the ancient hall survived.

HAMPTON COURT *Greater London*

Almost everyone has heard of the Maze at Hampton Court; it is the garden feature which has entered the folklore of a nation. And the palace itself is equally renowned, as a focus of pomp and pageant since Tudor times. Thomas Wolsey, a future cardinal and the most powerful of Henry VIII's subjects, acquired the site by the Thames in 1514 and built there a palace worthy of his status. Later, when the cardinal fell into disgrace, he presented the building to the king in an attempt to regain royal favour. The gesture was in vain. Henry enlarged the great residence as a monument to his own extravagant sovereignty – and Wolsey died on his way to the Tower.

Hampton Court lies on the north bank of the Thames some 7 miles upstream from Westminster. Today, the palace gardens and neighbouring parkland

WOLSEY'S FOLLY *When Thomas Wolsey (above), Archbishop of York, bought the manor of Hampton in 1514, he set about building a house. It ended up as the largest in England – the actual building covered nearly 4 acres – and to frame it, he enclosed a park of 2,000 acres. In 1529 he gave the estate to Henry VIII and it has remained in royal hands ever since. The centuries have obliterated the Tudor gardens, but some, like the Pond Garden (opposite), have been recreated in the spirit of the original.*

form a green, historic space in the suburban sprawl of Greater London. Yet the palace was conceived as a country retreat in a place where the air was of an 'extraordinary salubrity' after the squalor of London, and to which luxurious royal barges would come decked out for glittering entertainments. Tudor, Stuart and later kings and queens all contributed to its evolution.

It is known, for example, that Henry VIII's grounds included a pond, knot and herb gardens, with bowers and shady walks and a splendid Mount Garden topped by an arbour bristling with heraldic beasts borne high on painted poles. Little physical evidence, however, remains of the Tudor gardens. The Mount Garden was levelled in the 17th century, and a tiltyard where knights once jousted is now stocked with roses and shrubs. Only one small knot garden today illustrates the Tudor style – and this is a reconstruction, designed and planted in 1924.

More has survived from the Stuart era. Radiating from the east front, for example, are three majestic avenues of lime trees laid out in the time of Charles II. They extend like giant furrows ploughed through banked mountains of foliage, and a long canal conducts the eye down the central way. Overall, the three avenues form an effect beloved of baroque landscape designers: the *patte d'oie* (goose-foot) pattern in which splayed ways form the 'toes'.

BLACK PYRAMIDS OF YEW

By the palace, the 'heel' of the foot is a semicircular Great Fountain Garden designed by Henry Wise for William and Mary. Here huge conical yews cast dagger-edged shadows across the lawns. The trees were originally intended as slender obelisks, but 300 years of growth has turned them into the 'black pyramids' which Virginia Woolf once described.

In this historic jigsaw of a garden, some pieces were retained as the years passed; others were replaced or obliterated. Queen Anne added a red-brick orangery, and George III brought in Capability Brown. Happily, though, the landscapist did not sweep all away with his customary enthusiasm for naturalism. In fact, he made only two significant contributions. The first was characteristic: a terrace Privy Garden laid out by Wise was smoothed out to make grassed banks because 'we ought not to go up and down stairs in the open air'. The second has greatly enhanced Hampton Court's renown. In 1768, Brown planted a cutting of a 'Black Hamburgh' vine taken from a garden in Essex. That vine is still growing, and is now the most famous in the world.

More than 6 ft round at its gnarled base, the Great Vine twists its long, sinuous branches in weird knots, curves and arches round the walls of its vinery, yielding a crop of some 500 bunches every year. The monster is alleged to have spread its roots deep in the bed of the Thames. You can taste Brown's fruit too – the grapes are usually on sale to the public in late August or September.

Queen Victoria's great contribution was to open Hampton Court to the public in 1838. There was an

PALATIAL GROUNDS *The huge semicircle of lawn, segmented by avenues of clipped trees, gives some idea of the size of Hampton Court's gardens. Each of the avenues is 200 yds long. The tree-lined canal, stretching away at the top, runs for more than half a mile through the Home Park. The Pond Garden (previous page) is to the left of the white-roofed building, the Banqueting House, on the river bank near the boats.*

immediate and sensational interest evidenced by an influx of 120,000 visitors in the first year alone. Since her time there have been several additions: the new knot garden, for example, and two fine herbaceous borders. But it is the Maze above all which has captured the public imagination since visitors were first invited to explore its green corridors.

Labyrinths, of course, are as old as the tale of the Minotaur, but the craze for hedged mazes as intriguing garden features seems only to have developed in the 17th century. Charles I planted one at Wimbledon, and Hampton Court's example was established somewhat later, during the period of Henry Wise's alterations. For King William, Wise laid out a large geometrical garden (inappropriately called the Wilderness) of clipped box, hollies and yews. One of its features was a circular labyrinth design called Troy Town. The Maze seems to have been planted by Wise in the reign of Queen Anne.

The overall design is triangular, and the hedges are maintained at 6 ft high by 2 ft wide. Some complained from the outset that it was not difficult enough, but the Maze has retained its capacity to baffle and perplex.

HAREWOOD HOUSE *West Yorkshire*

It might be likened to some great open-air opera house. The royal box, as it were, is a huge balustraded terrace laid out in florid and opulent style by the Victorian architect Sir Charles Barry. But the stage beyond was set by an earlier master who worked with woodland, water and rolling hillside. This was the incomparable Capability Brown, and Harewood's is one of his finest backdrops.

Harewood House was built in 1759, and its 300 acres have been owned by the Lascelles family for more than two centuries. Three great arbiters of 18th-century taste contributed to the building's air of distinction. While Robert Adam and Thomas Chippendale furnished much of the interior, Lancelot Brown was commissioned in 1772 to model the parkland.

The landscapist worked at Harewood for nine years, for a fee of £6,000. And the 1st Earl of Harewood was rewarded with what Dorothy Stroud, Brown's biographer, called 'one of the most delectable landscapes'. Where rough gritstone farmland had been, smooth lawns emerged, sloping to a 30 acre lake, curving around scenic tree groupings and stretching through encircling woodlands to far distant horizons. Today, the overall impression remains much as Brown planned it. Disaster occurred in 1962, when 20,000 trees were destroyed in a storm. But though many beeches and oaks grown to a huge maturity were lost in the calamity, they have since been replaced.

In Brown's scheme, though, suave lawns were brought right up to the walls of the house. Today, the great terraces extend from the front, providing a platform from which to take in the long views. Sir Charles Barry, architect of the House of Commons, built them in the 1840s in the grand Italianate manner. The main level is backed by a herbaceous border which runs for 150 yds – somewhat more than the width of the house – with urns and statues grouped around.

You can spend a lot of time on the elaborate platform, admiring both foreground and landscape. But to fully appreciate Harewood's attractions it is worth coming down from the terraces. A wealth of interesting trees and shrubs have been planted in gardens and parkland. Immediately below, for example, you come upon a tall *Eucryphia × nymansensis*, palely petalled and nectar-rich with creamy blossom in August; there is also a maidenhair tree (*Ginkgo biloba*).

Down towards the lake, paths lined with azaleas lead to a waterfall, and a rocky dell where ferns, primulas and similar plants thrive in the moist soil. Here, too, the weird rhubarb plant *Gunnera manicata* unfurls its great umbrella leaves. Rhododendrons flourish in abundance: the hardy *R. racemosum* of Yunan is among the most widely planted, flowering in spring in shades of pinkish-white. A rustic bridge leads to an old-fashioned rose garden and the entrance to the walled garden which houses part of the national hosta and astilbe collection.

HARLOW CAR *North Yorkshire*

In choosing an ideal site for a garden you might well look first for good soil, mild climate and a sheltered position. When, after much consideration, the Northern Horticultural Society selected Harlow Car as a plot they plumped for the reverse of each attribute.

Lying some 500 ft above sea level and prone to whipping south-westerly winds, the site is both cold and exposed. The soil, moreover, is a very heavy and acid loam overlying beds of dour millstone grit – the rock of the neighbouring moorlands which is impermeable to water and so offers no natural drainage.

Harlow Car was founded in 1948, precisely for its challenge. The aim of the society was to study the problems of gardening in the north of England; to discover what could endure and give value in a typically uncompromising setting. If a plant could be coaxed to bloom in these Yorkshire acres the chances were that it would survive almost anywhere in the north.

From the outset, certain plants were favourites to succeed. Rhododendrons, for example, enjoy an acid

soil and, growing naturally among the snows of the Himalayas, are no strangers to extremes of cold. Today, some 450 species and hybrids enrich the garden with their opulent colours, and they have been especially widely planted in the woodlands. One of the first to appear is the hardy, large-leaved *R. calophytum* of Western China. It blooms through the mad March days, bearing speckled trusses of pink-and-white flowers with a deep red blotch at the base. Month by month, other luxuriants follow in crimsons, yellows, creams and mauves. The season ends only in July with, among others, the very late flowering 'Polar Bear' hybrid, a white rhododendron whose name belies its taste for summer sunshine.

Heathers also prosper at Harlow Car. They, too, are acid lovers, though much peat has been required to provide a truly acceptable habitat for them. The main heather garden is concentrated around an old lily pool and the neighbouring area of Tarn Meadows, recently landscaped with artificial rockwork. Over 300

SEASONAL HUES *At Harewood House the visitors can usually tell the season by the colour of the flowers in the herbaceous border beneath the terrace on the south front. This is June – when blue is the predominant colour. In July, shades of pink are in the majority.*

heather species and cultivars are represented – tree heaths as well as low, spreading shrubs – and the collection is one of the best in the country.

Although plants are labelled and studied for garden value, Harlow Car has also been laid out for ornamental effect. And it has been fascinating to see what has flourished. A wide variety of Japanese maples, for example, provide splendid colour in both spring and autumn, and the Chilean fire bush (*Embothrium coccineum lanceolatum* 'Norquinco Valley') has been an outstanding success, bearing sensational orange-and-scarlet blooms in May and early June.

A formal trials and demonstrations area has been laid out, in which horticulturists are invited to test their wares. You can judge for yourself the comparative performances of new and established varieties: for example, of dahlias, chrysanthemums, delphiniums, roses and slow-growing conifers. The failures are as interesting as the successes. In 1978, for example, the International Camellia Society tried out 140 species and cultivars of this lovely shrub. Almost every one died in the hard winter which followed. All had been one-year-old plants, and the lesson for northern camellia growers was that, for safety, only more mature specimens should be planted.

In this garden for gardeners, many different habitats have been created. There is the Stream Garden, for example, planted with moisture-lovers, and the Peat Garden whose abundant primulas include Harlow Car's own popular hybrids. To make raised beds for alpines, the soil has been lightened with leaf-mould and gravel; a Limestone Rock Garden provides a fascinating contrast. Here the alkaline soil permits saxifrages, campanulas, dianthuses and helianthemums to flourish. Elsewhere there are Bulb and Foliage Gardens, a youthful arboretum and a display house for alpines. Harlow Car also contains one of Britain's four vegetable sanctuaries where old and endangered cultivars are nurtured.

HARRINGTON HALL *Lincolnshire*

Come into the garden, Maud,
For the black bat, night, has flown,
Come into the garden, Maud,
I am here at the gate alone...

So sang many a Victorian tenor, inviting perhaps some particular member of his audience to a rendezvous amid the musk of roses and the dozing pimpernels. The music of the famous song cycle was by Arthur Somervell, but the words were those of the young Alfred Tennyson. And the garden which inspired the lyrics was that of Harrington Hall in Lincolnshire.

The house is a Caroline manor, built of mellow red brick and standing in tranquil countryside on the edge

SUCCESSFUL CHALLENGE *Lush foliage runs riot in the stream-side garden at Harlow Car. The vigour of the plants proves how successfully the Northern Horticultural Society has met the challenge of creating a fine garden on an exposed site in North Yorkshire.*

A QUEEN'S HOME *When Anne Boleyn (below) died in 1536 by the executioner's sword, her family's fortunes declined – and Hever Castle, her childhood home, entered its Dark Age. Rescue came in 1903 when William Waldorf Astor bought the castle, and embarked upon a massive restoration programme – employing 1,000 workmen over four years. Roses spread soft colours through the new gardens (opposite), soothing away memories of a bitter past.*

of the Lincolnshire Wolds. Tennyson was born at Somersby near by and, as a young man, fell in love with Rosa Baring who lived at the hall – it was she who became the 'Maud' of the poem.

Some 19th-century features have gone. An elaborate display of carpet bedding has, for example, been grassed over to make a croquet lawn. The old kitchen garden now contains a selection of white and silver plants backed by hedges of purple-leaved plum, but still today, as in the Victorian era, 'the musk of the rose is blown' in Harrington's 5 acres. Climbers bloom in wonderful profusion against the stonework of an 18th-century walled garden, and there is an especially fine Banks's rose (*Rosa banksiae*) which clothes the south face of the house. A brick-paved terrace walk is overgrown with rock roses, lavenders and rosemary which contribute fragrances of their own to the 'spices wafted abroad'.

Among many interesting plants and shrubs, Harrington contains two handsome specimens of an unusual variegated holly. They flank a herbaceous border below the terrace, and their leaves bear spines on their upper surfaces as well as round their edges. This form of the common *Ilex aquifolium* well deserves its nickname 'hedgeholly' and its Latin name of 'Ferox Argentea' – ferocious and silvery.

No such prickly curiosities intrude in Tennyson's dream imagery of lily, passion flower and casement jessamine. But if you visit Harrington in midsummer, when the roses are in full bloom, you can experience something of the poet's enchantment.

HEVER CASTLE *Kent*

Two different traditions rub shoulders at Hever. One is the romance of English history embodied in the moated castle; and the other is the American spirit of enterprise which inspired the lavish present-day gardens.

Rising four square from a lily-strewn moat, Hever Castle dates back to the 13th century. It was acquired by the famous Bullen family and is renowned as the birthplace of a daughter of the house – Anne Bullen (or Boleyn), the wife of Henry VIII. But when the luckless queen's head fell to the executioner's sword in 1536, the family fortunes declined. And the little castle declined too, so much so that by the turn of this century it was being leased out as a farmhouse. Bacons and hams hung from noble beams and potatoes lay heaped in the chambers when, in 1903, Mr William Waldorf Astor acquired the castle and its 640 acres.

Born into a fabulously wealthy family, William Astor had served as American Ambassador in Rome. And there he acquired a life-long love of European culture. He became a naturalised British subject and brought to Hever both wealth and energy. For four years over 1,000 workmen laboured to transform the grounds. A whole mock medieval village was erected near the castle to house his staff and friends. Acres of flood-prone meadowlands around were drained, and a new outer moat was dug for the castle. Additionally, Astor

had a 35 acre lake excavated to the east, into which the River Eden was diverted; this project alone required six steam diggers and 7 miles of private railway track. And while Hever's map was being redrawn with water, towering Scots pines were transplanted from Ashdown Forest, 12 miles away. It took teams of four horses and ten men to move each individual tree.

As for the gardens proper, they were laid out in varied styles. Close to the castle, a Tudor atmosphere was recreated with formal courts, rose gardens and a croquet lawn. Also within the outer moat, Astor established a Maze, and a topiary feature unique to Hever: this is the Chess Garden, in which golden yews have been clipped to form a set of giant pieces. Castle walls and pergolas in this area are hung with wisterias, clematises, honeysuckles and jasmines which, with the drifts of water lilies, contribute a delightfully mellow aura.

Very different in mood is the vast Italian Garden which William Astor had laid out some distance from his castle. The great walled plot lies beyond the outer moat, and was built to accommodate an enormous collection of antique statues and sculptures – Greek, Etruscan, Roman and Asiatic – which he had amassed in Italy. They stand today like weatherworn exhibits in some extraordinary roofless gallery: altars, sarcophagi, marbled busts and porphyry columns. The high south-facing wall of yellow sandstone stretches for more than 200 yds, and besides the sculptures in its niches, it shelters a wealth of shrubs and perennials: ceanothuses, magnolias and purple-leaved vines, fragrant lavenders and verbenas. At the eastern end, an immense loggia, hung with wisterias, looks across a magnificent bay-fronted piazza which swells into the lake like the prow of a ship, commanding views down the water.

South of this great walled domain is a rose garden and a rock garden shaped from mighty slabs brought from Chiddingstone Causeway. Among the boulders grow many blue-flowering shrubs – rhododendrons and hydrangea varieties, for example – which have earned the area the name of Blue Corner. Elsewhere in the grounds there are grottoes, ponds and falls, a grand Chestnut Avenue, a Rhododendron Walk and a balustraded Golden Staircase which leads to a fine viewpoint.

HIDCOTE MANOR *Gloucestershire*

Glance through any modern plant catalogue and you come upon products of this garden. There are popular 'Hidcote' varieties of lavenders and hypericums for example. But the name is known equally through a whole approach to modern gardening which has become a byword of 20th-century taste. Uniting formal planning with informal planting, it is known

ARCHITECT'S GROUNDPLAN *Clipped hedges of box and yew define the structured spaces of Lawrence Johnston's garden. An ordered framework underlies the informal planting schemes, echoing the principles of his architectural training.*

to gardeners everywhere as the Hidcote style.

The garden lies on the scarp of the Cotswolds some 4 miles from Chipping Campden. It covers, in reality, no more than 11 acres, but its fame – and complexity – are such that the physical scale means little. For this is a garden of many compartments, divided by bricked wall or clipped hedging, each enclosing its own design scheme. There are plots agleam with water, for example, or heady with roses, or sculpted with evergreen topiaries, and almost everywhere at Hidcote, borders brim with subtly blending or contrasting combinations of tree and flower and shrub. In all, the garden has been one of the most influential ever laid out.

Hidcote was bought for Lawrence Johnston by his mother in 1907. At that time there was no garden at all; only one fine old cedar by the house and a clump of good beeches a little way off. Johnston terraced his undulating domain, which stands fairly high on the Cotswolds. The now-famous hedges were planted in part as shelter against chill winds. But they served other purposes too: providing open-air rooms for different effects, firm verticals to hold the eye, and pure ornament in themselves. Apart from conventional yews, for example, Johnston made hedges of euonymus – the spindle tree – and others of combined evergreens. The most inspired creation was a 'tapestry' hedge composed of hornbeam, yew, holly and beech, which offers varied blendings of colour and texture throughout the year.

Johnston was an architect by profession, and had an architect's instinct for structuring space. But within the ordered framework he planted with great originality. It was a time of turmoil in gardening style. A wealth of new plant material was pouring into Britain, and the Victorian habit of organising brigades of plants in severe bedding schemes was being challenged by gardeners such as William Robinson and Gertrude Jekyll. They wanted to see the exotics blend into the English scene; effects should recall the chance harmonies of natural woodlands and cottage gardens.

Lawrence Johnston absorbed their enthusiasm. In fact, Hidcote has been likened to a whole series of cottage gardens, and it proved an inspiration to contemporaries. Victoria Sackville-West (creator of Sissinghurst), for example, noted how 'flowering shrubs mingled with roses, herbaceous plants with bulbous subjects, climbers scrambling over hedges, seedlings coming up wherever they have chosen to plant themselves'.

The central vista at Hidcote extends from the old cedar by the house, through a cottage-style garden to a circle of lilacs and hellebores. It then enters a corridor of red-foliaged and red-flowered plants and leads on up steps to a pair of gazebos. Above, is a walk flanked by hornbeams grown like hedges on stilts. The squared masses of foliage are borne on bare stems in the formal French manner – a memorable and much photographed effect. The walk leads eventually to great wrought-iron gates and tremendous views out across Shakespeare country.

This, though, is only the main axis. Among the diversity of small gardens leading off, you come upon repeated surprises. There is, for example, a paved fuchsia parterre enclosed by tapestry hedges. From it you enter a circular pool garden whose raised waters almost fill their enclosure, reflecting both sky and surrounding vegetation.

One enclosure, Mrs Winthrop's Garden, is named after Lawrence Johnston's mother. It is planted in shades of blue and yellow, drawn from pansies, veronicas and many others. Another, the Pillar Garden, is dominated by the solemn forms of columnar yews; tree paeonies and rare old double tulips contribute to its miscellanies of colour.

For spare elegance, nothing could compete with the Theatre Lawn, a vast expanse of immaculate greensward which rises at one end to a turfed stage. From the platform rise two huge beeches, acting out their own silent drama. The Stream Garden offers the greatest possible contrast, thickly planted with drifts of lilies and azaleas.

The Hidcote style has been copied since Johnston's day, in plots both large and small. But like all great works of art, the garden survives as a masterpiece outside its context in time. You can come simply to admire the roses, for example, planted in abundance to bring colour and fragrance to the borders. Johnston favoured especially the old French varieties.

Modern hybrids were also included, blending into the colour schemes. There is, for example, a little area under the old cedar devoted to white-flowering and silvery plants; here the hybrid rose 'Gruss an Aachen' contributes its creamy blooms. Additionally, two yellow hybrids are especially associated with Hidcote. One is the climber 'Lawrence Johnston', named after the owner by a French hybridist. The other is 'Hidcote Gold', a bush with fern-like leaves, which was raised in the garden itself in 1948.

The garden's own creations, of course, hold special interest. There is the 'Hidcote' hypericum, for example, a now-popular evergreen shrub bearing bright yellow, saucer-shaped blooms. And there is the 'Hidcote' lavender, widely valued for its compact form and rich purple flowers. (Adorning many a suburban garden today, it serves in its Cotswold home as a wall flower among other things, rooting in cracks between stones.) Additional delights include 'Hidcote' varieties of fuchsia, verbena, campanula and penstemon – all much prized and internationally known.

The garden has been managed by the National Trust since 1948, and its hybrids date chiefly from the period since Lawrence Johnston's death. But the Hidcote style, the tradition of aesthetic excellence which he established, these have remained enduring legacies of a garden-maker whose gifts amounted to genius.

HODNET HALL *Shropshire*

Water is the theme of these 60 Shropshire acres, water tumbling in flights through informal woodlands and dammed at different levels to form chains of pools and lakes. Yet, when the garden was started in 1922,

COTTAGE HARMONIES *Smooth thatch and graded topiary overlook the cloudy profusion of a cottage garden (opposite). Designed as a collection of open-air rooms, each with its own theme of colour or mood – Hidcote has been likened to a series of cottage gardens. The airy exuberance of form and hue defied the rigid gardening codes of the Victorians, and helped establish the more natural gardening style of the 20th century.*

FLOWERS COME FULL CIRCLE
Encircled by flowers, a stone statue at Hodnet Hall stands at the heart of three beds, with grass-mown paths between. Paeonies fill the outer circle in spring, giving way to the warm summer colours of the inner beds. Shades of yellow floribunda roses fade into a central pool of creamy Hydrangea paniculata.

Hodnet had no more than a muddy stream and marshy hollow. It was Brigadier A. G. W. Heber-Percy who, with modern earth-moving equipment, contoured the lush, liquid vistas seen today.

A scenic Broad Walk runs along the south front of the Victorian house, and looks down to the main lake below. Beyond you can see a red-brick dovecote of 1656, and the views extend as far as the distant Long Mynd, Shropshire's strange lump of wild moorland. The panorama, like the pools, was brought into the garden by clearing many trees to open up the far horizon.

Hodnet's soil is lime-free, a stiff clay overlying red sandstone, and it favours acid-loving plants. Rhododendrons, azaleas, camellias and magnolias shock with colour in season. Thirsty hydrangeas have also been planted in masses, and enjoy fairly high rainfall and moist conditions. It is thought that the abundance of water has moderated the garden's temperature: the pools rarely freeze over, and mists rising from them tend to keep off severe frosts. The tender *Phygelius capensis*, or Cape figwort, of South Africa, is just one among many unusual shrubs which have profited, bearing its scarlet-lobed blooms in late summer.

As might be expected, the margins of pool and stream abound in primulas, irises, astilbes and gunneras – moisture-loving denizens of damp places which have been planted at Hodnet in great drifts. The white-petalled *Trillium grandiflorum* is conspicuous in many a shady nook, blooming in spring among the bluebells and kingcups which lend native enchantment to the scene.

Flowering cherries, lilacs and laburnums splash their colours in season, and for autumn warmth there are Japanese maples. Amid these profusions, one unexpected touch of formality is supplied by a large circular garden, fashioned out of a sheltered sandstone pit. It is designed in concentric beds, the outer ring planted with mixed paeonies and the inner with pale floribunda roses. From the central bed rises dense white clusters of *Hydrangea paniculata*, edged with the mauves of lavender and *Caryopteris*.

INVEREWE *Highland*

The headland lies at a latitude further north than Moscow's, in terrain strewn with peat hag and eroded rock. *Am Ploc Ard* – the old Gaelic name for the Inverewe peninsula – captures something of its former brutish austerity. It means the 'High Lump', aptly describing the mass of red Torridonian sandstone which forms the core. In this corner of Wester Ross the soil is acid and shallow, and for much of the year round the area is exposed to the salt lash of vicious south-westerlies. Until 100 years ago, practically nothing grew there at all.

Yet today Inverewe is a paradise where Chusan palms and the tree ferns of Australia grow tall in the company of silvery eucalyptus, Moroccan broom and the giant Himalayan lily. In all, its 24 acres contain some 2,500 species of tree, flower and shrub drawn from both hemispheres of the globe.

Inverewe is a man-made wonder, the invention of Osgood Mackenzie who bought the property in 1862. But a compassionate Mother Nature has played her part too, contributing one asset without which the enterprise would have been impossible. This is the warm flow of the Gulf Stream, that kindly North Atlantic Drift which caresses Cornish headlands as well as the *Ploc Ard*.

Gale-torn, rock-strewn and thinly soiled, Inverewe may have been, but Mackenzie realised that it was almost entirely free from frost, the plant killer that destroys more readily in Kent than on Mackenzie's northern headland. In fact, in his book *A Hundred Years in the Highlands* (1922), the Scot was to claim that he could grow in the open air at Inverewe as many plants, and as good, as was possible at Kew under glass. And though the north-western climate may have worsened somewhat since his day, that claim remains largely true.

The first problem was to counter the gales and driving rain, and against them he planted an outer windbreak of Corsican and Scots pines. Within, thick hedges of *Rhododendron ponticum* were established, while many foreign and native trees contributed to the screen: a few *Sequoia gigantea* from California, for example, and many common silver birches.

Additionally, soil was brought to the site in creels, the large wicker baskets used by Scottish fishermen, to improve the soggy carpet of black peat.

The official guide to Inverewe acknowledges that the garden does not lend itself to a formal conducted tour. Overall, the impression is of some luxuriant woodland jungle through which paths wind according to their own secret logic. Inverewe has been likened to 'some wild corner in Burma or Northern China', an impression which owes much to the profusion of rhododendrons.

The garden profited by the 20th-century discovery of many larger-leaved varieties, and one tremendous specimen of *Rhododendron giganteum* was raised from seeds sent home by the Scotsman George Forrest. But they bloom in all shapes and sizes and the collection has been expanded over the years to include, for example, Exbury hybrid azaleas and plantings of the tender *Maddenii* group of rhododendrons which are normally grown under glass. There are remarkable camellias too, one over 200 years old which was bought by Osgood Mackenzie at a local sale. Though reputed never to have flowered before, it was moved to Inverewe, where it is smothered with pink-and-white flowers in most seasons.

Among the many richly lined pockets of interest, one is especially rewarding. This is an enclosure to the north-east of the garden, and some distance from the windswept shore. It is pleasingly known as Bamboosalem after its sheltering plantations of bamboos, and the centrepiece holds pride of place among all of Inverewe's denizens. This is a magnificent 40 ft *Magnolia campbellii*, a plant of Himalayan origin whose flowers, borne on leafless branches, are especially tender to frost. Inverewe's specimen, though, flowers safely almost every year in early April, bearing hundreds of great pink chalices 8 in. across.

Grouped around in Bamboosalem are scarcities culled from far and wide. There are hoherias from New Zealand, for example, and the climbing *Hydrangea petiolaris* from Japan. Chile's exotics are well represented here as elsewhere at Inverewe, and among them a rare *Gevuina avellana*, or Chilean hazel, is conspicuous for its lustrous green leaves and white flowers. In spring, Bamboosalem is remarkable for its American trout lilies (*Erythronium revolutum*) which have spread throughout the garden.

MAN-MADE WONDER *The barren hills on the far side of Loch Ewe are the measure of Osgood Mackenzie's achievement at Inverewe. Palms flourish and all manner of flowering plants luxuriate in the garden he created by bringing soil and shelter to a spot that was once as bare as the hills across the water.*

KEW *Greater London*

It is Britain's great plant zoo, a 300 acre giant of a garden containing over 25,000 species and varieties. At Kew you can see cacti and carnivores, rare orchids and primeval trees, flowers in every shape and size from the tiniest star-like alpine to the giant aquatics of the Amazon. Famed internationally as one of the finest botanic gardens in the world, Kew even requires its own station on the London Underground to accommodate the floods of visitors who come, like the plants, from the four corners of the earth.

Yet the Royal Botanic Gardens offer more than a collection of exhibits. In a complex history spanning more than two centuries, Kew has acquired temples and pagoda, woodland gardens and formal bedding schemes, tree-lined vistas and landscaped lake. This great national institution is also, more simply, a very beautiful garden.

Sir Joseph Banks, the botanist who accompanied Captain Cook on his first famous voyage of exploration in 1768–71, was one of the early directors. And he brought back from his travels many thousands of exotic specimens, notably from the Australian coast where Botany Bay was named after its wealth of plants. Capability Brown was among the head gardeners, ruling with such authority that even George III dared not quibble with his plans. When the landscapist died, the king greeted his second-in-command with the words: 'Mellicant! I hear Brown is dead. Now you and I can do as we please!' (What the king pleased became odder and odder as the monarch's mind lost its balance. He once planted some pieces of beefsteak at Kew in the hope of solving a meat shortage in England. Finding the steaks covered with snails the next day he mistook them for cattle and exclaimed to his queen: 'Here they are, Charlotte! Horns and all!')

Kew Gardens were handed to the nation in 1841, and continued to expand both their collection and acreage thereafter. And today some splendid landmarks testify to the expense that has been lavished upon them. There is the ten-storey, 163 ft high Pagoda, for example, erected in 1761–2. This was designed for Princess Augusta by Sir William Chambers, a pioneer of Chinese taste. The magnificent Palm House is the work of Decimus Burton, a Victorian architect who also designed the Temperate House. These and innumerable smaller monuments and plant houses make Kew fascinating for its garden architecture alone.

One of Kew's oldest inhabitants is a towering 80 ft tall maidenhair tree (*Ginkgo biloba*), thought to have been planted in 1762. Ginkgos are miraculous survivors from the primeval forests. Identified through fossil imprints, they are the sole representatives of a family of trees which flourished over 180 million years ago. The curious fan-shaped leaves have earned the tree its other name of maidenhair tree (after the maidenhair fern which the leaves resemble).

But this is a garden of remarkable specimens, descended from seeds culled from the Congo and Antarctica, from desert basin and high Himalayas. And

EXOTIC PLUNDER *Sir Joseph Banks (above) went round the world with Captain Cook, returning with thousands of plants unknown in Britain. Later, as director of Kew, he sent more plant collectors to scour the tropics. The treasures that they and their successors brought back were displayed at Kew. Among them was the legendary lotus (opposite), which now blooms in the humid sanctuary of the water lily house.*

PRESERVED UNDER GLASS
Climates other than our own are recreated under airy structures of iron and glass. The Temperate House (above) holds plants from countries only slightly warmer than Britain. Despite extensive repairs, it remains true to the original designs of Victorian architect Decimus Burton (below).

many a tale is told of their discovery. The explorer Archibald Menzies, for example, was attending a banquet in Chile in 1794. He was handed some nuts for dessert and, picking some odd-looking items from his dish, pocketed them. Menzies grew the nuts into seedlings which he presented to Kew – they became the first monkey puzzles ever seen in England.

For specialist interest, Kew has extensive gardens devoted to azaleas, bamboos, heaths and many other groups of plants. There is a superb rock garden and even a walled cottage garden. But for the first-time visitor what fascinates above all are the great glasshouses – cool, tropical, humid or dry.

In the great Palm House, for example, you discover a lost world of mysterious vegetation. The air is loaded with warm, luxurious scents, and strange fleshy forms greet the eye. Bananas, pawpaws, cocoa trees and yams are among the more familiar products of this glass-roofed jungle, while primeval cycads and weird screwpines, their leaves growing in spirals, contribute to the outlandish aura. The many rare ornamentals which lend their exquisite colours include the jade vine (*Strongylodon macrobotrys*); practically extinct in its Philippine homeland, it displays its lovely blue-green trusses for Kew's visitors. For sheer, rampant growth nothing could compare with the giant bamboo of Java which surges 45 ft – from the floor to the roof – every season.

In the reopened Temperate House you come upon such oddities as the sausage tree (*Kigelia moosa*) from East Africa (a plant whose name would surely have appealed to George III). In the Australian House there are kangaroos' paws (*Anigozanthos*). The ever-intriguing carnivores – pitcher plants and Venus's flytrap – are situated in a complex of glasshouses known as the 'T' Range and here too you come upon the most popular exhibit of all. This is the giant water lily *Victoria regia*, also known as *V. amazonica*. It bears flowers which turn from white to pink to purple. They last only two days, though, and unfold at the margins of the leaves. The leaves themselves are what most astonish, spreading up to 6 ft in diameter, they float on the water like vast green trays.

SNOW-BOUND JUNGLE *The majestic Palm House at Kew was Decimus Burton's masterpiece – built in the 1840s, it was then the largest glasshouse in the world. Caught in a frozen web (above), its icy exterior contrasts strangely with the jungle inside (right).*

KNIGHTSHAYES *Devon*

As with old music-hall artistes, high-Victorian architecture has now been around long enough to achieve a place in the English heart, and even examples like Knightshayes Court, with its gargoyles, heavily mullioned windows and pious, carved inscriptions, now inspire more affection than astonishment. The house was built in the 1870s on a lovely site above the River Exe for Sir John Heathcoat-Amory. It now belongs to the National Trust.

So far as horticulture was concerned, Sir John seems to have been content with the conventions of his day. For much of the house's history, its gardens depended for effect upon labour-intensive Victorian formality – conservatories, a bowling green, terraces, a programme of bedding-out and seasonal colour. There were also some magnificent trees, left over from the garden of a Georgian house that had stood, more or less, on the same site.

Many of the trees remain, including a Turkey oak whose 25 ft girth makes it the largest of its kind in Britain, some huge beeches, Scots and Monterey pines, and an awesome and handsomely shaped Wellingtonia. So do the terraces, though their intricately patterned beds have been replaced by grassy walks and topiary. But for the most part the garden was revolutionised by the grandson of the builder – another Sir John – and his wife.

It was a lengthy and loving revolution that began shortly after the Second World War with the planting of shrubs, perennials and climbers about the terrace and the house. Later, among the yew battlements, an old paved garden was re-created, centred upon an ancient pair of stone benches and an 18th-century lead cistern acquired from the Goldsmiths' Hall in London. The colour accent here is silvery or pale grey foliage with soft pink flowers to add a touch of warmth to the stone. Near by is what was once the bowling green, dug out in 1957 to form a lily pond in which fat goldfish twitch an occasional fin, guarded by an equally plump Victorian nymph.

This part of the garden is rounded off by an Alpine terrace, falling away to one of Knightshayes most original concepts; the Garden in the Wood. Each year, from the late 1950s to the early 1970s, Sir John and Lady Amory brought a piece of woodland 'approximately the size of a tennis court' into the garden by thinning the trees and planting among them magnolias, azaleas, rhododendrons, paeonies, a host of flowering shrubs and bushels of bulbs, as well as climbing roses that have been encouraged to clamber up among the branches. This enchantingly contrived wilderness now extends over 30 acres with three outliers – Holly's Wood, Sir John's Wood and Michael's Wood, the last named after the head gardener Michael Hickson. Another splendid innovation is the Willow Garden, in which a large number of willow varieties have been planted round a pond. Since these trees are relatively fast growing, the garden will soon reach maturity and provide a fine complement to the nearby groups of azaleas.

LANHYDROCK *Cornwall*

The best way to approach Lanhydrock is not by the obvious route from Bodmin, but by the road from Liskeard which climbs up over the moors – and, suddenly, there it is, the entire 200 acre estate, laid out among the dark woods on the far bank of the Fowey, with the pale granite of the house peering round the shoulder of a hill. From this distance, some 2 miles off, the visitor can absorb the entire prospect; the twin wide ribbons of the famous sycamore and beech avenue, the smooth turf, the meticulously planned specimen trees and, in season, the glowing rhododendrons and magnolias. It is a scene of great peace, permanence and Englishness precisely reflecting the family that created it. They were the Robartes, beginning with Lord Robartes, a Parliamentarian general and statesman at the time of the Civil War.

The road plunges down the hill to an old bridge and then to a lodge gate and the avenue, whose sycamores were planted by the general in 1648, and are therefore coming to the end of their long lives. A line of beeches was added in the early 1800s and, as the sycamores succumb, these too are replaced by beeches. Pricking the sky at the far end are the granite pinnacles of the delightful little gatehouse. The pinnacles are actually little stunted obelisks, each of which is topped by a ball. It is a motif that is repeated on the house, the garden walls and throughout the garden. Beyond the gatehouse, and in something of a contrast, is Lanhydrock itself, plain and perhaps severe.

The garden is unusually formal for Cornwall, a county that seems generally to prefer its great gardens to carry a hint of the wild moors. At Lanhydrock, 19th-century terraces are laid out around the house, and rose beds delineated by low box hedges in knot-garden style. Dotted about the smooth turf like

A GENTLE OPULENCE Paeonies bow under the weight of their own petals in a secluded corner of Lanhydrock (above). The mood is one of opulence, in a garden where magnolias bloom from spring through to autumn, and the woodlands shimmer with the rich colours of flowering shrubs.

PRECISE GEOMETRY An old bowling green is transformed by the curves of a lily pond, and the crisp angles of castellated topiary (opposite). The gardens at Knightshayes have shed the fussy formality of Victorian bedding schemes in favour of strong shapes, softened by trees and flowering shrubs.

COLOURWASHED FOREST *The ancient forest of St Leonard glows with a foreign fire – the warm tints of flowering shrubs introduced from the Orient in the last century. Sir Edmund Loder built his woodland garden at Leonardslee, around a chain of old ponds – the flooded pits of abandoned mines. The existing canopy of trees provided essential shade for new exotics – like rhododendrons, azaleas and camellias.*

sentinels are 38 Irish yews which look as though they have been shaved with a freshly honed razor, so smooth are their lines. They are accompanied by some magnificent bronze urns, the work of Louis Ballin, goldsmith to Louis XIV. They once stood in the garden of the Château de Bagatelle, Queen Marie Antoinette's mansion in Paris.

Plant choice tends to be opulent, with a strong accent upon magnolias, whose varieties have been carefully chosen to extend the season for as long as possible. Some of these, like the *Magnolia grandiflora* that flowers in summer and autumn, stand by the house, but most are in the shrub and woodland garden that climbs up the slope behind the church. Some are of astonishing size, but are matched in their grandeur and glory of colour by rhododendrons, azaleas, camellias, hydrangeas and ornamental flowering fruit trees – crab apple, quince, plum and cherry. Behind a curved yew hedge, the National Trust has put together a pretty little herbaceous garden of unusual combination, which features yuccas, green-flowering hellebores, paeonies, kniphofias and agapanthus. Over all is the backdrop of the Fowey Valley woods, through which a pair of beautiful walks have been carved.

LEONARDSLEE *West Sussex*

The ancient Forest of St Leonard in Sussex owes its name to the saint who is said to have slain a dragon in the woods. And wherever blood fell from the saint's wounds, lilies of the valley are supposed to have sprung up. Leonardslee Gardens also recall the saint in their name, and the plants are certainly found growing wild in abundance among the native beeches, birches and oaks.

But you could be excused for missing these traditional attractions at a first visit. Thick with exotica, the gardens burst in spring with the flamboyance of rhododendrons and azaleas; in autumn with the fires of countless rare trees. The kaleidoscope effects are magnified by reflections caught in the central chain of old hammer ponds.

The Georgian-style house at Leonardslee stands some 300 ft above sea level, looking down on the woodland valley garden and out across rolling countryside to the line of the South Downs beyond. The stream-fed hammer ponds, which contribute so much to the beauty of the scene, are distinctive features of the Sussex countryside. They date back to the country's 'iron days' some 300 years ago, when the

Wealden forest was more extensive than today.

The abundant trees fuelled the furnaces at that time, and they have left a valuable legacy for gardeners. Accumulations of leaf-mould have clothed the sandstone landscape around Leonardslee with a rich and fertile loam. Rhododendrons, azaleas, camellias and magnolias – all natural forest-dwellers – do exceptionally well in the lime-free soil.

The exotics came to Leonardslee after 1887, when Sir Edmund Loder began planting the property. An artist, scholar and traveller, he personally dressed the native woodland over 30 years, employing no landscape designer. A wealth of new flowering shrubs were just beginning to flood in from China, Japan and the Americas. They were, on the whole, creatures of the forests. Jungle shade and moist leafy soil were their natural habitat; they tended to perish all too easily in an open English landscape.

Woodland gardening was the solution, and Sir Edmund was a pioneer in the field. At Leonardslee he thinned the native trees somewhat to make space for his exotic plantings. But he took care not to destroy the valuable shelter which they provided, or to mar the natural beauty of the setting.

Rhododendrons were Sir Edmund's passion, and they flourish today in infinite variety in the 82 acre gardens. In April and May especially, the woodlands glow with spectacular banks and furrows of luxuriance deriving from both wild Asiatic species and modern hybrids. Among them, pride of place is held by the crosses which commemorate the founder. Sir Edmund raised many hybrids in his garden, but none has won more acclaim than the 'Loderi'.

The 'Loderi' rhododendrons were first raised at Leonardslee in 1901, by crossing *R. griffithianum* and *R. fortunei*. They have since proved invaluable to gardeners: vigorous, sweetly scented and free-flowering in shades of pink and white. 'King George' is perhaps the best known of the strain, but there are many other varieties: 'Pink Diamond', 'Sir Edmund' and 'Venus' for example. One area at Leonardslee is specially laid out as the Loderi Garden, and contains many of the original plants.

The present owner, grandson of Sir Edmund Loder, maintains the property at the highest standard; but it is a wild garden. The woodland is structured with masses of colour and foliage, and you meet few disciplined symmetries as you wander the winding paths.

Different areas, though, do have their own character. Camellias, for example, were a speciality of Sir Edmund. Many aged specimens grow around the walls and courtyard of the house, while a fine collection is housed in a cool greenhouse. And one semi-formal feature is a wide walk lined with large-flowering forms of *Camellia japonica*. But though known as the Camellia Walk, it is by no means bereft of other plant forms. Hardy Chusan palms mingle with the exquisites, while magnolias overhang the path.

Elsewhere the walks open into glades banked with gaudy drifts of azaleas. There is a streamside dell, for example, enchanting in May when the snowdrop tree (*Halesia carolina*) is hung with delicate white bells. Across the hammer ponds, paths lead to the Mossy Ghyl, a moist little ravine filled with yellow azaleas.

All around at Leonardslee are the great trees whose columnar trunks, leafy canopies and spires provide the essential architecture of the garden. Apart from the redwoods and Wellingtonias, there are superb cedars, firs, larches, oaks and many others, sometimes in unusual forms.

The main season at Leonardslee lasts from the end of April to early June. But long after the rhododendron blooms have died, the garden reopens for autumn colour. From a lawn by the house there rises one of the tallest tulip trees in the country. At 112 ft it is a truly majestic specimen whose leaves, turning bright yellow in autumn, contribute to spectacular foliage displays. As the evenings draw in, amelanchiers, liquidambars and Japanese maples light up the dragon woods and burnish its pool-chain with fire.

LEVENS HALL *Cumbria*

Some people feel uneasy about topiary, believing, like Joseph Addison, that they 'would rather look upon a tree in all its luxuriancy and diffusion of boughs and branches than when it is thus cut into a mathematical

CLIPPED IMAGINATION *Since the 17th century, succeeding gardeners at Levens Hall have expressed their whimsical visions in topiary – the trim and fanciful shapes of clipped box and yew. Waves of spring and summer flowers lap at the walls of their box-edged beds, isolated highlights of colour in a sea of green.*

figure'. But then, Addison was writing at the beginning of the 18th century, when the Landscape Movement was making its first stirrings, and topiary was consequently about to go through one of its periods of unpopularity. Nevertheless, the art has been around for a considerable time; the Romans clipped box and bay into geometrical shapes in their neat gardens, while *topiarius* was their term for 'gardener'.

The topiary at Levens Hall is composed of trees that were planted towards the end of that period, and now in maturity present one of the most fantastical gardening collections in the country. There are cones and corkscrews, circles and pyramids and peacocks, a group called 'Queen Elizabeth and her Maids of Honour', another known as 'Coach and Horses', and all made of dark green or gold box or yews, some of which have grown to great size. These giants are surrounded by little lawns and beds, each bordered by tiny box hedges that are as meticulously shorn as their 20 ft high neighbours. The beds are filled with the traditional flowers of the English spring and summer garden, and the surrounding outside border with swathes of pink roses. Looming benignly over all is the old stone house of Levens, whose youngest part dates from about 1580, and whose oldest is probably part of a medieval pele tower.

Though the topiary garden is the best-known feature of Levens, it is only part of a unified plan of park and formal garden that was unusual in its years of conception – the last and first decades of the 17th and 18th centuries – and is now a unique survival. As with most great survivals, it is the result of a happy blending of circumstances. It all began with the 'Glorious Revolution' of 1688, when James II was deposed and William of Orange was made king in his stead. Simultaneously, the ousted monarch's Keeper of the Privy Purse and close friend, Colonel James Grahme (or Graham), came to the prudent conclusion that it was time to retire from public life and tend to his garden at far-off Levens Hall. He was accompanied by another casualty of the change of regime, the ex-royal gardener, Guillaume Beaumont, one of the most brilliant horticulturists of his day. Together, they transformed the estate.

The results of their labours can still be seen, not only in the topiary garden but in the other formal plantings as well, including a kind of gigantic cartwheel of clipped beech. The spokes are paths, one of which runs out to the park where it seemingly joins up with an avenue of trees. In fact, the two are separated by a ha-ha, or sunken wall, a device that prevents livestock straying into the garden, yet permits the impression, from the house at least, that park and garden are one.

A mile-long avenue of oaks has been planted along the valley of the Kent, leading the eye to a gorge that squeezes the lovely river almost to a torrent, and clumps of trees have been established to emphasise different features in the landscape. Such ideas were innovations in the 1690s and helped to make Levens a unique example not only of its period, but of an important halfway house in garden design.

LINGHOLM *Cumbria*

Beatrix Potter probably composed her famous children's book *Peter Rabbit* at Lingholm, but Lingholm's owner, Lord Rochdale, reports rather sadly that his garden is not the model for Mr MacGregor's plot where Peter went in search of lettuce; apparently that is Fawe Park next door. But Beatrix and her family did stay at Lingholm, which was certainly the home of *Squirrel Nutkin*.

However, there is little Beatrix Potter cosiness about Lingholm, for it is gardening on the grand scale. The outlook is to the wide sweep of Derwent Water and to the bold hills beyond, while the acid, peaty soil and reasonable protection from the most savage of the east winds makes it the perfect setting for one of the most extensive rhododendron collections in Britain.

It all started over 50 years ago with plantings in the surrounding woods, and this casual arrangement continues still. Rhododendrons and azaleas have been permitted to climb and expand to their full height and girth, often at some distance from the paths. Visitors who see a gleam of colour through the trees should explore farther; some of the loveliest shrubs have been established quite deep in the woods.

Spring is the best time to come to Lingholm, when the grass in the old orchard can hardly be seen for daffodils, and the rhododendrons and azaleas are beginning their cycle of colour. Nevertheless, species and hybrids have been carefully selected to extend the flowering season as long as possible. Early blooming plants may be flowering in January in a good season, while the white *Rhododendron auriculatum* is still in bloom in August. Several species, such as the white-and-pink *R. discolor* and the yellow *R. brachyanthum* emerge in June and July. (There is little trouble about identification, by the way; many shrubs are clearly named.)

LOGAN BOTANIC GARDENS
Dumfries and Galloway

Even if you are familiar with the Gulf Stream's benevolent effect on Scotland's west-coast gardens, Logan may come as something of a shock. Enter the walled enclosure and you immediately meet a number of towering cordylines – the cabbage palms of New Zealand – whose long stems soar high overhead to burst like rockets in explosions of spiked foliage.

Logan lies about halfway down the Rhinns of Galloway, a narrow peninsula joined to the mainland by a slender neck of land. It cuts like a ploughshare into the Irish Sea, and is the southernmost part of Scotland, washed on three sides by the warm Atlantic Drift. Temperatures are kindly and frosts are unusual.

The McDoualls of Logan owned the land from the 12th to the 20th centuries. The ruins of their medieval castle overlook the gardens from the west, while many sheltering walls of brick and stone have long screened plots from the wind. But it was not until the late 19th century, when subtropical gardening 'took off' on the west coast of Scotland, that Logan's potential was exploited.

James and Agnes McDouall, and their sons Kenneth and Douglas, assembled plants from the world over. And their work was continued by the late Mr R. Olaf Hambro, who owned the house and garden for ten years. In 1969, management of the gardens passed to the Royal Botanic Gardens at Edinburgh.

The complex of old walled gardens forms the core of the design, with extensive woodlands to south and west. And you get an early indication of what is to come in approaching by a stepped avenue of Chusan palms (*Trachycarpus fortunei*). These are the hardiest of all the true palms grown in Britain.

Australasian tree ferns have also proved successful at Logan. Resembling triffids with their broad-spread sheaves of fronds, they are natives of tropical rain forests, and rarely seen in Britain outside heated glasshouses. Two species, though, flourish in the open at Logan: *Dicksonia fibrosa* and *D. antarctica*.

While ferns, palms and cordylines confer their surreal forms on the gardens, a wealth of tender shrubs and flowers lend their hues. For conspicuous colour, the scarlet Chilean fire bush (*Embothrium coccineum lanceolatum*) probably holds pride of place, burning so fiercely in May that you feel it could really set light to its neighbours. But there are other competitors: a climbing berberidopsis, also from Chile, hung with rich red in late summer; and a sensational rata from New Zealand which flares with colour through its crimson stamens.

If your taste is for cooler colour temperatures, you might explore the nearby Water and Tree Fern Garden. In May it is remarkable for its drifts of *Meconopsis grandis*, a majestic, poppy-like plant from the Himalayas whose lovely blue flowers are borne waist high on their stems; and the white lily of the Nile (*Zantedeschia aethiopica*) contributes its pallor in season. At Logan, in fact, you can explore the whole colour spectrum. And there is even a shrub from New Zealand, *Pseudopanax laetus*, whose nectar-rich flowers are black.

These are just a few among the thousands of rare and tender plants for which Logan is renowned. In all, there are 11 separate gardens, one even maintained as a gunnera bog and crowded with the rhubarb-like Brazilian giants. Another is outstanding for its historic interest. This is the Peat Garden, laid out by Kenneth and Douglas McDouall in terraced banks of local peat to provide beds for dwarf rhododendrons. It was in fact the first terraced peat garden in the British Isles.

LONDON, CHELSEA PHYSIC GARDEN

Almost next door to the Royal Hospital with its tall cupola and scarlet-coated Pensioners, in the statelier part of Chelsea, is the lovely but near-invisible 4 acres of the Physic Garden. How a 4 acre garden manages to be so self-effacing in this busy part of the capital is something of a mystery, but there it is. It is shielded

from the Embankment's traffic flow by tall iron railings close-backed by trees, and on the other sides by a high red wall.

The Chelsea Physic Garden was founded in 1673 by the Worshipful Society of Apothecaries, and in appearance and spirit it remains a 17th-century garden to this day. The 'Physic' in its title was, and is, used in the older sense, meaning not only medicine but all things natural and physical, as opposed to things metaphysical, of the spirit.

Consequently, a vast collection of plants was assembled at the garden, growing ever larger as new lands were discovered and new species were brought back by explorers. Then, in 1712, Dr (later Sir) Hans Sloane purchased the Manor of Chelsea, so becoming the garden's landlord. He promptly let the site to the society at a rent of £5 a year in perpetuity, and at the same time suggested the appointment of Philip Miller as head gardener. Miller held the post for half a century, during which time Chelsea became the finest botanic garden in Europe. Miller himself published his great *Dictionary of Gardening*, whose 7th edition employed, for the first time, the Linnaean system of

HIDDEN HEALING Tucked away from London's traffic, behind high brick walls, the Chelsea Physic Garden guards its healing herbs and rare plants. A statue of Sir Hans Sloane presides over the garden he rented, from 1712 in perpetuity, to the Worshipful Society of Apothecaries. Plants gathered for their medicinal, agricultural or botanical interest have established a world of quiet dignity in the heart of a teeming city.

exotics as the cucumber tree, an Indian bean tree, a thornless honey locust, a rocky-barked birch-leaved pear from China and a 30 ft olive that actually manages to produce pounds of fruit in London's unsympathetic climate. These and dozens of others – see especially the magnolias – arch over the crunchy, formal gravel paths that lead to such unexpected corners as The Fernery, a small greenhouse, quiet and cool, where ferns sprout from mossy rocks. Embraced within the lawns is a parade of dozens of beds, all extremely attractive at most times of the year, and with underlying purposes that may not at first be apparent to the layman. There are, for example, corners devoted to the plants of Australia, South Africa and parts of the United States; beds ablaze with paeonies and others of more soberly hued plants illustrating the past and present work of the Society of Apothecaries; and groups of the more familiar culinary herbs, like rosemary, thyme, fennel, sage and the rest. Mingling with their scents in one entrancing bouquet are those of the perfumery plants such as lemon verbena, lily of the valley, lavender, apothecary's rose (rose of Lancaster) and nutmeg-scented pelargonium.

LONDON, QUEEN MARY'S GARDEN

Kensington Gardens has its magic, most especially on autumn evenings when mist-haloed lights blackly silhouette the trees, but for north Londoners at least there is nowhere at all like Regent's Park. Ken Wood and Hampstead Heath are impressive, a Capability Brown contrived landscape running into a real wilderness. But Regent's Park is all that a city park should be, and gives a glimpse too, in its surrounding architecture, of what all of London could be, if the world had its time over again. To the south there is the incredible colonnaded elegance of the Nash terraces, like gigantic wedding cakes in white-and-blue icing sugar. Then, to the north, there is the Zoo, with its browny-yellow concrete crags – the Mappin Terraces, built for mountain goats – from behind which, in summer dawns, there comes the thunderous roar of lions to shake the stucco of Primrose Hill and St John's Wood. In between, there is the Broad Walk, lined by aristocratic chestnuts, the lake, all islands, ducks and dinghies, and at the heart of the park there lies the Inner Circle and Queen Mary's Garden.

The Inner Circle consists of pretty, early 19th-century villas, most of which now belong to London University, and in their midst, a vast pair of black-and-gilt wrought-iron gates that were presented in 1935 by Sigismund Coetzee, a German artist who lived in the area, to mark the Silver Jubilee of King George V and his consort, Queen Mary. The exquisite little park beyond was also named in Queen Mary's honour when it was taken over by the Royal Parks Department from the Royal Botanical Society, some three years earlier. The garden has many attractive features, but in high summer the ones that first greet the senses are the blaze and near-visible perfume of 40,000 rose

MIDSUMMER REVERIE *The air lies drugged and still over Queen Mary's Garden, intoxicating with the perfume of 40,000 roses. Rank upon rank of fragrant blooms parade through the summer months, massed around the lawns, avenue and lake. This lovely garden, with its rockery and an open air theatre, lies within the vast expanse of Regent's Park – among the attractive 19th-century villas of the Inner Circle.*

botanic classification evolved by the Swedish botanist Count von Linné – still in international use to this day.

Botanical milestones mark the garden's annals. Chelsea sent the cotton seeds to found the staple crop of the American colony of Georgia, and built the first rock garden in Britain from old stones taken from the Tower of London. Dr Ward, Master of the Apothecaries in the 1850s, designed a plant travelling case that transported bananas from China to Fiji, tea from Shanghai to India, and rubber from Brazil to Malaya, so altering the economies of nations. Nowhere on Earth can there be four more fruitful acres.

Such a record should make the Physic Garden awesome, but indeed it is not. Rather, it is a place of peace and dignity, a place to stroll in, and in which to enjoy its infinite variety. (This happy odyssey has recently become available to the public, on Wednesday and Sunday afternoons from April to October, and during the duration of the Chelsea Flower Show, which takes place in the grounds of the Royal Hospital.)

The first things to strike the visitor will probably be the trees, a wonderful collection of specimens rare in this country, of which the most striking is the Chinese willow-pattern tree, like a gigantic refugee from an old-fashioned dinner service. Then there are such bushes. They are arranged in large beds down an avenue, about the lake and out into the lawns. As a general rule, each bed is devoted to a single variety and the plants crowded closely together to provide a showing of maximum grandeur. The roses are superbly tended, so that the beds blaze anew as each flowering peak is reached. Throughout the season, it is possible to walk each day through the garden and never see quite the same display twice. Many of the varieties shown are old friends, but the place is also a testing ground for new ones.

It can hardly be missed that roses are the garden's reasons for existence, but it has many other attractions as well, not least its sense of smallness and cosiness within the wide spaces of the surrounding park. There are winding paths, much favoured by strolling lovers, a rock garden of Far Eastern aspect and smothered with alpines, a couple of vaguely classical statues, a lily pond, some fossilised tree trunks (imported) and wild birds of remarkable tameness.

LYME PARK *Cheshire*

'What a strange cold place it is', complained a 17th-century gardener. The reason is easy enough to explain: set on the wild edge of the Peak District well above the fertile Cheshire plain, Lyme Park rises to an elevation of 1,220 ft above sea level. The splendid mansion in fact stands at a higher altitude than any other historic house in England and, with its classical façade, cultured lawns and parterres is deliciously improbable against the backdrop of rugged moorland.

The Leghs of Lyme occupied the site for exactly 600 years until 1946, when the estate was given to the National Trust. The property covers over 1,300 acres and was famed in Tudor times for its breed of red deer. Gardening seems to have flourished in the 17th century, when great efforts were made to get apples to prosper. It was clearly a struggle though; the same gardener who noted the cold also complained that 'he cannot have things soe early as his neighbours'. Fruiting and flowering were delayed, then as now, by the challenging climate and persistent cloud cover.

Yet the nurture of plants has succeeded at Lyme Hall, as a visit will amply illustrate. The 15 acre gardens seen today are chiefly the work of the first Lord Newton, who contoured the terraces in the late 19th century. One legacy of his time is a Dutch Garden laid out on a parterre surrounding a fountain pool. You can look down from above on the ornate beds where over 12,000 bulbs contribute to a dazzling springtime display. In summer, no fewer than 15,000 plants are bedded out every year: antirrhinums,

OASIS OF ELEGANCE *The Palladian mansion of Lyme Hall (left) remains serenely indifferent to the encroaching scrub of Cheshire's moors. The formal gardens around the house were largely the work of the 1st Baron Newton (above), who countered the surrounding wilderness with acres of cool lawns and elaborate parterres. Behind the protective walls of the Dutch Garden, spring and summer patterns are drawn out with thousands of colourful bedding plants – demonstrating the abundance of artifice in defiance of the barren hills.*

MASTERPIECE IN IRON *Scrolls, leaves, fruit and crescent moons embellish the wrought-iron pergola in the gardens of Melbourne Hall. Called 'The Birdcage', it is the work of Robert Bakewell, the 18th-century artist in iron.*

begonias, golden fuchsias, marigolds, verbenas, heliotropes and scarlet lances of *Lobelia cardinalis.*

Lord Newton also built the orangery to the east of the house. It is fronted by panel beds as vivid as those in the Dutch Garden and today shelters not oranges but fig trees. A rose garden and herbaceous border are other formal features, while a tumbling stream gushes down from the moors into a lake south of the house. It has carved a ravine, now informally planted with flowering shrubs and aquatics. In spring, primulas, rhododendrons and azaleas splash their colours amid the evergreens, while hydrangeas and hypericums follow in summer. The wild garden is scarcely 'wild' by the standards of the high moors, but provides a pleasing counterpoint to the sophistication of the Palladian mansion.

MELBOURNE HALL *Derbyshire*

This is a garden of light and shade. Melbourne's 16 acres form a lucid composition of broad sunny lawns and carefully aligned vistas executed in the manner of the early 18th century. But to one side there runs a sombre yew tunnel, 200 yds long and enclosed by centuries-old trees. And as if to demonstrate how light and shade may be united, there is an exquisite wrought-iron pergola, a masterpiece of repoussé

work which frames both the sky and the view back to the house with the utmost delicacy and grace. It was designed by Robert Bakewell, a celebrated ironsmith of the early 18th century, who lived and worked at Melbourne for many years.

Melbourne Hall itself is a greystone building constructed during the 16th century and much enlarged in 1721 by Thomas Coke, Vice-Chamberlain to Queen Anne. It was Coke, too, who had the gardens laid out in the French style associated with André Le Nôtre, head gardener to Louis XIV. The designer was an Englishman, Henry Wise, who was much influenced by the French master's work. Melbourne, like Versailles, was to be graced with formal symmetries of fountains, lawns and tree-lined vistas – albeit on a smaller scale.

Remarkably few examples remain in Britain of this once very popular style. Most were swept away in the landscaping fervour of the 18th century, and Melbourne is perhaps the finest of the survivors. Only Bramham in Yorkshire competes as a period piece.

The central vista leads the eye from the east front of the house, between shelving, rectangular lawns and down to a formal lake known as the Great Basin. Side vistas cross the main axis, and there is a second area which stretches at right-angles away to the south. Here bosky avenues extend between flanking limes and

UNCHANGED *Melbourne Hall still looks much as it does in this view of 1875.*

walls of yew hedging, converging at radial points. The whole was composed with set-square and compass, and at key intersections fountain pools and statuary focus the eye. There are many delightful cherubs and mythological features executed by the 18th-century Dutch artist John Van Nost. Among his ornaments, the most imposing is a majestic lead urn representing the Four Seasons, which look out as boldly as ships' figureheads from their massive decorative vessel.

Running back down the south side of the garden, there is the dark yew tunnel. It is older than the rest of the garden, and a path of mystery which is faintly disquieting to walk. No one knows quite when the yews were planted, though the records show that they were once supported by a wooden frame which had already decayed by 1726 and had to be removed. The stems of the aged trees lean and bend, tangles of branches jut weirdly at awkward angles. You could not ask for a greater contrast to the sunlit composition whose refined symmetries extend to the north.

NESS GARDENS *Cheshire*

If you think heather blooms only in shades of purple, then a visit to Ness will amaze you. Its heather garden is famous throughout Britain, and in high season becomes one vast rumpled patchwork of colour – whites, blush pinks and deep, fiery reds all mingling with dark green and burnished-gold foliage. The whole glorious display unfolds in late summer – and derives from *Calluna vulgaris*, the common ling or moorland heather.

The Merseyside area, long a centre of transatlantic shipping, might at first seem to hold little interest for the gardener. Yet the region has strong horticultural traditions in which Liverpool University's Botanic Gardens at Ness hold pride of place. They are situated on the Wirral peninsula, above the estuary of the River Dee which bounds the headland to the south.

Ness began as the private garden of a very remarkable man. Arthur Kilpin Bulley, who built the house in 1898, started out as a Liverpool cotton broker with an abiding passion for gardening. It was he who founded the famous seed and plant firm of Bees Ltd, and to obtain foreign specimens he wrote to both businessmen and missionaries abroad. The first experiments were disappointing. 'Ness,' said his wife, 'could

claim to possess the best international collection of dandelions.'

But Bulley persevered, eventually hiring a young Scotsman named George Forrest to seek seeds in western China. Bulley financed the great plant hunter's first two expeditions of 1904 and 1910; in 1911 he was to launch the equally renowned F. Kingdon-Ward on his career. The Bees seed catalogue became ever more exotic as successive expeditions, which Bulley helped to fund, returned with their botanic treasures. And the whole gardening world profited.

At Ness, several of Bulley's original plantings may be seen today. Shelter belts of trees – poplars, holm oaks and Scots pines, for example – still screen the

gardens from gales, while a fine azalea border, planted in 1900, is stocked with venerable specimens. In the extensive collection of rhododendrons is *R. roxieanum* grown from seeds sent from China by George Forrest.

Among the older plantings, another Forrest original holds pride of place at Ness. This is a *Pieris formosa* 'Forrestii', an evergreen whose name commemorates its discoverer. Ness's specimen stood 12 ft high until the hard winter of 1962–3, when it was cut right back to ground level. Undaunted, the plant has returned almost to its previous proportions. It is spectacular for its youthful foliage of flaming scarlet and, in spring, while those fires are still flickering, it becomes quite astonishing. Hosts of drooping white panicles come into bloom, like snowfalls on a burning bush.

Arthur Bulley died in 1942, and his garden suffered neglect during the war years. Much that is seen today has in fact been achieved since 1948, when his daughter generously presented the whole estate to Liverpool University for a botanic garden. A condition of her gift, though, was that a specified area of ornamental ground should be kept open to the public. Ness, then, is young for a botanic garden. Though much changed and expanded since Bulley's day, it retains the character of a private garden.

The new features at Ness include herb and terrace

HEATHER MIXTURE *The uniform purple of Scotland's heather-clad hills in August gives no hint of what can be seen at Ness. The heather garden there, one of the finest in Britain, is a mixture of colour from white to scarlet offset by the greens and golds of the foliage.*

GOLDEN WALK *In early
summer golden chains of
laburnum hang from the
curved pergola which
leads to the rock garden at
Newby Hall (right). The
variety grown is 'Vossii',
chosen for its extra-long
pendants of blossom.*

gardens, herbaceous borders and a good collection of roses laid out to show their development from European and Far Eastern ancestry. A young arboretum is interesting for its specimens of *Betula jacquemontii*, the purest of the white-stemmed birches in cultivation – the true albino of the family. Arthur Bulley's original rock garden has been almost entirely remade, but includes among its colourful attractions of early summer the *Primula bulleyana*. Orange budded and opening to gold, it was collected by Forrest and named after the owner.

The more strictly scientific enterprises include a native plant garden, whose specimens have all been raised by seeds or cuttings from plants growing wild in Britain. Here you can see the purple *Primula scotica*, unique to Scotland in its wild state, the rare blue *Gentiana verna* of England and a white tufted saxifrage (*Saxifraga caespitosa*) culled from the slopes of Snowdonia. Seeds from these and many other scarcities are supplied to the Seed Bank at Kew – and also replanted in their native habitats.

Above all, the heather garden at Ness is outstanding, its plants quilting a slope above the Dee in their thousands. The tender tree heath (*Erica veitchii*) is among the first to flower in spring, its white blooms borne freely on long racemes. Month by month the garden quickens with colour until the grand set-piece of late summer and early autumn. It is then that *Calluna vulgaris* reveals its rainbow hues. A vast range of cultivars is represented: the white 'Alba plena', silvery-pink 'Elsie Purnell', the more deeply rouged 'Peter Sparkes' and the crimson 'Darkness' are among the most conspicuous. The tones of golden-leaved ericas contribute to the fantastic patchwork, and several of the callunas themselves have bright foliage. There is 'Robert Chapman', for example, which flowers in a soft purple and whose leaves change with the seasons from gold in spring, through orange to a red of glowing embers in midwinter. Sprawling in tufted drifts down the slopes, the whole tribe lights its setting with a vivid, improbable radiance.

NEWBY HALL *North Yorkshire*

To view herbaceous borders conceived on the grand scale you could do no better than visit Newby Hall. The central axis of its gardens is a grass walk 350 yds long, extending from an Adam house to a landing stage by the River Ure. This broad green gangway is framed on either side by immense drifts and swells of flower and foliage, backed by clipped hedges of yew.

Newby Hall has been the home of the Compton family since 1748, when an ancestor, William Weddell, bought it through a legacy from his uncle. Robert Adam was commissioned to make extensive alterations to the building, which has survived as one of the finest in a county noted for its historic houses. The superb gardens, though, are almost entirely of this century. The late Major Edward Compton, father of the present owner, was responsible for their design. 'I found I had inherited an exceptionally beautiful home,' he said, 'but no garden to speak of – a lovely picture but no frame.'

Beginning in 1923, Major Compton spent over 50 years in developing his 25 acres to provide the required frame. Much skill and taste were needed to create a setting worthy of the elegance of the house. And these qualities the owner had in abundance. He was greatly influenced in his approach by Lawrence Johnston's innovations at Hidcote in the Cotswolds. Newby, too, was to be laid out with a sound formal structure, but planted informally to soften the lines of the design. The great walk with its double herbaceous borders was Major Compton's first creation, planned to connect the south front of the house with the river below, and to form a main axis for the entire garden. It begins and ends with stone balustraded terraces.

Off the main axis he planned a series of formal gardens, each to show a particular season's plants at their best. First came Sylvia's garden, named after his wife, a sunken garden with early flowering plants which are at their best in April and May. Then came the rose garden, converted from a grass tennis court. This he filled with June-flowering old-fashioned roses – Albas, Damasks, Gallicas and Mosses – the whole surrounded by a copper-beech hedge. An excellent foil for the delicate colours of the roses.

Next came the July garden for midsummer; then the famous borders for late summer and, finally, the autumn garden filled with a host of rewarding plants for the tail end of the season. The gardens he designed are a major contribution to 20th-century gardening.

When the present owners, Mr and Mrs Robin Compton, came to Newby in 1977 they found a large and magnificent garden in a sad state of neglect. Renovation and food were vitally required, and the whole garden needed simplification. The daunting task has been successfully tackled over the last seven years by Mr and Mrs Compton.

To enable visitors to see the best of Newby, whenever they come, three separate leaflets have been written for spring, summer and autumn with an arrowed map. The suggested walks differ according to season, but their main features are the same – starting with Sylvia's garden, now completely replanted by Mrs Robin Compton with her favourite plants, many to be at their best in the spring. An old Byzantine corn grinder holds the eye at the centre, while many low-growing plants cushion its paving and beds. The lady tulip (*Tulipa clusiana*), white with pink streaks, is especially attractive in April. Other plants have been carefully sited for foliage effects throughout the year, they include artemisias, salvias and that silver gem *Chrysanthemum haradjanii*.

The walk continues to the rock garden planted by the famous Ellen Willmott at the turn of the century, enormous in scale and full of wild charm. The Victorian waterfall has now been restored to splash down and fill the peaceful pools below. From here a curving pergola, whose pillars are covered in spring with the long golden racemes of *Laburnum × wateri* 'Vossii', leads up to the rose garden. This is now

planted with the old-fashioned roses for which it was designed, and underplanted mainly with blue flowers, including baptisia, the false indigo; *Hebe perfoliata*, the diggers speedwell from Australia; and herbaceous clematis. They all flower together in profusion, an unforgettable sight in June.

The rose garden leads on to the great borders. Many of the old favourite herbaceous plants are to be found here, but shrubs too have been introduced to give variation in height and form, notably *Viburnum plicatum* 'Mariesii' with its horizontal branches giving the effect of a snow-laden bush when in flower.

Cross the great central vista of the herbaceous borders and you come to a garden of equal proportions to the rose garden. This is the autumn garden, laid out just before the Second World War on the site of an old croquet lawn. When the evenings begin to draw in, this garden is a riot of colour with buddleias, fuchsias, hydrangeas and many unusual and late flowering salvias – protected all round by a wattle fence over which climbers romp; clematis give colour and honeysuckles lay their scents on the air.

The walk ends with the orchard garden, a sun trap surrounding apple trees, and the tropical garden, so called because it is filled with plants whose leaves and habits resemble those thriving under tropical conditions. Last but not least is the white garden, which was planted in 1980 by Mrs Compton with her favourite white plants – a grand finale to one of the most varied gardens in the north of England.

NEWSTEAD ABBEY *Nottinghamshire*

Some time in the 12th century, a community of Augustinian friars set up a priory in a corner of Sherwood Forest called Newstead. They remained there for almost 400 years, until Henry VIII dissolved the monasteries in the 1530s. It was then rebuilt as a country mansion which served many generations of the Byron family. The last of these was the romantic poet George Gordon, 6th Lord Byron – 'mad, bad and dangerous to know', as he was once described.

He loved the ruined cloisters, especially the battlements through which the 'hollow winds' whistled. Associations with the poet's life and work are to be found all around the 25 acre gardens and 300 acres of surrounding parkland. The Upper Lake, for example, is one of several waters fed by the River Lean which contribute to Newstead's beauty. It is commemorated in the epic poem *Don Juan* as a place of lucid depth, a haunt of nestling wildfowl where:

*The woods sloped downwards to its brink and stood
With their green faces fixed upon the flood.*

In the smooth lawns falling south from the house is the stump of an oak tree planted by Byron when he first inherited the estate (at the age of ten) in 1798. It never prospered much in the acid, sandy soil. East of the building you can see the tomb of Boatswain, Byron's beloved Newfoundland dog which died of rabies and is commemorated in the poet's inscription as the only friend he ever knew.

But there are much older echoes at Newstead. You approach the priory gates by the huge Pilgrim Oak, dating back to the time of the friars. A medieval fishpond bordered by dark and ancient yews was used by the brethren for breeding carp. From it, a narrow tunnel leads to the Eagle Pond, so named because the friars are said to have thrown an eagle-shaped brass lectern into it at the time of the Dissolution. It is a beautiful rectangle of water, edged by terraced banks.

Newstead Abbey in the 19th century.

EASTERN TOUCH *Byron, with his taste for the exotic, would surely have approved of the Japanese Garden planted at Newstead a century after his death.*

The poet Byron was not the only member of his family to leave his mark on the gardens. His uncle, from whom he inherited the estate, had been known as the Wicked Lord Byron after an assortment of infamies which culminated in his trial for the murder of a neighbour. Convicted only of manslaughter, he retired to Newstead where he continued in his depredations. He brutalised his wife, let the house fall to ruin, and felled trees all around it simply to spite his son. But the Wicked Lord did not only destroy. His

POET'S HOME *The ruined cloisters of Newstead Abbey, where the poet Byron played as a boy, may have helped inspire his love of the romantic.*

enduring monuments include two little mock forts on the Upper Lake where he used to hold sham naval battles with his brother (an admiral known as Foul Weather Jack). He also set up statues of a male and female satyr in a dark grove at Newstead, which superstitious villagers named Devil's Wood. The grove has gone, but the statues still stand, looking rather less satanic now that they rise from open green turf.

The poet was forced by debts to sell the estate in 1817, and several notable features date from later years. Most of the trees near the house, for example, are of fairly recent origin; so many had fallen victim to the Wicked Lord's axe. Among them you can see an especially fine example of *Davidia involucrata*, the pocket handkerchief tree, an introduction from western China.

The great Garden Lake, sweeping south of the house, also dates from a time after the Byron connection was broken. The outflow of water forms a cascade which flows down to the Japanese Garden, complete with tea house, designed early in this century by a Japanese landscape architect. Other Victorian and 20th-century features include rock, heather and iris gardens. Among the most recent introductions is a rose garden laid out in 1965 where the old kitchen garden had been. Its southern border is devoted to historical and shrub roses where the holy rose (*Rosa sancta*) is a conspicuous attraction. This is a plant of immense antiquity, whose large, single pink blooms delight the visitor as they did the Egyptians some 8,000 years ago. The rose makes a fitting flower for the old priory – even if it is rather less appropriate to the colourful family which for so long made Newstead Abbey its home.

NYMANS *West Sussex*

Drive from London to Brighton by the main road and at Handcross, about 5 miles south of Crawley, you will see Nymans signposted to your left. It is not a promising introduction, but if you leave the tarmac lanes with their hurtling capsules of humanity you quickly enter a very different world where the roar of traffic is muffled by trees grown tall in the fertile soil of the Sussex Weald. Nymans' 30 acres are tranquil and secluded. Though lying at about 500 ft above sea level the gardens are well sheltered, enjoy a mild climate and are blessed with a rich, well-drained soil. These conditions have been exploited for almost a century now in one of Sussex's loveliest gardens.

Mr Ludwig Messel started planting the property in 1885, and his son Colonel Leonard Messel continued to nurture it until 1954, when the gardens were bequeathed to the National Trust. The house, built in mock medieval style, succumbed to a disastrous fire after the Second World War and survives chiefly as a shell of grey stone. Remarkably, though, the flames hardly affected the choice plants growing against its walls. And today, embroidered with flowering shrubs and climbers, the picturesque ruins contribute to the romance of the gardens.

The heart of Nymans is a Wall Garden made out of

an old orchard situated to the west of the house. Some of the original apple trees still remain in the plot, but what catch the eye are the mature specimens of trees and shrubs assembled from all over the world. They were established by James Comber, head gardener for decades at Nymans, whose son Harold became a celebrated plant collector in the 1920s. James was a brilliant plantsman with a talent for coaxing the best out of the most delicate subject.

The results can be seen all around the Wall Garden in the splendid specimens of magnolia, nothofagus and davidia, together with stewartias from the southern United States, eucryphias from the Andes and camellias and rhododendrons from the Far East. Especially notable features include plantings of *Lilium giganteum*, the giant Himalayan lily, which bears its drooping trumpets on stems 8 ft long or more. These can be very difficult subjects, requiring copious feeding and a long time to settle in before flowering.

GREEN WALL *Looking as solid as a wall of stone, a close-trimmed hedge of yew flanks the lawn at Nymans. Its topiary obelisks rise towards the roofless gable of the old Great Hall, destroyed long ago by fire.*

The flourishing examples at Nymans were the pride of Leonard Messel.

The main paths in the Wall Garden meet at the central Italian fountain. It is framed by four topiary yews, finely sculpted to the shape of hollow globes, while the paths themselves are lined with old-fashioned herbaceous borders. They were designed under the influence of William Robinson, a friend of the Messel family who, like the equally renowned Gertrude Jekyll, was a frequent visitor to Nymans. Between them, they pioneered a whole approach to modern gardening, based on informal naturalism and cottage-garden effects. Nymans is an early – and outstanding – illustration of their principles. Plantings may include a wealth of tender, rare and exotic specimens, but the charm of the whole is unforced.

There are several distinct areas. Near the outset of a tour, for example, you can explore the superb pinetum, bristling with mighty conifers: cedars, hemlock spruces and redwoods among them. They form a shelter belt to the north, deeply shadowed but luminous through spring and early summer with the blooms of underplanted rhododendrons and azaleas.

There is a sunk garden and a heather garden – one of the first ever established. In the rhododendron wood, exotics from Burma, Tibet and western China clutch at the Sussex soil, matting the ground and billowing in great bushes as freely as in their native habitat.

Now and again, pleasing incidents arrest the eye: here, it is a pale classical summerhouse set against deep green foliage; there, a pergola drenched in season with mauve showers of *Wisteria floribunda*. For old-world enchantment you can explore the rose garden, laid out around an ancient well; or admire the stone dovecote from which white pigeons take flight to settle and coo amid the branches of the trees.

A laurel walk and an avenue of limes bound the garden to the north-east, the latter leading to a balustraded viewpoint which looks out across beautiful natural woodlands below. These, too, are part of the Nymans scene.

One area at Nymans is known as Tasmania, and is devoted chiefly to plants gathered from that land. Here, growing wild, you can see such unusual plants as *Drimys aromatica* and *Lomatia tinctoria*, both survivals from the original plantings in the 1920s. It

would be tedious to enumerate all the interesting plants which contribute to Nymans' distinction, but special mention should be made of a few. Besides its vast range of rhododendrons, the garden is famed for its choice specimens of camellias and magnolias. Several were raised in the garden itself, as their names bear witness: the original camellias 'Leonard Messel' and 'Maud Messel', for example, and the magnolia 'Leonard Messel'.

Eucryphias, too, are well represented and include the garden's most celebrated product. This is *Eucryphia nymansensis*, an evergreen raised by chance in 1915 as a hybrid of the Chilean species *E. cordifolia* and *E. glutinosa*. It blooms in late summer and early autumn, bearing white-petalled flowers with a central golden boss. The tree grows to 30 ft or more, and has been widely planted in its Sussex home. More than that it has proved a gift to the whole gardening world, valued both for its hardiness and its tolerance of some lime in the soil. It flowers today in many parts of the world very far from the favoured loam of the Sussex Weald – and further still from the Andean homeland of its ancestors.

OVERBECK'S *Devon*

Britain, of course, has no Mediterranean coastline; but for the feel of the Riviera you could do no better than to visit the Salcombe area. The resort is the most southerly in Devon and claims the mildest climate on the mainland. Sheltered in the Kingsbridge estuary, this favoured spot is screened from the winds which blast the Cornish headlands to the south-west. Orange and lemon trees grow in the open, and set high above the harbour, less than 2 miles from the yachting centre, is a garden of exceptional luxury.

Overbeck's 6 acres sprawl down a steep, south-east-facing slope, commanding superb views down the inlet, out to sea and across to Prawle Point on the horizon. And the garden fully exploits the potential of its position. It was established during the early years of this century, when terraces and retaining walls were built to support a wealth of tender and unusual trees. The older surviving rarities include one aromatic camphor tree, *Cinnamomum camphora*, which is probably unique for size in the British Isles. Olives grow near by, and there are many varieties of cornus,

RIVIERA VIEW *Palms frame a view of hot beaches and a sail-studded blue sea in a scene reminiscent of the Mediterranean. But this is Devon, and the garden is Overbeck's which looks out over the Kingsbridge estuary.*

including *C. capitata*, an evergreen species from the Himalayas.

The garden is known as Overbeck's , after Mr Otto Overbeck who owned the property from 1928 to 1937. He amassed a great collection of curios in the building, which is now maintained as a museum. His chief contribution to the garden, meanwhile, was to establish its many palm trees. The hardy Chinese Chusan palm is well represented in this pampered site, and you can also see the little *Chamaerops humilis* – a native of the western Mediterranean which is the only true palm indigenous to Europe.

Trumpets of crinum and amaryllis play from Overbeck's warm beds; tender fuchsias, hydrangeas, acacias and agapanthuses abound. But for sheer magnificence, one specimen holds pride of place. This is a large *Magnolia campbellii*, a native of the Himalayas, which was planted in 1901. It is now some 40 ft tall and in March bears thousands of vivid pink chalices in a sensational display which can be seen from almost a mile away.

OXFORD BOTANIC GARDENS

In Oxford, traffic can rumble with alarming speed beneath the noble tower of Magdalen College. Yet across the road is a little oasis of tranquillity. This is the Botanic Garden whose high stone walls offer sanctuary for footsore sightseers: the shade of aged trees, the splashing of a fountain and vision of lilies in a glimmering pool.

The Botanic Garden was founded by Henry Danvers, Earl of Danby, in 1621 on the site of a medieval Jewish burial ground. It is the oldest botanic garden in Britain. The walls which enclose the original 3 acre site date back to the 17th century, and you enter by a fine gate built by Nicholas Stone, master mason to James I and Charles I.

CITY OASIS *Tucked away from the roar of Oxford's traffic, the University's Botanic Gardens offer a haven of calm in the heart of the busy city. But there is more to it than that – its eight glasshouses contain a major collection of tropical plants that flourish more lushly than they could in any desert oasis.*

The first gardener was a German named Jacob Bobart, who had 4,000 loads of 'mucke and dunge' brought in to enrich the soil and raise it above the floodwaters of the Cherwell. A man of great energy and ingenuity, he also introduced some 3,000 different plants to the garden. Among them was the yellow Oxford ragwort (*Senecio squalidus*), whose seeds were first brought to Bobart from the slopes of Mount Etna. It proved too prolific for the venerable walls to contain, and now grows wild all over England.

The garden was initially designed to accommodate medicinal plants. It formed part of the School of Medicine, and was known as the Physic Garden until 1840. Today, both medicinal herbs and culinary plants still grow in formal beds, and a yew has survived from a central avenue planted in Bobart's time. The original squared design has, however, been modified and extended to include, for example, herbaceous borders, alpine rockeries and a historical collection of roses showing their evolution from wild ancestry to the cultured blooms of today.

College spires, perceived above the walls, are glimpsed through the foliage of the trees. Enter the complex of eight glasshouses, though, and you depart from the world of fine stonework and scholarship. In this enclosed domain the air is aromatic and the textures exotic. In the humid, luxuriant water-lily house, for example, a splayed clump of sugar canes greets you, while bananas, papyruses and the sacred lotus flourish in the beds around. The centrepiece is a swampy tank first built to house the giant Amazon water lily (*Victoria regia*), which Victorian visitors had to pay a shilling to see. Today, the tank holds 20 different water lilies which tinge the surface with red, pink, yellow and blue.

The succulent house has a quite different aura, like some pocket of Arizona, harbouring desert cacti and agaves. At the far end you come upon the furred gullets and tendrils of the meat-eaters: sundews, pitcher plants and Venus's flytraps. Peer into their sinister forms and the Oxonian images of sculpted bust and library fade from the mind. You are intimate here with exquisitely murderous vegetation. The sign reads CARNIVOROUS PLANTS – DO NOT TOUCH.

PACKWOOD HOUSE *Warwickshire*

They rise in brooding solemnity from Packwood's lawns – scores of yews clipped as giant cones and tapering cylinders grown in some cases to 20 ft in height. Who put them there and to what purpose? There is a tradition that Packwood's famous assemblage of topiaries was planted to represent the 'Multitude' at the Sermon on the Mount. And the congregation does in fact stand below a raised Mount Garden crowned by a solitary cone which might be delivering some voiceless address.

Lately, the legend has been questioned. But you cannot wander among these dark abstracts without projecting animate qualities on to them. Some stand erect, as if spellbound; others lean slightly as if in discussion. All contribute a unique fascination to one

of the most celebrated gardens in Warwickshire.

Packwood House and its 5 acre gardens lie among the fields and copses of the ancient Forest of Arden. The gabled building dates back to Elizabethan times, and was built for the Fetherston family who occupied the building for some 300 years. John Fetherston enlarged the house in the 17th century, and it was he who seems to have set up the raised Mount Garden – an eminence from which he could survey his domain. The work probably took place between 1650 and 1670, and 13 of the yews may date back to the original garden. Twelve flank a raised path leading up to the Mount and are known as the Apostles. A spiral path winds on up to the summit where a single, venerable specimen known as the Master, presides over all.

John Fetherston lived through the English Civil War, a time of deep religious turmoil. It may well be that he had a Biblical parallel in mind when he sited his 13 yews. But the Multitude assembled below are not of the original garden. They were planted in the 19th century, to replace an old orchard.

Quite apart from the famous topiaries, there is much at Packwood to fascinate. The main entrance in the 18th century was on the west side, where you can see a cold plunge bath, with steps leading down, which was built in 1680. The main gardens, though, extend to the south where you first enter the so-called Carolean Garden. It has gazebos at its corners. One, dating from the reign of Charles II, incorporates a furnace and flues used to heat an adjacent wall, against which peaches were grown.

Apart from a sunken garden, laid out in the present century, what next catches your eye is a wide terraced walk massed with colourful bedding plants according to the season. A superb decorative gateway of 18th-century wrought ironwork leads through to the great yew garden. But before exploring their weird topiary world pause to look at the arched alcoves in the terraced wall. There are 30 of them in all, not built to house marbled busts but wicker beehives – intriguing features in this garden of curiosities.

PITMEDDEN *Grampian*

Long ago, when dark forests were enemies and rugged rocks evoked only terror, people took no pleasure in 'wild gardening'. Raw nature was too threatening a reality to be toyed with. As far as is

VERSATILE TREE *Yews play a large part in the gardens at Packwood House. Here, they are used as hedging to protect herbaceous borders and shelter a pool. In another part of the garden they stand alone in an impressive topiary composition said to represent the Sermon on the Mount.*

known, the earliest gardens were all more or less formal affairs, laid out with comforting rows of fruit trees, vegetables, flowers and herbs. From the geometrical designs of the Roman era to the elaborate knot gardens of Tudor times, styles continued to express delight in controlling nature.

The tradition reached its height in the 17th century, when vast ornamental parterres were laid out with thousands of flowers, each planted to help make up a picture – of arabesques, heraldic emblems or even written inscriptions. Spread like vast living carpets before palaces and great houses, they seem to have celebrated something more than a love of colour or design; the quality, perhaps, of sheer human cleverness.

In Britain, almost all of the great ornamental parterres were wiped out by the 18th-century landscapists. And among the few gardens which still recall the scale of the 17th-century conceptions, Pitmedden is outstanding. Enclosed by massive greystone walls, the garden covers an area of 3 acres, enclosing four great rectangular beds. No fewer than 40,000 brightly coloured annuals are planted out every year to make up the intricate compositions. The sight is frankly amazing; it is as if giants had imprinted the level green turf with immaculate stamps of their grandeur.

The great floral beds at Pitmedden are in fact reconstructions, skilfully achieved by the National Trust for Scotland which acquired the property in 1952. But the designs are traditional, and the framework is entirely authentic.

The Great Garden was founded in 1675 by Sir Alexander Seton, who was clearly influenced by the French fashions of his day. He laid out his plot by the old castle of Pitmedden, on land sloping away to the east. This permitted a split-level arrangement: an upper garden with terraced extensions to north and south looks down on the Great Garden below. Today, as in the laird's time, visitors can see the whole composition spread out at the lower level.

You come down to the parterres by imposing pillared gates and a handsome divided stairway, while matching stone pavilions rise at each corner of the main terrace wall. All these features date from the founding of the garden, but little is known of the original floral patterns. When the Trust took on the property, the whole area was being used as a kitchen garden, and records which might have shed light were destroyed in a fire of 1818. Inspiration had to be sought elsewhere, and was found in a 1647 book of engravings of Edinburgh, entitled *Bird's Eye View*. Almost every garden represented in the book is laid out according to one geometrical design or another. Three of the Pitmedden designs are taken directly from examples in the garden at the Palace of Holyroodhouse, as shown in the book. The fourth (the

GIGANTIC GEOMETRY *Three miles of clipped box hedging, 40,000 bedding plants, hundreds of immaculately trimmed trees and acres of close-mown turf combine to recreate the 17th-century formality of the gardens at Pitmedden.*

107

LOOKING DOWN *The terraces at Powis Castle, framed by balustrades, urns and statues, are now nearly 300 years old. They were laid out on a south-facing slope where tender plants flourish at every level. Below the bottom terrace a grassy bank, planted with flowering trees and shrubs, leads down to the great lawn.*

south-west parterre) depicts Sir Alexander Seton's coat of arms flanked by the Scottish emblems of St Andrew's cross and thistle.

To reconstruct the parterres, the garden first had to be razed and grassed over. The designs were then marked out and planted with box hedging – 3 miles of it in all. In 1958 the first flowers were planted to block in the colours, and they have been planted out yearly in May ever since. The annuals used include alyssum, begonias and dwarf wallflowers – considerably gaudier subjects than would have been available to Sir Alexander Seton. They are raised in a complex of glasshouses near by, and the colour schemes are sometimes varied. In accordance with traditional practice, coloured pebbles are also used to fill in the designs.

The Great Garden is designed to create impact from a distance. But there is much to engage the eye as you tread the turfed paths between the beds. A shapely fountain provides the focus at the centre of the garden, incorporating seven sculptured stones cut by Charles II's master mason. The south-east bed (displaying the inscription *Tempus Fugit* – Time Flies) has a superb 17th-century sundial at the centre; it was found in the garden and may have formed part of the original design. Yews sculpted into pyramids flank the main path, while mammoth buttresses of the evergreen also extend from the walls. And if you should tire of so much disciplined flower and foliage there are two great billowing borders to admire. They were planted by Lady Burnet of Leys (co-creator of Crathes garden) and are massed with wands of aconitums, golden rods and red hot pokers – bold strokes which vie in high summer with the radiance of the patterned beds.

POWIS CASTLE *Powys*

A traveller visiting Powis in 1784 wrote: 'In the gardens, which were laid out in the wretched taste of steps, statues and pavilions, not even the fruit is attended to; the balustrades and terraces are falling down, and the horses graze on the parterres!'

The gardens then were little cared for, and it is easy enough to understand the writer's scorn for their neglect. But no one visiting Powis today would refer to 'wretched taste' in their layout. The dramatic medieval castle, perched high on a south-east-facing bluff, commands superb views across the valley of the Severn to the line of the Breidden Hills and the flank of the Long Mountain. And the foreground frame is a quite magnificent series of steeply stepped 17th-century terraces, supported by retaining walls all built of the same rose-pink stone as the castle.

Eighteenth-century landscapists abhorred formal terraces, which explains the writer's slighting reference. In fact, it is said that Capability Brown himself visited Powis and suggested that the stepped garden should be abolished and the whole slope returned to bare rock. Without diminishing the landscape architect's achievements elsewhere, we can only be thankful that at Powis his proposals were ignored.

Powis has a history stretching back over 700 years, but the gardens date from the reign of William of Orange (1688–1702), when the Dutch Rochford family acquired the castle. The great terraces, with their balustrades and niches, belong to their period of tenure, as do the yews which are such prominent features today.

The old bones of the garden were fleshed out after 1952 when the property was vested in the National Trust. It now contains a wealth of rare and tender shrubs not often seen at this height above sea level. The gardens reach an elevation of 450 ft and the drop of the slope is, moreover, so steep that cold and damp air drains freely away. However, the soil contains lime derived from the pink rock of the bluff, and is no friend to acid-loving plants such as rhododendrons or azaleas.

There are basically three levels of terracing, and the raw limestone is exposed at the highest where it provides the setting for a rock garden at one end. At the other is a fine statue of Hercules, backed by a 30 ft high wall of yew.

Below, the second or aviary terrace has at its centre a handsome brick loggia clothed with a lovely *Wisteria floribunda*; tender and fragrant Himalayan rhododendrons are grown inside, in specially prepared troughs of lime-free soil. From the balustrade, delightful lead figures of shepherds and shepherdesses look out over the incomparable views.

The third or main terrace incorporates an orangery in its retaining wall. The structure was heated by a boiler in the 18th century; the orange trees would be grown in tubs and trundled out into the open air during the summer months. Today, the walls are hung with roses and passion flowers, while the terrace borders billow with choice fuchsias, cistuses and ceanothuses.

Powis did not entirely escape the attentions of the landscapists. Below the main levels is a fourth or apple slope terrace leading down to the great lawn. Baroque fountains once played here, but were scrapped by the landscape gardener William Emes, a disciple of Capability Brown. He also laid out a serpentine walk on the ridge beyond, known as The Wilderness. Its soil is lime-free, supporting profusions of rhododendrons and azaleas as well as exceptionally sturdy growths of trees. Powis is renowned for its oakwoods, which furnished timber for Admiral Rodney's ships in the 18th century. Many aged oaks still abound in The Wilderness, mingling with more recently planted exotics and several outstanding conifers: cedars, redwoods and giant firs, for example.

Overtopping all is a Douglas fir which rises from its clump to the stupendous height of 183 ft. This has often been cited as the tallest tree in the British Isles. Though the *Guinness Book of Records* awards the title to a slightly taller giant fir in Strathclyde, the exact statistics seem hardly worth quibbling over. Suffice to say that Powis's claimant is very tall indeed, surpassing any tree seen in England.

To one side of the great lawn is a fern-edged pool overhung with the giant leaves of Brazilian gunneras;

LOOKING UP *The sword-like leaves of dracaena make an appropriately martial pointer to the battlements of Powis Castle, perched on a crag above its terraced gardens. The cones of yew that line the topmost level have stood guard there for more than 250 years.*

to the other, an old kitchen garden where apples and pears are grown in unusual pyramid shapes. But perhaps Powis's most memorable feature is the view back from The Wilderness to the castle, taking in the full splendour of the terraces.

PUSEY HOUSE *Oxfordshire*

Sometimes you have to destroy to create. When Mr and Mrs Michael Hornby came to Pusey House in 1935 they found an evergreen wilderness of a garden. Yet today, these 15 Oxfordshire acres have become as gaily tinted as any in England. 'We had bonfires every weekend', Mrs Hornby has written. Out came the impenetrable thickets of shrub, and on to the flames too went some sizeable Wellingtonias, trees which cast a pall of darkness over the views. Geoffrey Jellicoe, a noted garden architect, was brought in to design a terrace as a new axis for the garden.

Not everything, of course, was sacrificed to the Hornbys' garden pyres. They were careful to retain the best of the aged trees: gnarled old cedars and holm oaks, for example, dating back to the 18th century. These continue to lend an air of maturity to what is essentially a post-war garden. Outstanding among the survivors is a mighty London plane which is reckoned to be the second largest in Britain.

The clearances also made sense of some of the existing garden features. A superb Cotswold stone wall, 10 ft high, was revealed when one vast, shaggy box hedge was uprooted. Today, the wall provides a magnificent backdrop for one of the best herbaceous borders in the country. Pusey's silty lake was dredged and now sparkles in the sunlight, a perfect setting for

an old Chinese bridge, dating back to 1748.

You enter today through a corridor of double herbaceous borders, recently developed and conceived for rainbow effect. Strong reds greet you at the outset – from crimson salvias and scarlet spiraeas – but these fade, as you advance, into a succession of pastels: mauve, yellow, blue and white. Inside the garden proper, lovely views open up of the lawns, lake, pale bridge and woods beyond.

To left and right curves the great main herbaceous border with its backing of Cotswold stone. The whole bed extends for some 360 ft, and is so densely planted that few of its subjects need staking. Hollyhocks, delphiniums, slender wands of penstemons, scarlet potentillas, blue salvias and pink cushions of phloxes – these and countless others tuft and jostle one another exuberantly in apparent disorder, interspersed with roses, silver-leaved and variegated plants.

Being open at its centre, Pusey is best explored further by making a tour of the perimeter. Leading across the sunny south front of the house is the paved terrace whose retaining wall shelters many a choice climber. A path then leads down to the lake between beds of shrubs roses and a border devoted to orange-flowering and orange-foliaged plants. A grand old oriental plane rises near the water's edge, and if you cross the Chinese bridge you can explore the splendid water garden planted with arums and lysichitons.

Back from the water's edge is a little woodland known as 'Westonbirt' after the famous arboretum in Gloucestershire. Magnolias have managed to prosper here, though Pusey is not, on the whole, a garden for acid-loving plants. The soil is light and alkaline; no effort is made to force lime-hating rhododendrons or camellias to endure it. Here, as in the adjoining Pleasure Garden and the lavishly planted shrubberies near by, the colours come from a lime-tolerant community.

The far side of the lake offers exquisite views back across the water to the house and its great curving border. The huge London plane rises at the head of the lake, and a short walk back towards the house brings you to a domed greystone temple and an intimate little walled plot which is one of Pusey's most delightful attractions. This is Lady Emily's garden, named after the wife of a 19th-century owner of Pusey.

Its enclosing walls are of warm red brick tangled with roses, clematises and honeysuckles. From eight little beds, more roses load the air with fragrance, and flowering shrubs bloom around in abundance.

ROUSHAM PARK *Oxfordshire*

In its way, Rousham Park is a time capsule, a complete and unaltered statement of the philosophy and manners of the Age of Reason – at least insofar as gardening is concerned. It was created in a style that has come to be known as classical landscaping and was the first true breakaway from the geometrical, formal style that had held Western gardeners in thrall for so long. Its inspirations were the classical education that was the birthright of every English gentleman, the wide, sunlit countryside of Italy recalled from Grand Tours, and the paintings of such French artists as Lorrain and Poussin who depicted vast landscapes in which graceful buildings of antiquity were set in balance with trees and water and far-away hills – scenes in which the works of man enhanced those of nature. This should be the gardener's theme, argued writers like Alexander Pope, to supplement the landscape, not to obliterate it with flower beds:

> *To build, to plant, whatever you intend,*
> *To rear the column, or to arch the bend,*
> *To well the terrase, or to sink the Grot;*
> *In all let Nature never be forgot. . . .*

Pope took his own advice and created his own ideal landscape at Twickenham, complete with grotto, which is still there. Lord Burlington and Vanbrugh were also in the forefront of the movement, and soon temples, colonnaded bridges, ruined arches and classical statuary were dotting estates all over Britain. Classical landscapes need no longer be viewed in paintings or visited in far-off Italy; they could be built outside one's own front door. There were several designers of talent engaged in this work, but perhaps the greatest of them was William Kent. He it was who created Rousham Park and, apart from a certain mellowing, it remains much as he planned it in 1738.

The house was built in 1635 for Sir Robert Dormer – whose descendants still live there – and was later added to and Gothicised by Kent, who gave it a battlemented front, a cupola and some lead statues. An architect and an artist as well as a garden designer, he also refurbished the interior of the house, but it is his gardens at Rousham that have excited the greatest admiration.

Kent visualised a romantic landscape with a series of idyllic scenes, meant to be seen in a particular sequence, that would link the house and its terrace with the woods and the River Cherwell. From the terrace, the visitor should wander down into Venus's Vale, with its pools, cascades and statues. Then by way of a woodland path with a little stone-lined stream running beside it to a great basin of water called the Cold Bath. Beyond is a Doric temple, named Townsend's Building after the mason who built it in 1738. From there, the path runs past a statue of Apollo to the medieval Heyford Bridge and the Temple of the Mill, a romantic ruin created from an old mill. There is the Eyecatcher, another contrived ruin on the skyline, designed to lead the eye out to the countryside. Close by is the Lime Walk, a pleasant introduction to an arcaded terrace called Praeneste, which is decorated with handsome urns and a statue of a dying gladiator. Above the river there is an amphitheatre which used to contain a fountain, and across a lawn stands the Pyramid, a fine viewing-base.

PIGEONS AND ROSES *The Pigeon House Garden at Rousham Park is a maze of formal rose beds outlined by miniature hedges of box. It takes its name from the circular dovecote which was built in 1685 – the year that William Kent, designer of Rousham's gardens, was born.*

ROYAL NATIONAL ROSE SOCIETY GARDENS *Hertfordshire*

The Gardens of the Rose they are named, as though by some medieval troubadour. But the term is much more likely to be definitive than romantic, for this is the showplace of the Royal National Rose Society, the world arbiter of taste and fashion in all to do with that lovely flower. And what a showplace it is – 12 acres mostly of roses, 1,000 species and varieties of them, old roses, large-flowered varieties (hybrid teas), miniatures, shrubs, climbers, bushes, historical, modern, wild, and roses that so far exist nowhere else at all.

The gardens on Bone Hill, near St Albans, look as though they have been there for ever but, in fact, they were founded only in 1960, and upon soil that is far from ideal for roses. In this part of Hertfordshire the soil is thin, with gravel not far beneath the surface, and to maintain fertility, large quantities of manure must constantly be added. But, as the society points out, this poverty of soil does have certain advantages so far as rose-fanciers are concerned; they will know that any plant that does well on Bone Hill could do at least as well elsewhere.

The gardens are divided into two major parts – the Display Gardens and the Trial Ground. In the Trial Ground everything is strictly regimented, with the plants in long, straight rows to facilitate observation of their behaviour and growth. Scores of new roses are submitted each year from all over the world, and trials take three years, during which the plants are awarded marks out of a possible 100 for health (the premier consideration, carrying a maximum of 20 points), vigour, habit, beauty of form, colour, continuity of flowering, general effect, fragrance and novelty. The roses actually undergoing trial are set out to the east of the gardens waiting to learn their fate, which could be anything from the good pass mark of a Trial Ground Certificate to the supreme accolade of the President's International Trophy for the champion new rose of the year. All round the Trial Ground perimeter, presumably to encourage them, are swathes of newish roses, all of which have won some award from the society since 1963.

Fascinating though the Trial Ground is, the chief attraction for most laymen is the Display Garden, which is itself divided into several parts. Close by the entrance there are three small gardens, the first of which is devised as little more than an idyllic spot in which to eat one's sandwiches, being wooed the while by the sight and scent of roses. The next, however, is designed to show how roses can best be employed in a small garden. The centrepiece is a sundial, round which are gathered a splendid variety of plants. The most spectacular is the June-flowering shrub 'Scarlet Fire', but look here too for the silvery-pink 'La France', first raised in 1867 and very probably the very first of the large-flowered varieties. The third enclosure, a little sunken garden, is devoted to miniature roses – true miniatures, with flowers, leaves and overall size all in proportion. Around the bank are beds of herbaceous plants, providing another illustration of how well roses will mingle in a small garden.

NOT ONLY THE ROSE *In spite of their infinite range of colour, size and form, even roses need the foil of other plants to point up their beauty. At the Bone Hill gardens of the Royal National Rose Society, a lily pond spiked by stands of iris enhances the attraction of roses massed in formal beds.*

Beyond, the display becomes much grander, and is appropriately introduced by a stately brick and oak pergola that supports as many as 46 different climbing roses whose blooms tumble from the high beams in a great, happy abundance composed of every imaginable colour. The pergola leads to a pretty little pool fed by a tinkling fountain and aswim with lilies, while on every side there are the massed phalanxes of the rose beds. All these are labelled, so that, armed with a plan obtainable at the entrance lounge, any sought-after plant can be tracked down fairly rapidly. There are also a number of general groupings, as in the case of the 'Old' or 'Old French' roses. This is a fascinating collection, for these are the roses of history and of the poets – the Albas, Damasks, Gallicas and Mosses. Other delightful gatherings are those of the wild roses, which are dotted about the garden and provide a rich variety with their different foliage and brilliant hips when the blooming of summer is over. Then there are the great collections of the roses that everyone knows, the large-flowered, or hybrid teas, which began in the 19th century with hybrids of the China rose *Rosa chinensis*. Among the dozens of favourites you will see 'Grandpa Dickson', 'Silver Jubilee' and the rest, as well as cluster-flowered (floribunda) roses such as 'Iceberg', 'Southampton' and 'City of Leeds'.

Summer is obviously the most popular time to visit the Gardens of the Rose, when the whole place is vibrant with colour, but as the society itself points out, a wander among the beds in autumn is almost as rewarding. April, too, is a favourite time with true rosarians, for then, they say, just after pruning, you get the best idea of the bones of the plants, and of the extraordinary brilliance and variety of the new young growth.

RUDDING PARK *North Yorkshire*

Among the disciples of Capability Brown, Humphry Repton (1752–1818) held pride of place. As the leading exponent of 'landskip' design after the master's death in 1783, Repton perpetuated the taste for suave lawns and informal woodlands. But he was rather more flexible in his approach than Brown had been; among other developments, he planted more densely and used more varied trees and shrubs.

Rudding Park in Yorkshire is among the best surviving examples of Repton's work, and was the subject for one of his famous Red Books. These were slim volumes made for his clients, with text and watercolour illustrations often showing 'before' and 'after' views of his proposed alterations. Repton came to Rudding in about 1790, and the parkland vistas remain much as he envisaged them.

From the fine Regency house, standing on a slight eminence, you look over broad lawns dotted with aged trees. There are thick belts of beeches beyond and, eastwards, the eye travels right across the plain of York to the line of the wolds in the distance.

The gardens themselves are largely informal, although by the south front of the house is a patterned herb garden, outlined in hedging yew and box. The design is filled in with blue-leaved rue, purple-brown

THE VERSATILE ROSE *Beds of hybrid tea roses lead the eye to a pergola over which sprawl more than 40 varieties of climber. In all, more than 1,000 species and varieties of rose can be seen in the gardens of the Royal National Rose Society.*

113

sage, silvery lavender and golden senecio. Their quiet and refined foliage tones well suit the character of the house, which was owned for generations by the Radcliffe family.

A walled flower garden with long herbaceous borders has been scrapped in recent years. But colour is not lacking at Rudding. Grassy walks and exotic glades have been created in the extensive woodland garden. Magnificent rhododendrons are represented, including many of the large-leaved Chinese species rarely seen in the north of England. And the season is a long one, extended by such late-flowering hybrids as the white 'Polar Bear' and wine-red 'Beau Brummel' (a plant with a fitting Regency name). There are also extensive plantings of a wide range of azaleas.

The rhododendron woods are underplanted with varieties of primulas and poppies, and late in the season gaudy hydrangeas come into their own. Thickets of bamboos, glowing wands of kniphofias – such subjects had no place in the 18th-century landscape. But they have colonised Rudding's woodland acres without disturbing their stately calm, providing interest from April to October.

SANDRINGHAM *Norfolk*

Many fine gardens throughout the nation are stamped with the character of families which have loved them. To tread lawns where children have played, or come upon gravestones of favourite pets, adds a dimension of human interest which the loveliest plants cannot in themselves evoke. Sandringham has that lived-in quality – though the scale is vast and the family far from ordinary.

Rising from a windswept landscape some 2 miles from the Norfolk coast, Sandringham Hall was bought in 1861 as a private residence for Albert-Edward, later Edward VII. The boundaries of the estate enclosed some 7,000 acres of lean, sandy soil, with an undistinguished Georgian house as the centrepiece. But since that time the property has evolved as the much-loved private home of four generations of monarchs. Edward VII held lavish shooting parties, inventing 'Sandringham Time' to extend the shooting season (all the clocks in the house were fixed half an hour fast). It was from Sandringham that George V made his first Christmas broadcast in 1932, and it is to their Norfolk home that the present royal family still comes to celebrate Christmas and the New Year.

No one would call the vast mansion an architectural masterpiece. Much rebuilt from 1867, it is a stylistic hybrid of cupolas, turrets and gables, executed in red brick and chocolate-brown carstone. Sandringham, in fact, is one historic residence where the gardens redeem the building.

The great house is set amid lawns and gravel walks, scattered here and there with aged oaks as well as younger trees, some of them planted by royalty. The biggest of these owes its presence to Queen Victoria who, in her diary for April 25, 1889, recorded: 'Out with Bertie (Prince of Wales), Alix (Princess of Wales), Louise (their eldest daughter) and all the children, and I planted a tree in front of the house.'

Several members of the family have been enthusiastic gardeners, among them George VI. His rooms were at the north end of the mansion, and he wanted to see flowers from his windows. Accordingly, the formal North Garden was created, a long and narrow

ROYAL FAVOURITE *Albert-Edward, Prince of Wales and the Princess of Wales – later King Edward VII and Queen Alexandra – were the first royal residents of Sandringham. The estate was bought for the prince in 1861, and has remained a favourite residence of the royal family. King Edward first opened the gardens to the public in 1908, and they have been open ever since.*

compartment surrounded by box hedges and flanked by alleys of pleached limes. Roses and lavenders billow from the crisply edged beds, while a central path leads to a statue of Father Time.

The bearded statue wears a suitably weary air, in marked contrast to Sandringham's other memorable figure. This is 'Chinese Joss', a gold-plated bronze statue, shipped from China in 1869.

Sweeping around to the north of the house are belts of great conifers, planted to give shelter from North Sea gales. And they have served their function so well that a wealth of tender shrubs has been successfully nurtured in their half-shade: cornus, camellias and magnolias, for example, with wonderful varieties of fuchsias and hydrangeas. Swathes of polyanthus fill spaces between, and one glade in particular is flooded in spring with the colours of rhododendrons and azaleas. Their display lasts well into July when the white rhododendron 'Polar Bear' provides a triumphant finale.

Among several choice trees, a fine pocket handkerchief tree (*Davidia involucrata*) is conspicuous, growing close to the great Norwich Gates. These were presented in 1863 to the Prince and Princess of Wales as a wedding present, forming a fittingly magnificent composition in wrought iron shaped with interlacing flowers and leaves.

'Dear old Sandringham, the place I love better than anywhere else in the world', wrote George V. He lived from 1893 to 1926 in York Cottage, a lodge some distance from the main house which stands by the lower of two landscaped lakes.

CHARM OF THE LAKES

But the lakes themselves contribute much to Sandringham's attraction, whether seen from the house or glimpsed from the woodland belt. They were excavated in the 19th century to replace an older lake lying much closer to the house. The upper is especially beautiful: irises, astilbes and candelabra primulas line stretches of the waterside, while darker corners are overhung with gunneras and arums. At one side a dipping path leads into a dell, graced by a lovely *Magnolia denudata* which is 60 years old and bears hosts of white goblets in spring.

On the facing bank is a sizeable rock garden, now planted chiefly with labour-saving conifers (even royal families have to make economies; about 60 gardeners tended Sandringham before the Second World War. Today's staff numbers 15). One interesting feature is a boathouse built like a grotto from boulders of the local brown carstone. Another, is an enchanting summerhouse nestling among the conifers and commanding lovely views over the lake. Known as the 'Nest', this charming retreat was given to Queen Alexandra in 1913 by the Comptroller of her Household. It is, of course, one small ornament in a garden of vast size and great interest. And yet, looking across the lily-strewn water and the little island set in the middle, it somehow distils that intimate quality which you might not expect in Sandringham's royal acres, and which is all the more pleasing when you meet it.

SAVILL GARDEN AND VALLEY GARDEN *Surrey*

William, Duke of Cumberland, the portly son of George II, is chiefly known to history for his victory at Culloden and for his savage reprisals upon the Jacobites in its aftermath. A minor consequence of this was that the flower Sweet William was dedicated to him by Government sympathisers, while the Jacobites in retaliation christened the strong-smelling common ragwort Stinking Billy. That, so far as most people are aware, was his sole contribution to horticulture, so it comes as something of a surprise to learn that among his offices was that of Ranger of Windsor Great Park. With a battalion of his Culloden veterans as a work force, he created the splendid lake of Virginia Water in

WOODLAND GLADE *Dappled by sunlight, a group of exotic plants show a fantastic variety of leaf forms in a woodland glade at the Savill Garden.*

the park, and drained, landscaped and planted with trees the surrounding swampy Surrey wilderness. In 1932, the Savill Garden was begun in this area, and though it occupies no more than 35 of Windsor's 4,500 acres, it is, after the castle, the park's best-loved and most visited feature.

Sir Eric Savill, the Deputy Ranger of the time, saw the site as perfect for a bog and woodland garden. Ponds were dug, clearings made, and flowering and ornamental trees planted, beginning with a weeping willow that can still be seen near the Temperate House, and extending gradually to the north-east. By 1939 the garden's perimeter had been established, as had one of its most attractive features, the alpine meadow. With the Second World War, work in the garden came to an end, but recommenced in 1950 with the planning and planting of the more formal heart of the garden. Colour was the theme, as can be seen from the great herbaceous borders piled and vibrant with every hue in summer, and from the long, buttressed wall almost overwhelmed by many-hued clematises. The wall was built of bricks obtained from bombed ruins in West Ham, in London's East End; at its foot, raised beds with a mixture of soils provide a series of habitats for bulbs and alpines.

The restaurant, built in the 1960s, provides a fine platform from which to look across ponds and clearings fringed with rhododendrons and azaleas to a beech wood carpeted with silver moss, or outwards to the wide expanse of the park. Above a little bridge

withstand English frosts, are grown tender varieties of rhododendrons, mostly originating from Burma and China. A curiosity well worth looking for is *Rhododendron lochae* from Australia, the only species native to the Southern Hemisphere. In its native Queensland, it is found only on a few mountain tops. In the Savill Garden, they tend their award-winning specimen in the Temperate House where it is known, appropriately, as 'Down Under'.

Rhododendrons also provide the major theme of the Valley Garden, which occupies the slopes and valleys of the northern shore of Virginia Water, still dotted with the trees planted by the Duke of Cumberland. It contains a collection of rhododendron species gathered together over half a century at Tower Court, Ascot, before being brought here in the 1950s, and some wonderful massings of azaleas in the Punch

AZALEA TIME *It is difficult to pin down azalea time in the Savill Garden – except to say that it extends over a considerable period. April and May is the main flowering period but species and hybrids of azaleas and rhododendrons from round the world extend the flowering time through summer into autumn.*

near by, built in 1977 to mark the Queen's Silver Jubilee, the banks are covered with lilies, ferns and primulas reaching out to mingle with more rhododendrons and azaleas, or with forest trees underplanted with blue hydrangeas. Climbing up a slope to the west, and therefore less likely to be hit by spring frosts, are magnolias and camellias to bring visitors to the garden in the early part of the year; later, they will probably return to see the roses, vivid against the dark green of conifers and handsomely displayed in large beds lapped about by neatly edged lawns.

All the same, throughout the garden the strongest accent is on rhododendrons, great parades of them flanking the walks and rides and bringing early colour indoors to the Temperate House. There, among camellias and other plants not hardy enough to

Bowl – a large, natural ampitheatre – and in the Azalea Valley. In the midst of the garden is the Pinetum, whose collection includes some 200 dawn redwoods, among the first to be grown in this country. The pines and cypresses make a sober introduction to the Hydrangea Garden which flanks them. There, blocks of hydrangeas with florets of blue, purple, red, pink and cream sing their colours to the sky from July to October.

On the other side of the Pinetum is the Heather Garden, ideally suited to this acid soil and, in fact, a partly natural covering that crept across a gravel pit that was abandoned before the First World War. Native heathers have been supplemented by other species and varieties so that now, among the hummocks and hollows, there is not one day in the year when one cannot find a heather in bloom.

SCOTNEY CASTLE *Kent*

Most Picturesque landscapes in Britain – that is, those stately landscapes in which vistas of woodland, turf, sheets of water and artfully placed ruins are combined into a harmonious, dream-like whole – were created all of a piece by rich landowners and the great landscape artists of the 18th century. Not so at Scotney Castle. There, it all began in the 14th century when Roger Ashburnham, probably in response to the French raids on Rye and Winchelsea, fortified his manor house; 'castle' was always a highfalutin label for Scotney. By Charles I's reign, not much of this was left, apart from the moat, a small Tudor house and a sturdy tower to which the Darrells, the then owners, added a handsome mansion. Eventually the property passed to the Husseys, one of whom, Edward Hussey, when he inherited in 1836, found the old house too damp and gloomy for his taste and built a splendid Gothic Revival dwelling on a piece of level ground above. To obtain the stone for his new home he quarried deep into the hillside, so establishing the last key feature of the garden as it appears today.

Nevertheless, Edward Hussey was very much a man of his time and background, and he may well have sensed the possibilities of his estate before he engaged William Sawrey Gilpin, the veteran garden designer and arbiter of taste in all to do with the Romantic landscape. At any rate, they were in full agreement on the way the garden should develop. Where the lawn ran down to the lip of the quarry, a terrace was built to command the magical view over the old house and castle. While the yawning pit below was converted into a kind of enormous rockery filled with rhododendrons and herbaceous plants. The castle was draped with climbing roses, as was the 17th-century house, which was partially and cunningly dismantled to blend with the castle in a manner that was even more wildly Romantic than before.

Two more generations of Husseys lived long lives at Scotney before it went at last to the National Trust, who maintain it with exactly the same affection and feeling for period that was lavished upon it by the family. The view from the terrace has matured. The eye wanders over huge mounds of rhododendrons, mostly of the old, wild ponticum species, with muted, pastel colours that range from lavender to purple. Beyond are gigantic lime trees, tulip trees and tall, slim Lawson's cypresses – among the first to be planted in this country – to point attention to the rounded top of the castle tower standing above its still reflection in the moat. Then, on the crest of the far side of the valley, the view is completed by the outspread arms of a great cedar of Lebanon. Having ruminated upon the Romantic and the Picturesque, it

NO ILLUSION *Scotney Castle, with its wide moat, creeper-covered ruins and warm stone walls bright with old-fashioned roses, looks too picturesque to be real. But it is. Castle and gardens took 600 years to grow together into their present harmony.*

QUARRY GARDEN *Like many other features at Scotney Castle, the quarry garden was not planned – it just happened. Now a cool, green place where slabbed paths wander between ferns and shrubs, it was originally the pit from which stone was dug to build a new house back in the 1830s.*

SEZINCOTE *Gloucestershire*

'Exotic Sezincote! Stately and strange', Sir John Betjeman called it in his verse autobiography *Summoned by Bells*. As an Oxford undergraduate the poet would cycle to the house for Sunday lunch with the owners, the Dugdale family. The Cotswold lanes, then as now, were heavy with hawthorn scents in early summer, and the church towers were golden in the sun. But his destination was no ordinary Cotswold manor. Sezincote is a Mogul palace – complete with minarets, onion domes and peacock-tail arches – which rises like a mirage among the leafy oak woods of Gloucestershire.

The house was completed in 1805 for Charles Cockerell, who had served in the East India Company. With growing British interest in the subcontinent, 'Indianesque' building styles became fashionable at home. But Sezincote survives as something unique in Europe: a complete building executed in the Mogul style of the 16th century, which combines both Hindu and Muslim influence. And the 'Nabob's house', as Betjeman dubbed it, is all the more extraordinary for having a purely classical interior. Though perfectly Indian from the outside, it is 'coolest Greek within'.

The park and garden were landscaped with advice from Humphry Repton. Though the foremost successor of Capability Brown, he was more flexible than his predecessor, and not averse to toying with whimsical ideas. Besides providing the parkland with landscaped woods and a sweeping lake (made to resemble a river), he also helped to select some of the Indianesque ornaments. In the main, though, these were the work of Charles Cockerell's brother, the architect S. P. Cockerell, and an artist named Thomas Daniell.

The ornaments are to be seen in the old garden, which lies to the north of the house. Known as the Thornery, this area consists of a luxuriously planted pool chain. At the head is a temple dedicated to the Hindu sun-god Surya; below, the stream passes under an Indian Bridge topped by Brahmin Bulls. Lower still is the Snake Pool, taking its name from a three-headed metal serpent which entwines the trunk of a dead yew. The snake is ingeniously devised to spout water – though the stream's flow is so slight that constant use would dry it up. The Prince Regent (whose famous Pavilion at Brighton was partly inspired by Sezincote) was once treated to an erratic display; the snake is said to have stopped spouting out of distaste for the royal visitor's private life.

Yellow-flowering St John's wort (*Hypericum calycinum*) grows in mounds around the Snake Pool, and the plantings become ever more lush as the water descends to the Rock Pool and Island Pool. Betjeman, in his poem, recalls 'water splashing over limestone rock/Under the primulas and thin bamboo', and these moisture-lovers still flourish at the water's edge. Magnolias and flowering cherries contribute their spring colours to the Thornery. Irises and lilies enliven the summer scene, to be succeeded by massed blooms of hydrangeas. In autumn, fiery mis-

is a splendid idea to wander down through the quarry where, if you look closely, the footprint of an iguanodon may be seen, pressed into the sediment of which the rock was formed, millions of years ago.

At the end of the shady tunnels through the shrubbery, the ruins beckon brightly. Roses are piled everywhere, mostly old roses, and in the forecourt there is a small herb garden with an ancient well at its centre. The moat lies beyond, bright with drifts of water lilies, and on summer afternoons when the bees are booming in the limes and dragonflies hover on iridescent wings, there can be few more peaceable spots on earth. One additional touch of the Picturesque remains, and that is to look back to the newer house and its terrace, seemingly piled on the top of its wonderful, stepped garden.

cellanies of Japanese maples keep the colours alive in the garden. Few of these plants are specifically Indian in origin, but they lend a fittingly exotic air.

Large-leaved aquatics, together with weeping beeches, pears and willows all provide sculptural effects, and there are many aged specimens among the trees. A grove of tall cedars, for example, dates back to the garden's founding, and there is a swamp cypress which may also be some 180 years old. There is in addition a huge and venerable weeping horn-beam (*Carpinus betulus* 'Pendula') which is probably the largest in England.

Sezincote suffered neglect during the Second World War, and most of the younger plantings were established by Lady Kleinwort, whose husband bought the estate in 1944 and whose family still

nurtures the garden. Lady Kleinwort also laid out a new Indian Garden to the south of the remarkable house. Its layout is formal, organised around dividing paths and canals, and emulates the traditional 'Paradise Garden' favoured by Babur, the first of the Moguls. Irish yews here accentuate the design, rather than the sun-loving cypresses that Babur would have used. But there are many exotic touches to be found, especially in the splendid curving orangery. Here, rare jasmines, passion flowers and abutilons are nurtured in a frost-free environment.

Presiding over all is the domed roofscape of the great house itself. It is 'stately and strange' indeed, a thing which belongs in the landscape of Rajasthan but instead looks out across Repton's lake towards Moreton-in-Marsh and the Cotswold skyline beyond.

COOL GOD *A fountain plays in the pool before a tiny temple where sits a statue of the Hindu sun-god Surya. The atmosphere of cool is enhanced by plantings of white-flowered and silver-leaved subjects in the raised beds flanking the temple.*

TIMELESS *Long shadows cast by an evening sun halt the passage of time as they reach the sundial in the garden at Hall's Croft (opposite), once the home of Shakespeare's daughter Susanna. The same sun's rays strike colour from the flower-filled borders as if to emphasise the timeless quality of an English walled garden.*

SHAKESPEARE GARDENS, STRATFORD-UPON-AVON

Warwickshire

*I know a bank whereon the wild thyme blows,
Where oxlips and the nodding violet grows
Quite over-canopied with luscious woodbine,
With sweet musk-roses and with eglantine.*

Shakespeare's love of flowers must be evident to any reader of the poet's work. Lines like those above, from *A Midsummer Night's Dream*, convey an intimate affection for the woods and meadowlands of his native Warwickshire. And at Stratford-upon-Avon, the old market town where Shakespeare was born and died, five gardens in particular burst with petals and fragrances known to the poet, and which he commemorated with lyric genius.

Each of the gardens centres on a site rooted in Shakespearean lore. There is the Birthplace in Henley Street, for example, where the poet was born in 1564. In its garden you can see the most comprehensive plantings of trees, herbs and flowers mentioned in Shakespeare's plays and sonnets. All of the Midsummer Night enchanters are represented: wild thyme, oxlips, violets, woodbines (honeysuckles), Musk roses and eglantines (sweetbriars). And scores of other Shakespearean subjects have been informally planted, from 'lady smocks all silver white' to pomegranate, wormwood and yew.

The most famous, and most photographed, of all the Shakespearean sites is Anne Hathaway's Cottage at Shottery. It was in this picturesque thatched farmhouse with its latticed windows that the poet's wife lived before her marriage. And the colourful miscellanies of cottage plants growing in the garden do much to enhance its charm. Not every one is mentioned by Shakespeare, or even available in his time. But they provide a delectable confection: jasmine clothes the half-timbered walls while hollyhocks and foxgloves thrust their wands from crowded beds. Here you find 'hot lavender' in abundance, with rosemary 'for remembrance'. And beyond the garden is Anne Hathaway's orchard, where the gnarled trunks of venerable fruit trees seem to bend in spring under their blossom loads.

The garden at Mary Arden's House surrounds the half-timbered farmstead at Wilmcote where Shakespeare's mother lived when young. Ancient box hedges and old-fashioned roses are among the memorable attractions. Hall's Croft, in the old town of Stratford itself, is very different in mood. It was here that Shakespeare's daughter, Susanna, lived with her husband Dr John Hall. The fine old house has a spacious, walled garden which was designed as recently as 1950 by the Shakespeare Birthplace Trust. The layout is formal, with a long, paved terrace, smooth lawns and herbaceous borders.

What was Shakespeare himself like as a gardener? When he retired from theatre life in London he came to New Place, one of the largest properties in Strat-ford. Records show that it cost him £60, and it had an orchard and kitchen garden in which the poet may well have spent many happy hours. New Place was already famous by the mid-18th century, and visitors would throng to see an aged mulberry tree said to have been planted by Shakespeare. The then owner was so annoyed by the intrusions that in 1756 he had the tree cut down. But one cutting was kept, and from it a new tree has grown – over 200 years old in itself.

The venerable mulberry rises from a smooth expanse of lawn, with an equally old beech near by. From the grass below, daffodils 'come before the swallow dares', and there are long flower borders set among yew-hedged compartments. A special attraction at New Place is the knot garden, nurtured as a replica of one of those decorative plots which graced every important house in Tudor times. Just such a 'curious knotted garden' is mentioned in *Love's Labour's Lost*.

POET'S FLOWERS *A formal knot garden, embroidered with flowers that Shakespeare knew, is one of the attractions at New Place, the poet's Stratford home.*

The plot is an enclosed square, slightly sunken, and divided by paths into four patterned knots. The designs are picked out in time-honoured herbs, and filled in with colourful flowers. In effect, the knot garden is a wonderfully embroidered space, a place for lovers' dalliance whose enclosing palisade is covered with crab apples and where one oak tunnel recalls the 'pleached bower' of *Much Ado About Nothing*.

In all, the Shakespeare gardens are richly suggestive of the poet's world. Not every feature is a period piece, though there are many inspired touches – at New Place, for example, there is even a 'wild bank' where Shakespearean favourites have been naturalised. 'This garden has a world of pleasure in't', runs a line in *The Two Noble Kinsmen*. The play cannot be attributed with certainty to the Bard, but the sentiment is appropriate to the Shakespeare gardens.

SHEFFIELD PARK *East Sussex*

This is gardening on the grand scale, with great seasonal sweeps of colour that seem to illuminate the very air. And what is particularly remarkable is that the displays are composed for the most part of great trees, planted with the same attention to height, grouping and colour contrast that gardeners with lesser plots devote to a herbaceous border.

Sheffield Park is, in fact, two gardens, created 200 years apart and with one superimposed upon the other; yet so happily have they blended, that it is hard to imagine that the place ever looked other than it does. In 1769, John Holroyd, MP, who was shortly to become the 1st Earl of Sheffield, purchased the manor that had once belonged to Simon de Montfort and commissioned James Wyatt, a rising young architect, to build him a house. Wyatt chose the currently fashionable Gothic style, and the equally fashionable Capability Brown was engaged to do something about the park.

As quite often happened, Brown left no record of his work, but it is generally agreed that he constructed at least two of the four lakes and probably the cascade too. Humphry Repton also had a hand in designing the garden about that time. In the late 19th century the 3rd Earl of Sheffield enlarged the First and Second lakes – the ones nearest to the house – built the

waterfalls, and established the hallowed cricket ground on which for 20 years (1876–96) opening matches of Australian Test tours were always played against Lord Sheffield's XI.

In 1909 the estate was acquired by Arthur Soames, a gardener of great originality and distinction, and he it was who began the massive plantings of the exotic trees and shrubs that are the chief glory of the place today. Obviously, it was the flat, placid lakes that were his inspiration, for he piled about them rhododendrons, maples, dogwoods, hemlocks, birches, cypresses, feathery-headed pampas grasses and many other trees and plants to lay their images upon the mirror expanse of the waters. After the Second World War, the work was taken up by Captain Granville Soames and, later, by the National Trust.

The park is organised in the most artfully casual manner possible, into walks and viewpoints, each with its special features and carefully chosen supporting casts. Starting at the Storage Lake, there are two towering cider gums from Australia, while by First Lake, American red oaks and old Spanish chestnuts are surrounded by a court of rhododendrons, maples, dogwoods and pines, together with cedars and firs from western North America. At the beginning of South Garden Walk there is a large Monterey pine, one of several in the garden. And there, too, is a splendid view across First Lake to a weeping silver-leaved pear set off by the dark column of an incense cedar.

So the parade goes on through the park's 100 acres, along Woodland Walk, Red Walk, Queen's Walk, Women's Way – so called from the headless spectre that is said to haunt it – Big Tree Walk, with its majestic North American conifers, Palm Avenue with its startlingly tropical air, and the rest; an endless parade of rarities in beautiful if bewildering array. It must be admitted that for the layman the park is more easily digested from one of its superb viewpoints – Top Bridge, perhaps, with its wonderful vista of tree colours, shapes and textures and, in the background, the fairy-tale battlements of the house.

Best of all, of course, is to visit the place through the seasons. To see in winter the subtly hued conifers pushing through the dark, skeletal branches of the deciduous trees, then to walk through again in spring, when Lent lilies and thousands of daffodils push through the turf, to be followed by a breeze-tossed sea of wild bluebells. Then, as the year advances, comes the bright snow of cherry blossom and the rhododendrons and azaleas, astonishing splashes of vivid colours against the dark green palette of their foliage. Summer is the time for water lilies and the endless stirring of foliage against the sky. But autumn is the time when Sheffield Park really puts out its full panoply. Between mid-October and mid-November, it seemingly bursts into flame. Outstanding among all others is the soaring crimson of the maples, but their surroundings of clear yellow, russet, gold and crimson are hardly less breathtaking. Reflected in water stilled by the first frost, and arched over by the clear blue October sky, it is a scene to remember.

SEASONAL CHANGE *In spring (opposite) Sheffield Park displays a simple, rustic charm as bluebells carpet the woodland floor before the trees are fully in leaf. But in summer (below), when the forest giants put on their full panoply, the atmosphere is one of grandeur.*

SHUGBOROUGH *Staffordshire*

In 1744 George Anson, commander of a naval squadron and future First Lord of the Admiralty, returned in his flagship from an epic four-year voyage round the world. He brought with him a captured Spanish galleon worth, with its cargo, some £400,000. This fortune he and his brothers used to greatly enlarge their family house at Shugborough, erecting a host of monuments in its park and garden.

Shugborough lies beside the River Sow where it meets the River Trent. The broad valley is lightly wooded, and Victorian terraces today lead down to the river. At the water's edge are a group of mock ruins erected for picturesque effect; a footpath leads on along the bank to a Chinese House, near which grow Chinese shrubs and a pagoda tree.

This delightful little house was probably the first of all the garden buildings erected by Thomas Anson. It was completed in 1747, not long after the return of his brother, the admiral. His voyage had included a long call at Canton, and the design was done from sketches made in China by one of the admiral's officers. And on an island in the river is a charming monument, said to commemorate a ship's cat which circumnavigated the globe with the flagship. Elsewhere at Shugborough you can see a historic collection of Grecian-style garden buildings.

Apart from its noble ornaments, Shugborough holds much to interest garden-lovers. One of the terraces, for example, was redesigned in 1966 to make a Victorian-style rose garden. A sundial stands at the centre while, all around, ramblers and clematises have been trained to garland arches and pillars.

And towering around are fine beeches and cedars, which lend an impression of aged grandeur to the whole. For a sense of real immensity you should not miss the great English yew. At 72 ft it has reached a fair height. But the height is not what most impresses – it is the girth. The yew spreads its skirt at ground level to cover almost an acre of space.

SISSINGHURST *Kent*

The story has often been told: how the Bloomsbury writers Harold Nicolson and his wife Vita Sackville-West came to Sissinghurst in 1930. The Elizabethan mansion was then in a state of appalling dereliction, as it had been for 200 years. Vita Sackville-West, scouring the Weald of Kent to find a property in which she could start a garden, came upon the estate. The 6 acre garden was cluttered with 'old iron bedsteads, old plough-shares, old cabbage stalks, old broken-down earth closets, old matted wire, and mountains of sardine tins, all muddled up in a tangle of bindweed, nettles and ground elder'.

A GARDEN OF GARDENS *Looking down from the tower of Sissinghurst Castle, its 6 acres can be seen for what they are – a jewel among gardens set in the already beautiful landscape of the Kentish Weald, itself the Garden of England.*

JOINT EFFORT *Together with her husband, Sir Harold Nicolson, Vita Sackville-West (above) created the garden at Sissinghurst from a junkyard wilderness. Harold gave the garden its shape while Vita dressed it with flowers.*

And yet she fell in love with Sissinghurst at first sight: the romance of the castle with its pink-brick Tudor walls, the quiet water of the moat amid the shambles. It was, she wrote, Sleeping Beauty's garden – and it cried out to be redeemed.

It took the couple three years just to clear away the rubbish, and some seven more to plan and plant the garden. But after the Second World War, when Sissinghurst was opened to the public, it became known as a wonder among British gardens – and today it has matured into a modern 'classic'.

Sissinghurst lies in the farmlands of the Weald, some 130 ft above sea level. And despite all the problems that the Nicolsons acquired, there were also some notable advantages. The soil, for example, was a good friable loam well worked by generations of tenant farmers. The old walls and gatehouse buildings provided both shelter and the elements of a design. It was Harold Nicolson who laid out the bones of the garden, once the mess had been cleared away.

Vita Sackville-West, meanwhile, was of a romantic temperament and infinitely sensitive to mood. Of Sissinghurst she wrote: 'Though very English, very Kentish, it had something foreign about it, a Norman manor house perhaps, a faint echo of something more southern. That was why figs and vines and roses looked so right, so inevitable. I planted them recklessly.'

Between them they aimed for a harmony: 'the strictest formality of design with the maximum informality in planting'. This was the principle pioneered at Hidcote, a garden which deeply influenced the Nicolsons. They in turn were to help shape the thinking of countless gardeners of their generation.

Sissinghurst, like Hidcote, is a garden of compartments: some planned for seasonal interest and others according to colour themes. You are aware of the structural element of the whole as soon as you come to the entrance: a straight avenue of Lombardy poplars lines the direct approach. Inside the gatehouse, Sissinghurst's plan is a complex of squares and rectangles, intersected by long walks.

These symmetries beautifully suit the character of the central Tudor tower (in which Elizabeth I spent three nights in 1573). But for all its sophistication, Sissinghurst is no formal period piece. The loveliest of England's native wild flowers grace the garden in spring: daffodils, narcissi, blue sheets of forget-me-nots and nodding snake's head fritillaries.

Leading off the walk there is even a cottage garden set around the remnant of a wing of the Elizabethan house. Inside it is the room where Harold Nicolson used to write; outside, tree paeonies, columbines, rock roses and evening primroses flourish in dreamy profusions. The cottage front is clothed with the white climbing rose 'Mme Alfred Carrière', almost unbelievable for the vast expanse that it covers.

Also lying off the lime walk, for example, is the magnificent rose garden, widely famed for its old-fashioned and shrub varieties. Clematises run wild over the walls, while mingling with the roses in the plot are ceanothuses, caryopteris, lace-cap hydrangeas

and a host of other shrubs. Tulips and irises surge from the beds, while pansies seem to cover every spare inch of earth. Yet, at the centre of these billowing medleys, the eye is held by the firmest of features. This is the so-called rondel, a circular patch of turf which takes its name from the round floor of Kentish oasthouses. It is framed by a mighty broken ring of yew, trimmed with austere precision.

Every compartment at Sissinghurst is a delight. There is a nuttery, for example, whose aged nut trees are among the very few worthwhile plants which were there before the Nicolsons arrived. There is the azalea-bordered moat walk, and the paved herb garden richly stocked with aromatic plants. Artistic associations were never far from the cultured founders' minds when they planned their Wealden acres. The spring flowers in the lime walk, for example, were consciously nurtured to recall Botticelli's famous painting of *Spring*.

But among all the compartments, one is an acknowledged masterpiece. This is the white garden, devoted, as its name implies, to white or grey plants and flowers. A silver willow-leaved pear (*Pyrus salicifolia* 'Pendula') dominates the scene, overhanging a lead statue of a virgin. And an immaculate pallor greets you here in any season. On the hottest June day, the scented *Rosa longicuspis* will lower your temperature. Its snowy avalanches of white quite smother the central iron canopy while, later, the pale trumpets of

WHITE GARDEN *Cream and white flowers with silver and grey foliage combine to make the white garden the masterpiece of Sissinghurst.*

Lilium regale rise through mats of grey artemisias. Wands of white delphiniums mingle with occasional heads of Scotch thistles and, as the evening draws in, baby's breath (*Gypsophila*) blows white froth around.

The white garden has been called 'the most beautiful garden at Sissinghurst, and indeed in all of England'. It is not entirely white, of course: high above all rise the rose-pink walls of the castle while, through an archway to one side, you look out to the green bosom of the Weald.

SIZERGH CASTLE *Cumbria*

In all the Borders, there can be few more eloquent arguments for the Union of the Crowns than Sizergh Castle. Its oldest part is a pele tower built about 1350 as a defence against marauding Scots, and very likely against quarrelsome English neighbours too. Today, its warlike lines are blurred by a draping of Boston ivy, while below, the defences offer shelter and support to a large Turkey fig, buddleias, brooms and other flowering shrubs. At the foot of the tower, too, there is a bed of gentians of a blue so piercing as to make the spring sky seem washed out by comparison.

From the house, an 18th-century terrace and wall runs south, offering a haven to flowering shrubs and climbers – clematises, honeysuckles, vines and cotoneasters – then, below the wall, a precipitous bank falls away to a lawn. All summer long, the bank is covered by dog daisies, so that, with the old tower in the background, it looks exactly like a corner of a medieval illuminated manuscript brought to life.

The 17th century approach to the castle was by way of a beech avenue terminating in a pair of noble, urn-crowned gate piers. The gates still stand, but the beeches, having reached the end of their natural term, were replaced in 1963 by limes. All the park area about the avenue has been transformed into a great lawn that is dotted with 200-year-old yews and island beds filled with roses and a dazzling variety of flowering trees and shrubs, underplanted with bulbs and herbaceous plants.

But the most famous – and astonishing – feature in Sizergh's surroundings is its rock garden, built of the local stone for Lord Strickland in 1926. From a pool above the house, a waterway threads its quarter of an acre, pausing at pools and little falls, before it empties into the lake. When the garden was established, a large number of dwarf conifers were included for background effect, but many, though retaining their forms, are now very big dwarfs indeed. There are hummocks of spruces, 8 ft across and 4 ft wide, bushy pines, cypresses, yews and junipers, and a prostrate blue noble fir at least 15 ft across. In the damp earth beside the watercourse, primulas, polygonums, astilbes, globe flowers and, above all, gentians give patches and pockets of colour all season long.

Modestly intermingled with the other plants in this lovely dell is one of the largest collections of hardy ferns in the country – more than 100 species and forms, including rarities from North America and the Far East.

SPRINGFIELDS *Lincolnshire*

The flat fens of Lincolnshire lie, like much of Holland, only just above the level of the sea. Ancient trading contacts connect the two flatlands, and many old houses in Lincolnshire are built in Dutch style. And in the area around Spalding, analogies with the Netherlands are even more marked. For this is Britain's 'Tulipland', where more than half of the nation's bulbs are grown. In spring the level acres surrounding the

old market town come alive with vast sheets of primary colour. And the magnet for gardeners at this time is the great show garden at Springfields.

Springfields is situated just outside Spalding, where the soil is a sandy loam. It is an exposed site, suffering cruel winds which no sheltering ridge or slope helps to alleviate. The 30 acre site was established in 1964 by a branch of the National Farmers' Union. The designer was Carl van Empelen, who planted trees and shrubs to keep out the wind and excavated a lake. But the layout remains basically formal, organised around a series of rectangles.

The high season at Springfields is the six weeks in April and early May when the bulbous plants come into their own: tulips, narcissi, daffodils and hyacinths – well over a million bulbs and corms bear their blooms. The tulips, of course, hold pride of place and account for three-quarters of the plantings. They come in an astonishing range of varieties, from the smallest early flowering species to the most grandiose hybrids. Glorious battalions of yellows and reds are what first assault the eye, but Springfields' army wears a coat of many colours. Among the popular Darwin range, for example, hues range from the snowy white of 'Glacier' through a rainbow of shades to the dusky maroon of 'La Tulipe Noire'.

Although this kaleidoscopic display is the traditional glory of Springfields, there are other more recent attractions. In 1976 the season was extended to September with bedding plants and shows of dahlias. Over 10,000 rose bushes – mainly new varieties – have also been planted to continue the colour feast.

TULIP TIME *In Britain's own 'low country', around Spalding, a tulipland has grown up to rival that of Holland. Its showplace is Springfields, where every April and May a million bulbs burst into bloom in a vivid display of colour and form in a garden designed, fittingly, by a Dutchman.*

STOURHEAD *Wiltshire*

Looked at in one way, Stourhead is the Disneyland of 1744, a dream world furnished with the habitations of imaginary beings, and created purely for pleasure. In another, it is one of Britain's greatest national possessions, as important as a Turner or Constable painting, and having much in common with them – the same vistas, the same use of light and shade, the same mixture of landscape and gracious buildings. The main differences are that Stourhead is composed of real water, earth and light, and while the paintings are finished, the great garden is forever subtly changing.

Its creator was Henry Hoare of the London banking family, who, in 1741, inherited the house built by his father above Six Wells Bottom. To make the garden he first dammed the infant Stour, so making a series of lakes, the largest of which was to be the focal point in his creation. He established about it vast plantations of trees, mainly spruce and beech, taking great care, as he said, to site them 'in large masses as the shades are in painting, to contrast the dark masses with the light ones'.

Like most English gentlemen of his time, he was not so much well versed in the classics as soaked in them, so his perfect landscape had to contain a range of Arcadian groves and pastoral vistas. Among them there gradually rose a range of buildings; the Temple of Flora, followed by the Grotto, dedicated to the River God and to the Nymph of the Grot, out of whose basin the springs of the Stour bubble. The Pantheon, with its magnificent statue of Hercules, lesser statues and busts of other deities, was completed in 1754: the Temple of Apollo on its eminence overlooking the lake was added a decade later, as was the stone-built Turf Bridge, which carries a grassy path over a corner of the lake. About this time too, in obedience to the prevalent fancy for the Gothic, Henry Hoare added a medieval cross from Bristol and a rustic cottage.

Predeceased by his wife and children, he devoted the latter part of his long life entirely to the beautifying of Stourhead, and was succeeded at last by his grandson, Sir Richard Colt Hoare, in 1785. Sir Richard respected his grandfather's overall plan, but added to it by providing gravel walks and a much greater variety of trees and shrubs. This course was followed by his descendants down to the first decades of this century when Sir Henry Hoare, the last member of the family to live at Stourhead, planted the huge collection of azaleas and rhododendrons that are now at their somewhat overpowering peak. Thus, Stourhead is not the product of a single vision, but a grand canvas composed over nearly two and a half centuries.

Nevertheless, it is the spirit of old Henry Hoare, Stourhead's builder, that predominates. It was his

A DREAM COME TRUE *When Henry Hoare inherited his father's house he set about converting a large and untamed part of Wiltshire into his ideal landscape. How well he succeeded can be seen from this view of the lake which he created in the gardens at Stourhead.*

GOD'S RETREAT *Were Apollo to appear on earth, he might well choose to reside at this temple that Henry Hoare built for him in idyllic surroundings at Stourhead – rather than his old home at Delphi.*

notion that visitors should walk from the house to the lip of the valley, whence the Temple of Apollo appears to be floating between trees and water. From there, a path offering tantalising glimpses of the Pantheon and the Rustic Cottage crosses the northern end of the lake to the Grotto, whose mouth frames a perfect view of the Temple of Apollo on the opposite shore. The path then continues towards the Rustic Cottage and the Pantheon – with views of the Turf Bridge and the Bristol Cross – before climbing up to Apollo's temple and a grand panorama of the entire estate. Beyond, and by no means an anti-climax, the route crosses the Turf Bridge to the delightful village of Stourton.

At present, most people come to Stourhead by way of the village, and therefore take in their first view of the landscape from the low ground, exactly the opposite of what Henry Hoare intended. It does not matter very much. There are a dozen reasons for visiting Stourhead; its walks, its architecture, its trees, shrubs and flowers, its bird life, its peace and serenity.

STOWE *Buckinghamshire*

In the early years of the 18th century, Alexander Pope incorporated this advice to gardeners, large-scale ones anyway, in his *Epistle to Lord Burlington:*

Consult the Genius of the Place in all;
That tells the Waters or to rise or fall,
Or helps th' ambitious Hill the heavens to scale,
Or scoops in circling theatres the Vale,
Calls in the Country, catches opening glades,
Joins willing woods, and varies shades from shades . . .

The advice continued for some time, and might well be regarded as the hymn to, and the recipe for, the

FIRST MAKE A LAKE *With a lake you have something across which to build a bridge. This was how gardening on the grand scale was conceived – and Stowe was conceived on a very grand scale indeed. The Palladian Bridge (opposite) is copied from one built at Wilton in 1757. It spans the eastern arm of the Octagon Lake and is just one of 20 or more architectural features which embellish the landscape at Stowe.*

TEMPLE'S TEMPLES *No fewer than seven temples survive among the garden ornaments at Stowe. It is probably no coincidence that Temple was the family name of Lord Cobham, who had them built. The Temple of Ancient Virtue (above) was designed by William Kent in 1734 to match a now-vanished Temple of Modern Virtue, built as a ruin – a reflection of his lordship's view of the contemporary world.*

Landscape Movement. This curious phenomenon, composed of philosophy, a thorough grounding in the classics, wistful memories of the Grand Tour in Greece and Italy and a yearning for something new, struck many 18th-century landowners like a thunderbolt. They translated their ideals into grand vistas of 'natural' landscape. So convincing are some of these landscapes that now they have matured we have almost forgotten they were created, and imagine them to be the true and ancient faces of the countryside.

It is hard to say where the movement began, for there were stirrings everywhere. But Stowe was one of the first, and is unique in showing all the phases of the movement from its beginning to the end. It is unique, too, in being the place where the movement's greatest craftsmen – Charles Bridgeman, Sir John Vanbrugh, William Kent and Lancelot 'Capability' Brown – did some of their earliest and finest work.

In the reign of Queen Anne, Richard Temple, Lord Cobham, a distinguished soldier in Marlborough's wars, inherited Stowe, then a late 17th-century brick house surrounded by formal, terraced gardens. He seems to have been satisfied with the house, but he at once employed Bridgeman, a brilliant and original designer, to revolutionise his garden. Bridgeman's first act was to do away with the wall separating garden from park and install in its place a ha-ha, or sunken wall, so opening a grand view of the countryside to the house. He then established parterres, walks

and a canal; the world was not quite yet ready for the abolition of flower beds, but so far as was possible he dispensed with straight lines, making his paths curve around little blobs of woodland. At the same time Vanbrugh was engaged to design buildings suitable for the new, idyllic landscape. His answer was a number of temples dedicated to vague deities, which were later added to by James Gibbs, William Kent and several other designers, professional and amateur.

Kent's main contribution, however, was to extend Bridgeman's ideas and to use the ha-ha as a gateway or window upon a magical countryside, stretching to the blue distance and apparently little touched by man. In fact, it was touched fairly heavily; a lake was created, vistas artfully opened, and attention drawn to them by cunningly planted trees or temples. Among these were Kent's two perfect landscapes – of course with temples – the Elysian Fields and the Grecian Valley; he manipulated the countryside as an artist would work his oils and, in this sense, landscape gardening was invented at Stowe. Then, while the building was at its height, the staff was supplemented by a 24-year-old under-gardener named Lancelot Brown. His talents were quickly recognised, and promotion to head gardener followed.

In 1748, William Kent died, as did Lord Cobham in the following year. He was succeeded by his nephew, Lord Temple, who was at least as keenly devoted to building and innovation as his uncle. He determined

to build a house that was worthy of its surroundings and engaged the architect Robert Adam, who not so much rebuilt as encased the old house in stone, enlarged it and added a massive, pillared portico. Lord Temple then flung landscapes and buildings ever wider, working first with Brown until he left, then with his successor, Richard Woodward. By the time Lord Temple died, in 1779, the gardens at Stowe were much as they are today. At length, in 1923, the place was sold to become the home of a public school.

The house is never open to the public, but the gardens are, at weekends during the summer holidays, when they are really compulsory viewing for anyone who is interested in gardening history. The approach is by the 1½ mile long Grand Avenue, which runs up to the 60 ft square Corinthian Arch, then swings around to the Oxford Lodge and the pretty little bridge over the Oxford Water. Beyond, are the twin domes of the Boycott Pavilions, named after a little village that once stood on the site. An obelisk that pricks the sky from a hilltop on the left is a monument to General Wolfe, the hero of Quebec, while the equestrian statue that stands before the north portico of the house commemorates George I. But any visit to the gardens should certainly begin with the view from the south portico, since it is from there, with sudden and startling clarity, that one sees what the 18th-century designers had in mind. Great swathes of turf

fall away, punctuated by strategic plantings of magnificent trees, to a vast lake, on the far bank of which are two Lake Pavilions.

It is then recommended that, rather than plunging straight down into the view, the visitor should turn left and descend instead by way of the Elysian Fields. A short way down is the Grenville Column, a monument to a Temple relative killed in action against a French frigate, and close by, most unexpectedly, a 14th-century church. This is all that remains of the 'lost' village of Stowe, destroyed during the Civil War; Capability Brown was married in the church in 1744. Near by, the temples begin. A slim waterway is crossed by the Shell Bridge, actually a dam, and close to it there is a monument to Captain Cook and a white marble fountain, long dried up. Order is restored by the lovely Palladian Bridge, seemingly half-submerged in the lake, and by the ruinous Temple of Friendship that was dedicated to Pitt the Elder and his friends in the Whig Party in 1739.

Throughout the gardens, the monuments and temples continue, sometimes half-concealed by foliage that would certainly have been cut back in Lord Cobham's day, even if to modern eyes it lends a certain attractive mystery. Among those that should be visited is the Congreve Monument topped by a monkey gazing at itself in a mirror as a tribute to the dramatist whose speciality was the mockery of human foibles.

JAUNDICED VIEW *The Temple of British Worthies at Stowe, designed by William Kent, reflects Lord Cobham's disillusionment with his fellow man – none of his contemporaries earns a place.*

BROWN'S SCHOOLDAYS *There can be little doubt that it was at Stowe that Lancelot 'Capability' Brown learned many of the skills that made him Britain's greatest landscape gardener.*

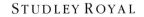

STUDLEY ROYAL *North Yorkshire*

Gardens have grown out of all kinds of circumstances, but few can have odder beginnings than the lovely landscape of Studley Royal. In 1720 the South Sea Company volunteered to assume partial responsibility for the National Debt in exchange for a trading monopoly in the South Sea Islands. With such collateral, the company attracted wide, even hysterical, investment. But, alas, no trade existed, and when the South Sea 'bubble' burst the following year, thousands of people were ruined. It was one of the gravest financial disasters in the annals of the City of London, and if any single factor was to blame it was the inept, or worse, handling of the affair by the Chancellor of the Exchequer, John Aislabie. He was expelled from Parliament, which seemed to many people to be a remarkably mild penalty under the circumstances, and he prudently retired to his Yorkshire estate.

Whatever his shortcomings as a Chancellor, he was a landscape gardener of genius and, in his enforced leisure, he was able to give his talents full rein. What he sought to do was to create out of the three elements of formalism, the romantic and the picturesque, a landscape that would both refresh and elevate the mind of the beholder. The canvas he used was the wild, wooded valley of the River Skell, which runs from above Fountains Abbey then through the Studley estate to join with the Ure beyond Ripon. He dammed the river to make a large lake, a canal and two other ornamental sheets of water, his Moon Pool and Half Moon Pool, overlooked by statues and the classical architecture so dear to the hearts of the period. By the Moon Pool, delicately emphasised by the surrounding velvety lawns, is the stately columned portico of the Temple of Piety and, above it, reached by a patch that runs through a grotto-like tunnel, is the Octagonal Tower, and the open rotunda of the Temple of Fame. Beyond this, suddenly revealed, is the Surprise View, the crescendo of the entire planned landscape. It is a surprise indeed, and one that never fails to take the breath away, for it is the soaring ruin of Fountains Abbey, with its great tower and gaping windows etched against the sky.

Built in the 12th and 13th centuries, and allowed to fall into ruin – and used as a quarry for nearby Fountains Hall – after its dissolution in 1539, it is one of the most perfect examples of a Cistercian monastery in Europe. John Aislabie was a true product of the Age of Reason, and it was a sense of the picturesque, rather than of piety or history, that led him to make the ruin the focal point of his garden. However, it was never actually a part of the Studley Royal estate during his lifetime, and it was not until 1768, after his son, William, had inherited, that the two estates were joined together. William Aislabie turfed the abbey's

A RIVER TAMED *Ornamental ponds linked by a canal were created by damming the turbulent River Skell at the beginning of the 18th century. The new discipline was enhanced by erecting a Temple of Piety which looks out on groups of classical statuary.*

surroundings, added some features to the joined parks and naturalised parts of the river banks in accordance with the ideas of Capability Brown, whose influence in garden matters was then at its height. But the general flavour is still very much the one dictated a generation earlier by John Aislabie.

One feature, though, has nothing to do with either father or son, and that is St Mary's, the splendid Gothic church erected in the park during the 1870s by the Marchioness of Ripon. It is by no means incongruous, but from the church the visitor should look back towards the east gate. From there, another planned and astonishing vista is carried through an avenue of ancient trees and out over miles of countryside to the precisely aligned view of Ripon Cathedral's twin towers. Whatever the wrath of the 18th century, posterity cannot but be grateful to the ancient scandal and for the unseasonable retirement it brought to John Aislabie.

SYON PARK *Greater London*

A ducal estate that time has surprised, Syon is now almost engulfed by the brick and concrete of London's western suburbs. Nevertheless, in the midst of its 55 acres it is quite possible to find the hum of insects drowning that of the traffic and to look over a landscape that wistfully reminds us what a lovely country Middlesex was before commuterdom was dreamed of. In the midst of it stands Syon House, a modest term used to describe the square Tudor palace with the stiff-tailed heraldic lion of the Percys balanced above its battlements and glaring over the Thames to Kew.

It was built in the reign of the boy king Edward VI by his Protector, the Duke of Somerset, on the site of a monastic house dissolved by Henry VIII. In 1542 it served as a prison for a few months for Queen Catherine Howard, before she was rowed downriver to the Tower and execution. Five years later, Henry's corpse was kept there overnight while on its way to Windsor for burial. But the servants deserted it, leaving it to be gnawed by the dogs, thus fulfilling, so it is said, a curse put upon the king when the monks were evicted.

The Duke of Somerset was able to enjoy his new house for only five more years, before he, too, made the melancholy journey to the Tower and the block. But in that time he also constructed the terrace and, with the aid of Dr William Turner, the father of English botany, he established the first botanical garden in the country. This garden has long vanished, but the mulberry trees that were planted at the same time – about 1550 – still thrive in the private area to the east of the house.

A succession of owners followed, at least two of whom also took the weary path from Syon to the Tower of London. Perhaps it was dangerous to own so grand a house so close to the capital. A number of these owners made important contributions to the gardens, but it was not until the 1st Duke of Northumberland inherited in the mid-18th century that they

GLASS PALACE *Ducal gardening is, almost of necessity, on the grand scale. The great conservatory at Syon is a case in point – the area under the great dome alone, 3,000 square ft, is bigger than many gardens. The conservatory, completed in 1827, was one of the wonders of the 'modern' world until Paxton went one better with his Crystal Palace in 1851.*

began to assume the appearance that they have today. Like many of his contemporaries, he was entranced – for cost-saving as well as aesthetic reasons – by the new idea of natural landscaping. In consequence, he swept away the formal Tudor beds and walled enclosures of his predecessors, and replaced them instead with vast lawns that lapped to the very windows of the house. Still not satisfied, he employed Capability Brown who, as usual, attacked the landscape with the enthusiasm of a general setting about an occupying foe. First, he excavated over a million cubic feet of earth to make a pair of lakes, and about them opened up great vistas of turf dotted with shrubberies, a botanical garden and plantings of cedars, limes, oaks, chestnuts and beeches.

This was by no means the end of creativity at Syon. In the 1820s, the 3rd Duke commissioned the architect Charles Fowler to build the Riding School – now the Garden Centre – and the great, domed conservatory. Nearly 400 ft long and 65 ft high, it was the wonder of the horticultural world. At the same time, the 3rd Duke engaged Richard Forrest, one of the greatest gardeners of the day, to make further improvements and to supervise a collection of rare plants and trees.

Syon Park is therefore the product of many men's love and care over the centuries, which makes a pleasant reflection to accompany the visitor on a stroll about it. Many of the trees by the lake were planted by Capability Brown, but among them are later plantings of weeping willows, dogwoods and swamp cypresses with their writhing, aerial roots, all united by artfully casual clumps of irises, day lilies, primulas and other moisture-loving plants. Flora's Lawn – so called from a statue of the Roman goddess of flowers that stands on a 55 ft plinth in its midst – was also one of Brown's creations.

By contrast, the conservatory is fronted by a garden of stately formality. There, the statue is of Mercury, forever on the point of flight from the centre of a round, still pond, while about him are geometrically curved beds, shaven topiary and a splendid backdrop of azaleas and magnolias. The conservatory itself contains, as might be guessed, a fine collection of exotic plants, but not quite so foreseeable is their use as a background for an aviary and an aquarium, whose inhabitants make a vivid foil for their lush surroundings. Also at Syon is the world's largest collection of live butterflies that flutter freely among greenhouse gardens. Happily, an equally impressive collection of giant spiders and scorpions is kept enclosed.

One of the great glories of outdoor Syon is the 6 acre Rose Garden. Brown's ubiquitous hand was here too, as may be seen by the presence of the oaks and cedars. But the original terracing and layout was planned by the Duke of Somerset more than 400 years ago. There are more than 8,000 roses in the garden, which are preceded in spring by an overture of massed daffodils, narcissi and crocuses. Spring bulbs, too, are a particular feature of the woodland garden, where they are naturalised among a mature and highly varied collection of trees and shrubs.

TATTON PARK *Cheshire*

'There is a noticeable lack of scandal and intrigue in the family history', observes a brochure to Tatton Park. The family in question are the Egertons, a historic dynasty in Cheshire and South Lancashire, who were masters at Tatton for 380 years. Apart from Maurice, the last lord (a big-game hunter and pioneer of aviation), they were little given to eccentric behaviour. For colour, drama and whimsy you should not look to the family's chronicles but to their superb 60 acre gardens.

The Tatton gardens are owned today by the National Trust, and are remarkably varied in character. Set in a vast parkland landscaped by Humphry Repton, they include terraces and mixed borders, ornamental lakes, fountains, a classical temple and orangery, a complete Japanese garden and the largest fernery in Britain outside of a botanic garden.

The Egertons acquired Tatton in Elizabethan times, and occupied the site until 1958. The oldest feature of the gardens is a long, straight Beech Avenue which once formed the main approach to the house. Planted in the early 18th century, it is all that survives today of the early formal gardens. The rest were swept away by Humphry Repton, the gifted disciple of Capability Brown, who was brought in to landscape Tatton in 1791. He advised breaking up the Beech Avenue to leave only informal clumps of trees. In the event the advice was ignored, though a new curving drive was introduced.

Repton's lovely parkland today provides only a background for the gardens proper. The viewing platform is a fine series of stone balustraded terraces and parterres at the south front. They were designed in the mid-19th century by Sir Joseph Paxton, famed for his work at Chatsworth and the Crystal Palace. Elaborately adorned with fountain, steps and marbled vases they are grandiose in style, but not so ornate that they clash with the misty perspectives of lake and woodland beyond.

The terrace borders are massed with perennials in pastel tones: blues, pinks, mauves and yellows mingling with fragrant lavenders and rosemary. Paxton's Italianate parterre below is equally quiet in tone; it is hard to believe that Maurice Egerton could have used it as a firing range to test out his new hunting rifles.

The fine orangery up by the house was built in 1818, and still shelters oranges and lemons – as well as papaws. But the nearby fernery dates from Paxton's time, and may even be his design. Victorians disposed the green fronds of ferns lavishly around halls and drawing rooms. The fashion died out during the Edwardian period, and Tatton's glass-roofed building is a unique period piece.

Within the building are a gurgling pool and arrangements of mossy rockwork. The heart of the collection is formed by lofty New Zealand tree ferns (*Dicksonia antarctica*), brought to Tatton 130 years ago by a brother of the 1st Lord Egerton. Spreading their weird sheaves from truncated stems, they have an outlandish appearance. Around grows the more

ORDERED KINGDOM *Neptune commands the Italian garden at Tatton Park. From a pool, set at the centre of a formal arrangement of geometrically precise flower beds, he looks out on the informal world of Repton's park beyond.*

elegant *Woodwardia radicans*, while the creeping fig (*Ficus radicans*) clothes the walls. The atmosphere is kept warm, and the mood is loaded with remembrance of a bygone taste.

The long Beech Avenue bisects the great pleasure grounds below the house, leading to a tall, narrow classical temple. At the outset of a walk down the straight way, a Brewer's spruce (*Picea breweriana*) will catch your eye. In spring the magnolias grouped around provide luminous delights, while starlike chionodoxas spangle the ground. On the other side of the way is a little tower garden, named for an old brick tower from which watch was once kept for sheep-stealers in the park. Here, among the hostas, you can see such unusual plants as the blue-podded *Decaisnea fargesii* of China, and the rare Kentucky coffee tree (*Gymnocladus canadensis*).

Explore the gardens further and you will be arrested time and again by fine specimen trees and little-seen shrubs. Banks and thickets of rhododendrons and azaleas conceal many a surprise: secret pools, a beech maze, a walled rose garden and even – improbably – a heather-thatched African hut which recalls the last lord's hunting days.

Perhaps the most pleasing of all these features is an authentic Japanese garden, created in about 1910. It lies off the Golden Brook, a lovely stretch of water landscaped out of old marl pits, and was made by Japanese workmen brought to England specially for the task. From a small island at the centre of the lake there rises a Shinto temple, also brought from Japan, while a low and shapely arched bridge connects it with the garden itself.

The calm fantasy is watered by spring-fed streams coming down from a glade of bamboos. Conspicuous features include a thatch-roofed tea-house, a miniature stone pagoda, and a steep mound of earth contoured to resemble Mount Fuji with white snow stones at the summit. Lanterns and symbolic figures are carefully grouped around, while every plant is of Japanese origin. Wands of irises line the water's edge, for example, while cherries, plums and magnolias rise above.

The effect is more than picturesque. Prisms of light in the lily-strewn water, the quiet harmonies of flower and branch – all summon that tranquillity of spirit which is the essence of Japanese gardening. The mood, like the material, is authentic.

THREAVE *Dumfries and Galloway*

In centuries past, the great gardens of Britain were tended by armies of gardeners. Horticultural skills, passed on from generation to generation, provided a pool of experience for landowners to draw on. Today, very few gardens offer training facilities for youngsters. But Threave in Scotland is one of them – it was conceived from the outset as a teaching garden.

The Threave estate covers some 1,500 acres, including five farms, extensive woods, and areas of wetland adjoining the River Dee which are maintained as a wildfowl reserve. Migrating greylag geese come here in their hundreds every year, and whooper swans are regular visitors. Conserving their habitat was something that the late Major A. F. L. Gordon had very much in mind when, in 1948, he presented the whole estate to the National Trust for Scotland.

The major continued to live in the turreted mansion until his death in 1957. Apart from one small walled garden, his main horticultural legacy was the planting of a myriad daffodils in the woodlands, which welcome visitors with their radiant display in spring. But he also conceived the idea of making Threave the site of a School of Practical Gardening, so that the skills and traditions of the great Scottish gardeners should not be lost in a changing world.

The school was opened in 1960, and the 65 acre gardens date from the same year. At the gaunt house, students learn a range of subjects from ornamental gardening to soil science and plant genetics. The gardens themselves serve as a field of study – but they are far from academic in their appeal. Plantings are largely informal, and include woodland and glade where choice shrubs have been established among beeches, larches and firs. Rhododendrons and azaleas are well represented and, though still young, thrive in the heavy, damp loam.

TINTINHULL *Somerset*

The house, like Topsy of *Uncle Tom's Cabin*, 'just grow'd'. In 1600 it was a Somerset yeoman's farmhouse, then about a century later acquired new dignity with the addition of a rather grand west front with tall latticed windows, and a porch with pillars and steps to enhance the front door. When, a few years later, it was given a forecourt and piers topped by stone eagles, it had clearly become the residence of a country gentleman or prosperous farmer. And so it remained until the end of the 19th century.

That it is now one of the most important small gardens in the country is due to the efforts of Tintinhull's last two owners, both of whom, by happy chance, were gardeners of considerable merit. In 1898 the house was purchased by Dr Price, a clergyman and distinguished botanist, who laid out the handsome series of little gardens that stretch out from the west front. The first of these is the forecourt, or Eagle Court, as it is rather splendidly called. From there, a paved path and steps guarded by large busbies of yew, run through the next area, the azalea

garden, and so to the fountain garden with its pool and fountain surrounded by yew hedges. At the very end there is a seat from which one can look back down the path and admire the softly glowing stone of the house centred in its framing of garden.

The next owners were Captain and Mrs Reiss, who acquired the place in 1933, and at once set about developing and enlarging the garden. In general, they followed the principles of Dr Price, maintaining a series of gardens enclosed by hedges and made to look, in that somewhat flat part of the country, as though the whole had been created from different levels. This is achieved by the inclusion of a sunken garden in the plan, and the cunning placing of steps. Other features are a wide expanse of lawn pinned down by a vast cedar and a formal garden with borders, a large rectangular pool and a summerhouse.

The Reisses made many other additions and improvements, including the building of the terrace, but their greatest flair – and especially Mrs Riess's – was for planting. She planned her borders in the manner prescribed by Gertrude Jekyll, the great garden designer at the turn of the century, who sought always for overall and continuing effect rather than the display of outstanding single plants or species. Thus, at Tintinhull in spring the accent is upon massed bulbs with a supporting cast of flowering cherries and a few evergreen shrubs and plants. Then, in summer, one border might be filled with bright colour such as red and white roses mixed with brilliant yellow verbascums and Spanish brooms, while another near by would be in more muted shades, with pale yellow roses, and pale pink and mauve flowers predominating. All of the borders are mixed, an orchestration of shrubs, plants for flowers and foliage, bulbs, and even a low fronting of alpines, while each garden is brought into a pleasantly disciplined whole by its surrounding of dark yew. Tintinhull is a delight at any time from spring to October, but an especially good time for a visit is July, when great tubs of Regale lilies are placed upon the terrace to flaunt their white

ROSES AND YEWS *The rose-covered west front of Tintinhull House looks out on the Eagle Court – a walled garden laid out on formal lines but planted for the most part with a lush informality. Trim bushes of yew stand in file beside the path, while roses, shrubs and herbaceous plants tumble over one another in a riot of colour in the surrounding beds.*

DOWN TO EARTH *A model of an armillary sphere – an ancient navigational aid for calculating distances between the stars – adds emphasis to the deliberate choice to 'go small' at Tintinhull. The garden is divided into many separate compartments, each with its own character, like the one glimpsed here through an arch in its enclosing hedge of yew.*

trumpets and sulphur-yellow interiors, and to fill the air with their somnolent fragrance.

Tintinhull is a gardener's garden; therefore, the National Trust, who now own the place, have made an inventory of all its plants and their positions to ensure the continuance of the effects so carefully composed by Mrs Reiss. Copies of the inventory are available for visitors.

TRELISSICK *Cornwall*

You expect to find hydrangeas in a Cornish garden. They are plants which tend to prosper in coastal areas, and especially relish the mild climate ushered in by the Gulf Stream. In summer, the common varieties seem to cluster every cottage wall with their densely flowered heads, shading from blue-mauve to pale pink according to the soil.

Trelissick Garden, above the estuary of the River Fal, is remarkable for its range of tender shrubs: choice magnolias, camellias and rhododendrons, for example. But if one family of plants has to be singled out as a speciality, it must be the hydrangeas. They are everywhere, from common Lace-caps and Hortensias to the rarest and least seen species. In all, over 130 different forms are represented, making the collection as complete as any in the British Isles.

Trelissick lies at the head of Falmouth Harbour, and at different points commands superb views, framed by hanging woods, down the deep-water anchorage and out to sea. But though graced with spacious lawns, the 25 acre garden is not open in every direction. It needs its protective plantings of conifers and Holm oaks to combat savage prevailing winds. (Many trees were

SPLENDID SITE *The gardens at Trelissick occupy one of the finest sites in Cornwall. From high above the Fal Estuary, Trelissick looks out to sea over green parkland and hanging woods of oak, beech and pine, which run down to the water's edge.*

brought down in one particularly wild storm of December 1979, when hurricane-force winds reached 120 mph.)

John Lawrence, a captain in the Cornwall Militia, built a house on the site in about 1750 and was remembered, enigmatically, for his 'good nature, convivial habits and wild eccentricities'. Remnants of his villa survive in the porticoed mansion seen today, though it was substantially rebuilt at different periods. The property changed hands many times over the years, and the garden grew in stages.

The Gilbert family owned Trelissick from 1844 to 1913, and their squirrel crest can be seen at the top of an old water tower in the garden. They were probably responsible for planting many of the screening trees, but the exotics were chiefly established by the Copelands, a husband and wife team who nurtured the garden from 1937 to 1955. Their plantings were culled from all over the world. No sooner are you inside the entrance gate, for example, than you meet a tall *Hoheria sexstylosa* from New Zealand. The evergreen is smothered with white flowers in summer, while the tender *Solanum jasminoides*, the jasmine nightshade of Brazil, climbs through its branches.

Similarly luxuriant associations of plants are met throughout the garden. One magical spot is a quiet dell sheltering beneath Japanese cedars. In this lush hollow, Australian tree ferns spread their green fronds among plantings of *Musa basjoo*, the hardy banana of Japan. Beneath them spread a wild carpet of primulas, hostas and astilbes, while tall Himalayan rhododendrons loom behind.

Hydrangeas, of course, have been lavishly planted throughout the garden, lining paths with ramparts of summer colour, or planted singly as specimens. Among the host of species and cultivars there is, for example, a spectacular *Hydrangea paniculata* 'Grandiflora', which bears its freight of great white panicles throughout the summer; and a prominent mauve *H. villosa*. Among the curiosities, pride of place is probably held by *H. maritima* 'Ayesha', with its cupped petals of lilac-grey.

North of the main garden area is a large stretch of rising ground specifically devoted to hydrangeas of the widest possible variety, planted among ornamental trees. It is reached by a bridge, and is known as Carcadden from old Cornish meaning 'fortified place'. This area was an overgrown orchard when the National Trust acquired the property in 1958. Though it has since been developed for decorative effect, it still retains a Victorian summerhouse which offers lovely views back from the young to the older garden.

Apart from the hydrangeas, rhododendrons have taken to Trelissick as they have to so many Cornish gardens. The coaxing climate and lime-free soil have permitted a splendid miscellany to flourish. A tall clump of the tree-like *Rhododendron altaclarense* 'Cornish Red' is just one of many eye-catching plantings, and the garden also has its own rhododendron hybrids: 'Trelissick Salmon' and 'Trelissick Port Wine'.

THE PROTECTORS *Tall evergreen trees provide protection from the fierce Atlantic winds which whip over Trelissick in winter. Secure beneath the trees, their charges – including tender azaleas, rhododendrons, camellias and magnolias – can relax into bloom.*

Add the springtime freshness of camellias and magnolias, the autumn fire of maples and oxydendrums, and you have a true garden for all seasons. Nor do Trelissick's attractions end at the boundaries of the garden proper. Below the exotics are many acres of woodland where miles of carriage drives wind among the beeches and oaks. They were laid out by Ralph Allen Daniell, a tin-mining magnate of the early 19th century. Owner of the Trelissick estate, he was said to be the richest man in Cornwall in his day, and known as 'Guinea-a-minute-Daniell' after a single mine which was said to furnish him with that sum.

The walks lead down to the tide-lapped shores of the estuary, following the bank of secluded Lamouth Creek. It is a haunting inlet, richly evocative of a more ancient Cornwall than the garden's – of Druidic mystery and Arthurian romance, and of the smugglers, too, who would bring their own contraband exotica by moonlit paths from the shore.

TRESCO ABBEY GARDENS

Isles of Scilly

In a corner of Tresco Abbey Gardens is an area known as Valhalla – named for the resting-place of heroes in the Norse heaven. In it you can see a collection of figureheads and other objects salvaged from ships that foundered on the Isles of Scilly. There are Saracen heads and gilded eagles, women in billowing robes – all victims of the salt gales which shriek about the islands and the wind-driven rollers which burst against their shores.

The Scillies' winds are wreckers' winds – root-wrenching, stem-snapping swashbucklers which ought to make gardening impossible. But of course it is not. Screen off the vandal air currents and you detect a special radiance in the sea-cleansed air, and a mildness of climate found nowhere on mainland Britain. Apart from tourism, flower growing is the islanders' main source of income. Bulbs, planted in sheltered, pocket-handkerchief fields, yield daffodils for Christmas.

And on Tresco, the second largest of the isles, much more than daffodils are grown. There are date palms from the Canaries and blue-plumed echiums from Australia, South African proteas and coral-red Mexican beschornerias. Strange spiky foliage, colours rich and rare – all jostle for attention in an atmosphere of unimaginable luxuriance. Tresco has been called a plant-lover's Treasure Island, and it holds Britain's most exotic paradise garden.

Tresco lies out in the Atlantic some 30 miles from Land's End. Though its line of latitude is fractionally to the north of the Cornish Lizard's the island is washed on all sides by the warm Gulf Stream, which accounts for its exceptionally mild climate. And it was Augustus Smith, a 19th-century Hertfordshire gentleman, who first saw Tresco's potential.

In 1834, Smith acquired the lease of all the Scillies, taking up the title of Lord Proprietor of the Isles. And he made Tresco the capital of his little Atlantic empire,

HIGH AND DRY *Neptune looks out to sea from his resting place on the top terrace of the Tresco Abbey Gardens. Between him and his kingdom lies a garden where 3,000 species of plants from all parts of the world flourish together in harmony.*

building a granite house for himself on the site of Tresco's ruined Benedictine priory.

Tresco was treeless then, boasting no plant taller than a gorse bush. But Smith knew what might be done in its practically frost-free climate. Immediately on arrival he built a complex of walled garden enclosures to fend off the wind. Later, terraces were gouged out of the south-facing slopes below the abbey, and shelter-belts of conifers were established to extend the storm-proofing. By the time of his death in 1872, Tresco Abbey Gardens covered some 17 acres, with considerable woodlands around.

The purpose was, from the outset, to nurture tender exotics which would not survive on the mainland. It has been said of the Scilly Isles that they know only two seasons: spring and summer. Though slight frosts do occasionally occur at Tresco, winter temperatures very rarely drop below 50°F (10°C); very high summer temperatures are equally uncommon. Into this balmy, ever-coaxing climate, Smith brought rare specimens from Kew as well as seeds gathered from all over the Southern Hemisphere. And many of the southerners had their own inverted calendar, flowering in December rather than July.

The result was a garden vivid even in midwinter, a marvel among those of Smith's contemporaries. In 1851, Smith could write on Christmas Eve: 'My garden was left in high colour, the Clianthus just bursting into flower and the *Acacia lophantha* also covered with yellow blossoms.'

In Smith's day a visit from the mainland was akin to an act of pilgrimage – and an arduous one at that. Today, it takes less effort than you might think to reach Tresco Abbey Gardens. Apart from regular ferry services, the island also claims the world's only Garden Heliport; visitors are brought from Penzance almost to the garden gate by a British Airways helicopter.

Whatever route is chosen, your surprise on arrival will be unfailing. The plants which flourish here with such exuberance might be familiar to a Maori or a Mexican – but what place have they in an English garden? Great sheaves of palms and cordylines do much to set the tone, with the sharp-leaved desert agaves, aloes and opuntias which abound. But so much contributes to the subtropical mood. Take the mesembryanthemums, for example. These gaudy natives of South Africa were one of Smith's first introductions at Tresco. Today, they have seeded themselves throughout the Scilly Isles.

There is *Kennedya nigricans*, a West Australian climber whose petals are black as ebony; dasylirions from Mexico like huge green sea urchins with their bristling spheres of spikes. Correas, puyas, gazanias and dimorphothecases ... over 3,000 species and varieties of plants are represented. More remarkable still, as you explore Tresco's paths, it seems that every

ABBEY WALLS *The ruins of the old Priory of St Nicholas, which once sheltered Tresco's community of monks, now provide support for climbing plants and a roothold for stonecrops and other succulents.*

major planting has had to earn its place as a rarity.

Among the eye-catching trees is a sensational *Eucalyptus ficifolia*, the red gum of south-west Australia, which bears richly rouged flowers in September. This splendid tree has fig-like leaves and does not grow outdoors anywhere else in the British Isles. Another prize specimen is a *Banksia integrifolia*, flowering in greenish-yellow and at 70 ft the largest known example in the world.

But of all the exotics in this garden of rarities, one specimen holds pride of place. This is a rata from New Zealand, *Metrosideros tomentosa*. Sometimes known as the New Zealand Christmas tree, it belongs to a species all too easily killed off by frost. Tresco holds several examples, and the giant among them towers to some 80 ft. It is a breathtaking sight in summer when the branches burgeon forth in a myriad crimson blooms which glow like red-hot lava against the sky.

The tree is also remarkable for its aerial roots, which hang like cables to the ground – cables so thick and strong, moreover, that they help to prop up the branches. You can actually walk a path between the roots – a weird, unforgettable experience.

The giant metrosideros grows just off the Lighthouse Way, which divides the garden in half. At the lower end is a 17th-century lighthouse cresset, a container in which coal fires were burned to warn passing ships of danger. At the higher end, a stone head of Neptune looks down a flight of steps flanked by Canary Island palms.

For all its luxurious diversity, Tresco is not a hard garden in which to find your way about. The sloping site is roughly rectangular, and the other main axis is a so-called Long Walk which crosses the Lighthouse Way at right-angles. Between them they divide the garden into four quarters, within each of which different areas display their own character. One, for example, is known as 'Mexico'; another is a rockery devoted to cacti and succulents from Arizona. The garden ornaments include an ancient Roman sacrificial altar which stands at the end of the Long Walk. Near by is a planting of the Chilean myrtle (*Myrtus luma*), yet another outstanding attraction. The smooth and slender orange trunks of these distinctive trees leave a memorable impression.

And then there is Valhalla of course, with its splendid display of painted figureheads. It lies down near the lighthouse cresset at the exit, and you can read here about the maritime history of the isles before leaving the paradise gardens behind.

VENTNOR BOTANIC GARDEN *Isle of Wight*

Among Britain's leading Botanic Gardens, the name of Ventnor may not have the resonance of, say, a Westonbirt or a Kew. Covering some 22 acres of the Isle of Wight, the garden was only started in 1969, and it was opened as recently as 1972. It is, in fact, Britain's youngest Botanic Garden – though you might find the claim hard to believe on a visit.

One reason is the size of the trees. At Ventnor you can see towering thujas, Monterey cypresses and other handsome relics of a garden established here in the Victorian age. Another is the sheer exuberance of the more recent plantings: there are rampant ceanothuses, and mimosas grown to 25 ft high; flaming orange gazanias, bright yellow calceolarias and white-flowering hoherias. These and many other tender introductions have flourished in a kindly south-coast climate augmented by Ventnor's unique geographical advantages.

The Botanic Garden lies in the Undercliff – a curious 6 mile ledge in the downs. It was formed by ancient landslides, and completely protects the garden from chilly north and east winds. Salt gales from the south and west, meanwhile, have already been largely screened by youthful shelter belts of trees. Climatically, this warm pocket is as favoured as Scilly and the Channel Islands. Olives, pomegranates, oranges and the hardy Japanese banana (*Musa basjoo*) all fruit in the open at Ventnor, as in only the most privileged gardens in Britain.

If the south-coast sun trap has a problem, it is the high alkaline content of the soil. You would not expect to find acid-loving plants in a downland setting. Yet in this, as in all else, Ventnor has been fortunate. In one area, natural deposits of peat overlie the local limestone. Camellias and magnolias thrive there, along with such rarities as the tender camphor tree of the Far East.

Ventnor includes a good selection of rare conifers, and a very well stocked Rose Garden. But for the most heightened tropical effects you should visit the Palm Garden, where many types of palm and cordyline spread their spiky fronds all around. Crotons, aspidistras and New Zealand tree ferns contribute to the mood of pampered luxury, and here, too, you can see the curious *Beschorneria yuccoides* of Mexico. It is a striking plant which seems somehow colour-schemed the wrong way round: the 6 ft high stems are a vivid coral red – while the flowers are a brilliant green.

WADDESDON MANOR

Buckinghamshire

When Benjamin Disraeli was invited to witness the building of Waddesdon, he is said to have remarked that if only the Almighty had had a Rothschild to aid him, then the Creation would have been accomplished in considerably under seven days. As it happened, it took Baron Ferdinand de Rothschild rather more than seven years, from 1875 to 1883, to build the house and the elaborate park surrounding it. But considering it involved lowering a 10-acre hilltop by 9 ft over all, it was not too bad. A branch railway was constructed to bring the Bath stone and other materials from the main line at Quainton, while teams of Percheron mares were imported from Normandy for the last stages of the haul. Hundreds of mature trees were brought in on specially constructed carts, and telegraph wires were lowered along the roads so

ENTENTE CORDIALE *In 1875 Baron Ferdinand de Rothschild decided to bring a little bit of France to England. First he built Waddesdon Manor in the style of a French Renaissance château, then he called in a French landscape gardener to lay out the grounds. The result (above) would fit just as well – or even better – into the environs of Paris as it does into the landscape of Buckinghamshire.*

as not to impede their passage. The trees were then dropped by a system of chains into holes in the bare hillside. Acres of turf, paths and drives were laid, statues and fountains set up, beds planted, the aviary and pergola constructed, and there it was, the park virtually complete.

At its heart was the towered and turreted manor house, and there the baron lived, among his beloved collections of 18th-century art, until his sadly early death in 1898. The estate then passed to his sister, Miss Alice de Rothschild, who is still remembered in the district for her kindness and strength of character. She was also a gardener of note, and added considerably to the numbers of rare trees and shrubs in the park. When she died in 1922, Waddesdon passed to her great-nephew, James de Rothschild, who served with distinction with the French army in the First World War, and as a junior minister in the British government in the Second. In accordance with his grandfather's wish that the manor should never be broken up or allowed to deteriorate, he left it to the National Trust in 1957, together with all its magnificent collections of paintings and furniture.

Waddesdon Manor is a deliberate compromise between a French château and a great Victorian country house, and a similar comment might be made about the park. The outlying area, with its deer pens, artfully 'genuine' caverns (for wild sheep), its apparently random distribution of grand trees and shrubs and its wonderful views over the Chilterns to the

south, is very much a Victorian adaptation of the landscape notions of the previous century. But the northern approach to the house, standing proud on its eminence where it can see and be seen, is far more reminiscent of the great gardens of France. The introduction is a large gravel circle, in the midst of which is an awesome group of 18th-century Italian statuary – Triton and the Nereids – spouting water. From there, no fewer than five parallel drives reach up, ruler-straight, to the house. All about are fine trees, a Chinese maidenhair tree, for example, silver limes and blue cedars, and groups of statuary depicting classical themes.

About the house are majestic terraces, laid out by Baron Ferdinand de Rothschild himself. To this day, the terrace beds require some 5,000 tulips and 4,000 wallflowers to fill them in spring, and about the same numbers of geraniums and ageratums for summer colour. On the south terrace there is another group of fountain statuary, this one portraying Pluto and Prosperine. In the early 18th century it was united with the group by the north entrance to form, amazingly, only part of a fountain for a ducal palace near Parma.

A stroll in the park presents all kinds of delights. There is the vast bowl of Daffodil Valley, for instance, given additional depth by the tall conifers gathered upon its rim, and pushing forth a sea of daffodils in the spring. And certainly, no one should miss the aviary, a large semicircle of delicate metalwork beautifully set off by hornbeam hedges and 'Iceberg' roses.

WAKEHURST PLACE *West Sussex*

However lovely it may be, it must still be a considerable accolade for any garden to be coveted by Kew; but so it was at Wakehurst. It is a very old place, with a robust history of abducted medieval heiresses and 18th-century rakes, but the story of its garden begins little more than 80 years ago when the estate was purchased by Gerald Loder, later Lord Wakehurst. A gardener of brilliance, he began the famous collection of trees and shrubs at Wakehurst. His work was continued by his successor, Sir Henry Price, who bequeathed the estate to the National Trust. Then, in 1967, it was acquired on a long lease by the Royal Botanic Gardens as a kind of out-of-town Kew.

The emphasis at Wakehurst is upon wild species collected from all over the world, and they could not have a finer setting than the wooded slopes and valleys of the Sussex Weald, where so many great gardens have been created. The grounds are magnificently laid out, and a number of garden trails have been devised. Whether these are followed or not, there is a large number of 'must-be-seens'. Among them is Rhododendron Walk with its large number of rhododendron species and hybrids, including one whose native habitat is some 8,000 ft up in the mountain woodlands of Szechwan. Beyond Rhododendron Walk is a pond, mirroring the old house, which contains exhibition rooms and a restaurant. Watch out hereabouts for some fine specimen

trees, among them a magnolia planted in 1908, some Japanese maples and a giant sequoia. Just to the north of the house is the Memorial Garden dedicated to Sir Henry Price. The Pleasaunce, near by, is another small and intimate garden with clipped yew hedges and an ornamental pond with a fountain.

One of the oldest established parts of Wakehurst is the Heath Garden. It was here that Gerald Loder established his collection of Australasian and Latin American plants at the beginning of the century. There are myrtles and waratahs with flowers like red claws, beautiful white-flowering hoherias and a Tasmanian conifer (*Athrotaxis selaginoides*) that closely resembles fossil trees discovered in the Isle of Sheppey. The Slips, not far off, is an idealised Sussex Valley, with a little stream running through it. Here is another memorial, a sundial commemorating Gerald Loder and his gardener, Alfred Coates. It bears the words:

Give fools their gold and knaves their power,
Let fortune's bubbles rise and fall,
Who sows a field or trains a flower
Or plants a tree, is more than all.

The Slips comes to an end with the Water Garden, a series of ponds round which grow a wide variety of marsh and water-loving plants, including a Florida swamp cypress. Downhill is another valley, Westwood Valley or The Ravine, with steep, heavily wooded sides and a broad scattering of rhododendrons showing through the trees. In spring, they look for all the

MEMORIAL GARDEN *A walled garden, close to the house at Wakehurst Place, has been dedicated as a memorial to Sir Henry Price, who left the estate to the nation in 1963. It is stocked with old-fashioned cottage-garden flowers in pastel shades and includes old roses, pinks and clematises.*

world like an avalanche of colour breaking down the slopes. There, too, are some wonderful specimen trees – a 60 ft tall pink-flowering magnolia, a handkerchief tree with its curious fluttering white bracts and a western hemlock.

About Rock View, a natural outcrop of the local sandstone, is the Himalayan Glade containing a collection of plants – rhododendron species, mountain gentians and cinquefoils among them – that would more normally be found about 10,000 ft up on the shoulders of the Himalayas. Beyond is the Pinetum, a splendid, 12 acre gathering of conifers, many of which are rare in Britain. Horsebridge Woods, Bloomer's Valley and Bethlehem Wood, by contrast, seem much more like native woodland; at least at first glance. But among the more familiar trees there are also some handsome strangers, such as California redwoods, Wellingtonias, a giant fir and a monkey-puzzle tree from Chile. Throughout the woods, the bluebells grow, thousands of them, producing in spring an acres-wide carpet of misty blue. At the head of Horsebridge Woods, the highly picturesque Rock Walk begins. A place of massive sandstone outcrops, over which writhe and flow the roots of yews, beeches and oaks.

DUTCH DISCIPLINE *High walls and neatly trimmed hedges keep untidy nature at bay in the gardens at Westbury Court. They were laid out in the late 17th century in the formal Dutch style which became popular – if not obligatory – after the accession of William of Orange. Only one constituent remains free – the water lilies, which spread haphazardly across the geometrically confined waters of the canal.*

WESTBURY COURT *Gloucestershire*

An early 18th-century engraving shows Westbury Court as a Tudor house with the tall spire of a church near by and, in the middle distance, an imposing summerhouse or pavilion standing at the head of a long, straight waterway. Much of the surrounding landscape consists of formal flower beds, further rigidly drawn waterways, and row upon row of immaculately spaced trees and shrubs.

The spire still stands, and so does the summerhouse, but Westbury Court itself has long vanished as have two houses that succeeded it. Which makes it all the more remarkable that through a number of lucky accidents, a generous and anonymous donation and some very hard work on the part of the National Trust the garden has survived and is now the most perfect – and the oldest – example of an enclosed Dutch-style garden in the country.

It was laid out in the closing years of the 17th century by Colonel Maynard Colchester in response to the enthusiasm for things Dutch that swept over the country in the wake of William of Orange's accession to the throne of Britain. There were dozens of gardens like it at the time, almost all of which were to be obliterated by Capability Brown and his fellow landscape gardeners.

Westbury Court is the very antithesis of the landscape garden. Like other Dutch gardens of its period, it depends for effect not upon the outside world – which in Holland's case is fairly uneventful anyway – but on organised prettiness close at hand. Nature was ruthlessly kept at bay by high walls, woodlands replaced by nearly 5,000 yews and hollies carved into hedges or topiary figures, and babbling streams by straight-cut waterways whose limpid surfaces faithfully reflected statuary and the tall, white windows of the summerhouse. Flower beds too were straight-cut, outlined by miniature hedges of box and interspersed with geometric shapes in topiary.

It was a place of great charm and elegance, but its survival was due not to preservation, but neglect. For most of the 19th century it was deserted by the Colchester family, and though they moved back and built another house there in 1895, they sold the estate in 1960 to a speculator who intended to build ten houses on the site of the garden. The local council refused permission, however, and instead decided to build a home for the elderly on the site of the old house and to offer the garden to the National Trust.

The problems seemed insurmountable, but thanks to a public appeal and donations from various sources, sufficient money was raised by 1967 for the National Trust to begin a serious programme of restoration. All was done to conform as closely as possible with the 18th-century engraving and with information gleaned from Colonel Colchester's account books and planting records. Perhaps the most delightful aspect of the restoration is that the gardens have been replanted almost entirely with species and varieties known to have been present in England prior to 1700.

WESTONBIRT ARBORETUM

Gloucestershire

King Midas, according to the old Greek myth, suffered from a curse by which everything he touched turned to gold. Visit Westonbirt in October and you may feel that autumn stalks the woodlands with the same glorious affliction. In the Acer Glade especially, fires of sensational brilliance burn all about: glowing pinks and crimsons, furious oranges and sheaves of yellow that flash so bright they seem to be lit from within.

Westonbirt is a marvel at any time of year. The cathedral spires of its mighty conifers change little month by month, and the blooms of innumerable interplanted shrubs lend colour in spring, summer and even winter. But October – the month of the Japanese maple – provides a quality of experience all its own.

The great arboretum was founded in 1829 by Robert Holford of Westonbirt House. His family had occupied the Gloucestershire estate for many generations. But what was to become the best tree collection in Europe started only when the owner began planting in pasturelands west of the park. The existing layout, with its formal avenues, broad rides and meandering paths, dates chiefly from 1855 when many oaks, beeches, pines, larches and yews were established.

The whole enterprise was designed for private pleasure and interest. From 1870 the owner's son, Sir George Holford, joined his father in amassing a wealth of ornamental trees brought to Westonbirt from all over the world. The decorative plantings were extended to cover some 247 acres in all. And the tradition established by the Holfords and their successors is now continued by the Forestry Commission, which acquired the property in 1956.

Westonbirt lies on a broad Cotswold ridge at some 400 ft above sea level. But though situated in a limestone landscape, pockets of sandy loam are sufficiently free of lime to allow acid-loving plants to root comfortably. Some fine magnolias, for example, grace the woodlands in March, and by May the blossoms of flourishing rhododendrons and azaleas provide wonderful shows of colour among the trees.

The arboretum is managed today for purposes of teaching and research. But maintaining the tradition of ornamental planting has been much in the minds of the administrators. Westonbirt was after all conceived for private enjoyment. Now open all the year round, it invites the attention of the public. 'For us,' claims the guidebook, 'every day is an open day.'

You can wander at will throughout the entire collection with its 13,000 catalogued trees and shrubs. And the authorities are not fastidious about how you choose to view the specimens. 'For a change,' it suggests, 'put some foliage between yourself and the sun – you could not believe the colour and the effect you will see; get down on your hands and knees if you have to, we don't mind!'

Come to Westonbirt in any season and you will first

be awed by the sheer scale of the trees, some of them dating back to the first plantings. Their mighty trunks provide the architecture for the scene.

One tremendous group of old incense cedars (*Libocedrus decurrens*) stands near the house, and elsewhere all the great conifers are represented: Wellingtonias, coast redwoods and Douglas firs, for example. But there are giants, too, among trees not normally noted for height. Take the Italian alder (*Alnus cordata*), for example: this is a bright green, pyramidal tree from southern Europe which rarely grows to more than 30 ft or so. Westonbirt's specimen is more than treble that height – at 93 ft, the largest of its family in Britain.

There are several such record-breakers at Westonbirt. Others include outstanding examples of silver maple, paulownia, caucasian oak, whitebeam and Chinese lime. They make a fittingly diverse crew for this garden of variety, and with 17 miles of pathways winding among the woodlands the attractions are impossible to digest in one visit. The answer of course is to plan your explorations according to the time of year. The official guidebook is helpful in suggesting different areas for different seasons.

The Westonbirt calendar begins in the dark days of

AUTUMN GOLD *If a single term covers the glowing miscellany of Westonbirt in October, it can only be Autumn Gold – the gift which dying leaves bequeath to the gardening world before they fall.*

January and February. At a time when most English gardens are languishing, the arboretum is flecked with the colours of winter-flowering cherries; shrubs such as Christmas box (*Sarcococca humilis*) and *Viburnum farreri* load the air with their fragrance.

From the bluebell days of spring through to June's lilac time, Westonbirt is radiant with colour. In the heat of high summer you can escape to any number of cool, shady walks, and then, with September and the ripening of fruits, autumn comes with its Midas touch.

By October, the Acer Glade to the north of the entrance becomes a place of magnetic attraction. The focus of interest is a fireworks display without parallel in any English garden. The fireworks, of course, are entirely natural phenomena caused by the retreat of sap from the dying foliage of the maples. The so-called Japanese maples (*Acer japonicum, A. palmatum* and their cultivars) are famed for the brilliance of their autumn colours; but the selection at Westonbirt is unique for its range and magnificence – almost every known form is represented. Several of the specimens are over 100 years old, and there are record-breakers here as elsewhere in the arboretum. But you do not look especially for statistical marvels. Maples are not tall trees, and a 50 ft specimen is exceptional.

The colours are what quicken the pulse. For the most sensational effects, *A. japonicum* 'Vitifolium' holds pride of place, its foliage turning from yellow in September to a whole mosaic of tones, suffused with smoky purple as well as pink, crimson and gold – all on a single tree. In contrast, *A. palmatum* and its cultivars tend to turn colour in uniform sequence: the elegant 'Osakazuki' – a perfect scarlet – is the most prized for its purity of hue. These and a host of others, including the native field maple and common sycamore, provide one of the finest sights known to British gardeners.

In reality, it is more than a 'sight'. With the foliage glowing all around, shaken by gusts and carpeting the ground with their fiery leaves, you could call it an experience – a vision even – of autumn itself.

WESTON HALL *Shropshire*

The oriental plane (*Platanus orientalis*) has one of the noblest pedigrees of all European trees. It was a favourite of Xerxes, King of Persia in the 5th century BC; the Greeks and Romans used to plant it for shade. Broad-spreading and with a handsome rounded crown, the tree is capable of living to a great age.

Britain's largest and most magnificent example grows at Weston Hall in Shropshire. Rising to 70 ft in height, with a trunk of immense girth, it spreads its branches over a circumference of more than a quarter of an acre. Some of the lower boughs growing close to the ground have to be propped up because of their great length and weight. But the whole remains superbly proportioned, forming one tumultuous dome of green foliage.

The house was built in 1671, and the great oriental plane seems to have been planted at the same time. But the rolling landscape which extends to south, east and west was contoured in the next century by Capability Brown. He was commissioned in the 1760s and worked his customary magic on the terrain, filling in the middle distance with a glimmering lake, and planting trees singly and in clumps to provide serpentine views towards the horizon.

A series of wide terraces looks from the house to the parkland beyond. Embellished with topiary and ornamental urns, they end at a beautifully balustraded arc which encloses the great plane tree in the middle. A Victorian orangery stands to one side of the house, with an Italianate garden spread before it.

Out in Brown's landscape there are lovely walks to be had through what Disraeli called Weston's 'scenes so fair'. Temple Wood, especially, is magnificent in early summer when rhododendrons bloom at the feet of venerable chestnuts and oaks. The long, narrow woodland was laid out by Brown as a backdrop for a Temple of Diana designed by James Paine, an architect who often collaborated with the landscapist.

The building is among the finest examples of Georgian garden architecture, the shapely arches of its tall glass-paned windows surmounted by a domed roof to the rear. But it was never designed to house a shrine. The temple takes its name from decorative panels which grace a circular tea room within; they show scenes from the Roman goddess's life.

North of the building, though, is the secluded Temple Pool, overlooked by a little domed temple of its own. This is a place of sylvan mystery, and when breezes crinkle the water and rustle among the leaves you really can imagine that it is haunted by the woodland gods of antiquity. At the far end is Paine's Roman bridge, pale against the trees which cast long shadows on the water.

WINKWORTH ARBORETUM

Surrey

The National Trust's only true arboretum, Winkworth consists of 96 acres of wooded hillsides curled about a pair of stilly, reflective lakes in the Surrey 'Alps'. Most of it is the work of Dr Wilfrid Fox, a distinguished physician and horticulturist, who bought a large piece of neglected woodland in 1938 and devoted the last quarter-century of his life to making it a place of beauty that would be enjoyed in perpetuity.

It was a magnificent accomplishment, a skilful blending of exotic trees and shrubs with native woodland to produce a round-the-year cavalcade of colour and interest that is all the more delightful for its apparent casualness. This is, one feels, what all British woodland might have looked like had nature not distributed some of the most colourful trees in other parts of the world instead. However, a goodly number of these have now been assembled at Winkworth among the native trees, to spring out in their seasons in wild displays of foreignness.

Autumn is the crescendo, when the sky is clear and the water is polished by the early frosts. Then the hillsides above flame, in the manner of the hills of

New England, with the luminous yellows and oranges of snake bark maples, the deep red of American oaks and the clear, singing yellow of birches. Among them are crimson-berried cotoneasters, the coral of ornamental cherry trees, fiery Japanese maples, bronze North American sweet gums and the incredible scarlet of disanthus, a Japanese relative of hamamelis (witch hazel). At one point, there is a line of tupelo trees from the eastern United States, whose leaves flare scarlet, yellow and orange; among them, holding the brightness down, as it were, is the steely blue-grey of Atlantic cedars.

But lovely though autumn is, spring and early summer could hardly be termed an anticlimax. In May and June, the splendid collection of mountain ashes and whitebeams put forth their white flowers to provide a background for the vibrant colours of flowering cherries, rhododendrons, and the clearer, waxy white of magnolias. This, too, is the time to visit the Azalea Steps; there are 93 of them climbing the hillside, lined on either hand by joyous masses of azaleas, giving this remarkable feature the air of a triumphal stairway. Those who prefer spring with less drama should visit the arboretum in March, when vast areas of the woodland flower are white with wild anemones, and then again in April, when they give way to a soft ground-mist of bluebells.

In the midst of the garden there is a simple monument to Dr Fox, designed by Sir Hugh Casson and guarded by a pair of evergreen eucryphias that bear large white flowers towards summer's end. Altogether a memorial that seems particularly apt.

WISLEY *Surrey*

One of the joys of visiting any garden is to discover some plant or ornamental effect which might grace your own plot at home. Wisley, in this context, offers a range of ideas without compare in the British Isles. In these Surrey acres almost every type of gardening is practised, researched and displayed. Wisley is a great puzzle-solver – a treasury of possibilities.

If your own garden tends to go through a dull patch after June you can visit the summer garden. Here a host of bulbs, herbaceous plants and flowering shrubs demonstrate what a vivid palette you can draw on for colour. Suppose that some corner of your garden needs a tree for height: which has the fastest growth rate? Which offers the best tones of foliage or bark? You can visit the Jubilee arboretum where 32 acres are being developed to answer such questions.

Wisley can advise you on what is tender, what is hardy, what to use for ground-cover and how to clothe a wall. It has bog garden, rock garden, herb garden, heath garden, wild garden, pinetum … there is no space here to describe all the attractions. But there is space at Wisley – 240 acres of it – for their display on the grandest scale.

World famous today, Wisley was founded in 1878 when Mr George F. Wilson bought a 60 acre estate of neglected woodland in Surrey. He was a talented amateur gardener and former treasurer of the Royal

making glades and ponds as settings for flowering shrubs, lilies, irises and a wealth of other plants. After his death, the estate was given in 1903 to the Royal Horticultural Society. It was to be developed and extended to make an experimental garden where every form of scientific and practical horticulture could be encouraged.

You approach Wisley today through a heathland lightly wooded with birches, oaks and pines. The soil is not in fact favourable to gardening, being generally lean and sandy, so that water drains swiftly away. With an average annual rainfall of only 26 in., keeping the plants mulched, fed and watered is a full time occupation for the staff. But you could be forgiven for failing to notice the difficulties on a visit. Wisley is as beautifully maintained as it is fascinating.

On entry you discover the laboratory building where subjects from propagation to pest control are studied. It is not, though, the stark construction you might expect. This functional building is a picturesque creation, half-timbered, rose-hung and with magnolias and ceanothuses among the tender subjects which billow from its red-brick lower walls. Near by are terraced lawns, a formal pool and pergola. The area typifies the spirit at Wisley.

Scores of gardening styles are represented, Wisley's index running from alpine meadow to winter garden. And though each holds its own fascination, some are famed in their own right as gardens of exceptional quality. Take the alpine meadow, for example. This is a sloping expanse of grass which shimmers in early April with the tiny nodding heads of a myriad yellow *Narcissi bulbocodium*, self-seeding and spreading all the time. Later, the pastels of wood anemones and dog's tooth violets will spangle the turf. Spotted orchid succeed in June and, before winter comes, purple autumn crocuses will splash the grass with colour again.

The meadow merges to one side with Wisley's

generally thought that autumn is the time to come to Winkworth, when maples, gums, oaks and birches flare into luminous imitation of a New England fall. But it is apparent, too, that glorious though the Winkworth autumn is, it is almost equalled by the springtime pageant, when the azaleas put forth their near-incredible range of colours against the young green of the trees.

celebrated rock garden, where slabs and boulders of Sussex sandstone are threaded by a chain of pools and waterfalls. It is a glory in spring when a pink weeping cherry blossoms on the summit mound and pale mauve ramondas from the Pyrenees raise their heads from the shadiest of crevices. Near by is the equally renowned wild garden, one of the oldest attractions at Wisley, where trees and shrubs planted by George F. Wilson have matured amid the native oaks. The soil is more moist and peaty here than is typical in the gardens. Rhododendrons, magnolias and camellias prosper in the shade, while all around rise the trunks of noble trees like the dawn redwood, for example, a primeval conifer with its fissured red-brown bole.

These informally planted areas comprise only a part of Wisley's attraction. Elsewhere there are acres of rectangular plots developed for specialist interest: herbs, border plants, fruit trees and so on. One which will absorb every town-dweller is a plot laid out with three model small gardens. The smallest is designed with the young married couple in mind, and at 72 ft × 24 ft is typical of the kind of area which many a first-time housebuyer acquires. The second, somewhat larger, is a family garden complete with playing space for children. The third and largest shows what the ambitious gardening enthusiast can achieve – still in a fairly constricted space. And as if these were not enough, an adjoining plot has been thoughtfully developed as a garden for disabled people.

Simply listing the enticements does them scant justice, and that in a sense, is the whole point. This, supremely, is a garden to be visited.

THE GARDENER'S GARDEN *Wisley is designed to show what any English garden could look like – given a century of the Royal Horticultural Society's expertise, enshrined in the Surrey 'Tudor' laboratories (above) and in the splendour of the summer borders (right).*

POET'S CORNER Rydal Mount, which became William Wordsworth's Lakeland home in 1813.

GAZETTEER

An A–Z guide to a further 136 fine gardens open to the public in Britain. Few gardens are open all the year round, so it is advisable to enquire in advance about opening times. Details are obtainable from the organisations listed at the end of this gazetteer.

ABINGTON PARK *Northamptonshire*

On Northampton's eastern fringe, a landscaped park studded with lakes and ornamental gardens offers respite from urban noise and bustle. Abington Park reveals its full splendour in autumn, when avenues of majestic trees parade in gold and crimson foliage. One of the gardens, designed for the blind, concentrates on elements of sound and fragrance – with a raised fountain and an aromatic camomile lawn. The park once belonged to Abington Manor, now a museum. It was the home of Shakespeare's grand-daughter Elizabeth Nash, and legend relates that she hid his manuscripts there, but they have still to be found.
LOCATION *On Wellingborough Road, Northampton.*

ACORN BANK *Cumbria*

Sheltering on the floor of the Eden valley, the gardens at Acorn Bank remain relatively unscathed by the winds that scour the surrounding moors and fells. The milder climate encourages the glorious display of spring flowers for which the gardens are famous. Rose beds and well stocked herbaceous borders bring abundant summer colour. Behind high walls the former kitchen garden harbours one of the most comprehensive collections of culinary and medicinal herbs in the country. The house – once lived in by Una Ratcliffe, the Yorkshire dialect poet, is now let by the National Trust as a Sue Ryder home for the disabled.
LOCATION *Off the A66, 6 miles E of Penrith.*

ARBIGLAND *Dumfries and Galloway*

The land of this rocky promontory was reclaimed from gorse and scrub in the 17th century, and a garden was begun in the 1730s. John Paul Jones, a founding father of the American navy, was born here in 1747. He was the son of the head gardener, and worked in the grounds as a boy. Major developments were carried out on the gardens early this century, using an existing framework of mature trees. Small paths break away from the 17th-century Broad Walk, and pass through unexpected changes of scene. The delicate colours of a sunken rose garden make demure contrast with the fiery-leaved shrubs of the oriental garden, known simply as 'Japan'. There are breathtaking views of the Solway coast from the terraces, below which the garden runs down to a sheltered sandy bay.
LOCATION *On the A710, 2 miles S of Kirkbean.*

ARDTORNISH *Highland*

Ardtornish lies on a hilly slope that has views to inspire an artist or poet. To the south-west the waters of Loch Aline stretch away to the Sound of Mull, and in the far distance are the hills of Mull. A London distiller chose this setting in 1856 to build himself a house, and his grandson created a garden of lawns and streams, rockeries and flowering shrubs. In this century the range of shrubs has been extended, and planted with less formality – lending the gardens the untrammelled air of natural woodland. Rhododendrons bloom in infinite variety, followed by eucryphias, hoherias and bright-berried sorbus. Variegated hostas, gunneras and blue meconopsis join the legions of primulas in the bog garden. In the south-west corner of the garden is an avenue of self-sown birches, and a glorious specimen of the rhododendron 'Polar Bear', with huge scented flowers of Arctic white.
LOCATION *Off the A884, 3 miles NE of Lochaline.*

ARLINGTON COURT *Devon*

The house and grounds at Arlington still reflect the many enthusiasms of Miss Rosalie Chichester – artist, photographer, traveller and collector – who lived there from 1865 until her death in 1949. Behind 8 miles of high fences she created a haven for animals and plants – introducing the Shetland ponies and Jacob's sheep whose descendants now roam the park. Close-mown grassy walks meander through woods where buzzards and ravens nest. The waters of Arlington Lake echo the call of ducks and herons, secure in the bird sanctuaries Miss Chichester established. Nearer the house, the herbaceous borders and lawns of the flower garden retain a Victorian elegance, while the conservatory proves a treasure-house of colour and fragrance, with cannas, lapagerias and the sweet-scented jasmine. The stables house a fascinating collection of 19th-century carriages.
LOCATION *Off the A39, 7 miles NE of Barnstaple.*

ASCOTT GARDENS *Buckinghamshire*

Ascott was taken over as a hunting-lodge in 1874 by Leopold de Rothschild – racehorse owner and son of the great financier, the first Baron de Rothschild. With sweeping views over the Vale of Aylesbury, the gardens combine intriguing artifice with great natural beauty. Imaginative topiary, like the vast sundial sculpted out of golden box and yew, ensured variety in winter when the house was occupied. In contrast, the oval pond with its veil of water lilies seems altogether uncontrived. A circular garden enclosed by yew hedges frames a magnificent fountain sculpture of Venus in her chariot, drawn by sea-horses with faithful cherubs in tow. The smooth lawns of the main garden are planted with ornamental trees, including glowing specimens of scarlet oak and copper beech.
LOCATION *Off the A418, half a mile E of Wing.*

GARDEN GODDESS *Venus rides through the garden at Ascott in a waterborne chariot drawn by sea-horses and attended by winged cherubs.*

ASHRIDGE HOUSE GARDENS
Hertfordshire

In 1813 the most notable garden designer of his day, Humphry Repton, began work on the commission he later prized above all. He devised a fantasia of 17 gardens around Ashridge House, a new mansion built by the Earl of Bridgewater. Repton's death in 1818 prevented the full realisation of his dream, but successors were faithful to his concept. A dozen intimate gardens, some linked by avenues of yew or Wellingtonia, provide interest for every season. Against a background of evergreens, the bedding plants make colourful spring patterns, while summer heralds the glory of rhododendrons and roses. The autumn visitor is rewarded by flamboyant displays of dahlias and begonias.

LOCATION *On the A41, 3½ miles N of Berkhamsted.*

ATHELHAMPTON *Dorset*

The Tudor love of intricate design is reflected in Athelhampton's series of walled gardens, framed in mellow Ham stone. Each offers new variety as cascades and fish ponds alternate with terraced lawns and formal topiary. Although the gardens date from 1891, the style remains true to the Tudor character of Athelhampton. Walks of lime and yew lead on to less formal vistas of magnolia trees and flowering shrubs. Old varieties of British apple thrive in the kitchen garden, as do the more exotic plants kept in the spacious glasshouse.

LOCATION *On the A35, half a mile E of Puddletown.*

BALMORAL CASTLE *Grampian*

'All seemed to breathe freedom and peace, and to make one forget the world and its sad turmoils', wrote Queen Victoria. Her words still describe Balmoral, where a white granite castle stands beside the River Dee in a circle of hills. It has been a retreat for the royal family since 1848, when Queen Victoria first went there. Begun by Prince Albert and improved by his successors, the gardens have a formal grace, with wide herbaceous borders leading the eye on to wild moorland scenery beyond. The wooded valley has delightful walks, past monuments erected to commemorate people and events important to Queen Victoria.

LOCATION *On the A93, 8 miles E of Braemar.*

BARRINGTON COURT *Somerset*

These delightful gardens reflect the style of Gertrude Jekyll, writer and garden designer, who submitted designs for them in the 1920s. Flowers in bright profusion soften an essentially formal structure. Barrington Court was built in 1514 without gardens, and the open lawns around the house leave uncluttered views of its magnificent Tudor façade. The 16th and 17th-century outbuildings provide the setting for experiments in floral magic. Honeysuckles, roses and jasmine clamber over the brick pillars and arches of ancient cattle stalls. In the raised beds of the lily garden, crinums, crown imperials and azaleas crowd around a pool of water lilies. The soft blues and purples of the iris garden are sustained through the year by the lavenders, clematises and Michaelmas daisies.

LOCATION *Off the B3168, 3 miles NE of Ilminster.*

BATH – ROYAL VICTORIA PARK
Avon

Bath has survived as the best preserved Georgian city in England. And some of the country's loveliest public parks and gardens contribute to its air of distinction. The Royal Victoria Park, not far from the city centre, was one of the first of its kind to be established and remains queen of the city's green spaces. The park, which covers 57 acres, was opened in 1830 and named to

GEORGIAN FORMALITY *Order prevails in Bath's Royal Victoria Park – from clipped lawns and precise beds to the Royal Crescent beyond.*

honour a visit by Princess Victoria. Urns of golden Bath stone and marble are disposed around the main area of the park, and tree-lined walks provide glimpses of the famous Royal Crescent. But the park's chief attraction is the 7 acre Botanical Garden established in 1887 to receive over 2,000 specimens from the garden of a local botanist, C. E. Broome. Much developed over subsequent years, it is arranged more for visual delight than for scientific study. One winding path, for example, threads its way through a splendid rock garden overhung by a fine hemlock spruce. There is a small pinetum and a traditional herbaceous border, but perhaps the most beautiful feature is a spring-fed ornamental pond. Willows and maples embower banks underplanted with primulas and irises. The spot is especially dreamy in spring, when blue drifts of forget-me-nots appear.

LOCATION *Royal Crescent, Bath.*

BATSFORD PARK ARBORETUM
Gloucestershire

In the totally English and rustic setting of the Cotswolds, with the Vale of Evesham spreading out below, Batsford Park unfolds like a sequence from some oriental dream. Over 1,000 species of trees and shrubs create a panorama of ever-changing shapes and hues. Many were brought here in the late 19th century by Lord Redesdale, former British Ambassador to Japan. His zeal as a collector embraced ornamental statuary as well – a pair of bronze deer step shyly from a dark copse, and a Buddha contemplates the peace of an English wood.

LOCATION *On the A44, 1½ miles NW of Moreton-in-Marsh.*

BEAULIEU PALACE HOUSE and ABBEY *Hampshire*

Once described as the 'beautiful place of the King', Beaulieu Abbey was founded in 1204 by Cistercian monks, on lands given by King John. These lands were reclaimed by Henry VIII during the Reformation, and sold to the ancestor of the present owner – Lord Montagu. In the ruined abbey cloisters, a medieval herb garden echoes the industry of those banished monks. Flowering shrubs border the wooded walks by the river and Monk's Mill Pond, and April brings yellow waves of daffodils to cover the lawns of Palace House. The admission fee covers a visit to the famous National Motor Museum within the grounds and to

PALACE *A creeper wandering across the face of Beaulieu Palace House softens the discipline of cropped lawns and gravel paths.*

the Palace House and Abbey, with its exhibition of monastic life.
LOCATION *Off the B3056, 7 miles SE of Lyndhurst.*

BENINGTON LORDSHIP GARDENS
Hertfordshire

Not content with the existing Norman keep in the grounds of his manor – or 'Lordship', as it is called in Hertfordshire – one of Benington's Victorian owners added a gatehouse and curtain wall to the 18th-century house. Against this romantic backdrop of real and simulated ruins, the gardens have been developed. In springtime, a pale flood of snowdrops fills the old moat, followed by scillas. In the keep itself, *Stachyurus praecox* unfurls soft yellow pennants in a garden devoted to winter-flowering shrubs. Past the Norman fish ponds, now stocked with golden orfe, the path leads to a rock garden, beyond which herbaceous borders stand bright against the brick wall of the kitchen garden.
LOCATION *Off the A602, 4 miles E of Stevenage.*

BETH CHATTO GARDENS *Essex*

A wilderness of blackthorn and bramble, rejected as barren by generations of farmers, has been transformed into a gardener's paradise. Since 1961, Beth Chatto – horticulturalist and writer – has worked miracles with a site that is waterlogged at one extreme, and arid at the other. The sandy soil of the 'Mediterranean Garden', with raised beds, steps and terraces, is host to multitudes of drought-loving plants. In dramatic imitation of its Sicilian namesake, the Mount Etna broom produces golden showers of blossom, their fragrance mingling with the warm southern scents of thyme and santolina. Yet within a stone's throw of this flowering desert are the cool, dark pools of the water garden, created by damming a spring-fed ditch. Here, many shades of green are broken early by bright flashes of marsh marigolds, followed by the rich colours of knotweeds and day lilies. Every step taken, every seasonal change, brings new variety to enthral both amateur and professional gardener.
LOCATION *Off the A133, 4 miles E of Colchester.*

BRESSINGHAM HALL GARDENS
Norfolk

Every species of hardy herbaceous perennial – from the tall-plumed acanthus to the ground-hugging periwinkle – seems to be represented at Bressingham Hall Gardens. Alan Bloom, a specialist producer, began his collection in the 1950s, reintroducing forgotten varieties and raising others of his own. At the lowest level of the gardens – created out of a sloping meadow – water lilies bask on the surface of a small pool. On the slopes above, wide grassy paths wend their way round oases of colour – the island beds of perennials for which Bressingham is famous.
LOCATION *On the A1066, 2½ miles W of Diss.*

BROCKHOLE *Cumbria*

The Lake District National Park Visitor Centre at Brockhole offers – through exhibitions and lectures – an introduction to the beauties of the Lake District National Park. The gardens seem to illustrate that introduction with a particular beauty of their own. The centre was once a private house, built at the end of the 19th century. Near the house itself are neat lawns and clipped box hedges, smooth 'boulders' of yew and patterned carpet bedding. The ground falls away in terraces, lined with roses and hydrangeas. Gradually the gardens lose their formality, merging into woodland beside the shores of Lake Windermere. An exotic note enters with a variety of unusual trees and shrubs – a tall Chile pine and the Chilean fire bush, New Zealand flax and the Californian snowdrop tree. Magnolias, eucryphias, clematises and buddleias add flower and fragrance in their season – and over it all are views of the distant crags of Langdale Pikes.
LOCATION *On the A591, 2 miles NW of Windermere.*

BRYMPTON d'EVERCY *Somerset*

An air of serenity envelops this 17th-century manor, and everywhere the gardens reaffirm the elegance of its architecture. The spacious windows of the south front overlook wide lawns, stretching down from the balustraded terrace to the edge of a placid pond. Trim shrubs and herbaceous plants shelter in the crook of lichen-covered walls, and ramblers embrace the old stones. Behind the house, ranks of orderly vines grow up a slope, their fruits yielding a pleasant wine which is sold on the estate – together with cider and produce from the kitchen garden. Hundreds of oak trees, now stately in their age, were planted in the 19th century by the owner, Lady Georgiana Fane.
LOCATION *On the A3088, 2 miles W of Yeovil.*

BRYN BRAS CASTLE *Gwynedd*

In the foothills of the Snowdonia mountains, the towers and parapets of Bryn Bras Castle look down on an idyll of flowers, shrubs and streams. The castle was built in 1830, and the gardens developed through the 19th century, in accord with Victorian romantic ideals. Azaleas and rhododendrons gather in colourful groups around the close-mown lawns. Diverted mountain streams form cascades and pools, where the snowy water-crowfoot and saxifrage lie in drifts by the water's edge. Larch and hazel, rowan and lime adorn the wooded slopes, leading on to the mountain walk through hardy gorse and bracken. As the climb progresses, glorious views of Snowdonia and the Isle of Angelsey unfold.
LOCATION *Off the A4086, 4 miles E of Caernarfon.*

BURTON CONSTABLE *Humberside*

Burton Constable combines the free vision of parkland, landscaped by Capability Brown, with the intimate husbandry of a courtyard garden. The fine Elizabethan house, with its intricate brick and stonework, needs no embellishment, and the flat lawns before it are austere and plain. A wide, gravelled path bordered by

shapely yews directs the eye to a distant statue of a stag, then on to other vistas contrived by Brown. Twenty-five acres of lakes are hidden within the undulating contours of the 200 acre park. By the side of the house, in the large courtyard garden, rudbeckias rise in golden starbursts over clusters of rosy phloxes, and globe thistles gleam purple against the brick walls.
LOCATION *On the A165, 7 miles NE of Hull.*

BUSCOT PARK *Oxfordshire*

Garden design at Buscot Park is on the grand scale, with majestic intersecting avenues of oaks and limes. To east and west of the 18th-century house the grounds stretch away to distant lakes. In 1905 the architect Harold Peto devised a water garden, linking the house with the eastern lake, some 250 ft away. He created a formal

LIQUID LINK *An 80 yd long chain of Italian-style water gardens links Buscot House with the 20 acre lake in the park.*

vista in the Italian Renaissance style, feeding a stream through symmetrical pools and canals of stone. Statues and fountains, bridges and cascades alleviate the severity of its geometrical lines. Water lilies break the surface, disturbing the reflected trees.
LOCATION *On the A417, 3½ miles NW of Faringdon.*

CAMBRIDGE UNIVERSITY BOTANIC GARDEN *Cambridgeshire*

Botanic gardens conjure up images of rare and exotic species, sinister succulents and carnivorous plants, and Cambridge Univer-

sity Botanic Garden has a considerable share of these. But there are also interesting collections of plants on various themes. A chronological bed charts the introduction of familiar species, from the ancient almond and woad to *Cytisus battandieri*, the pineapple-scented broom, introduced from North Africa early this century. The Ecological Area nurtures rare and protected species, like the snake's head fritillary, or the lovely spiked speedwell. Scented and winter gardens offer new inspiration to the amateur gardener. The rock garden is a botanical atlas of alpines – divided according to geographical distribution. A lake and water garden add the interest of aquatic species.
LOCATION *Trumpington Road, Cambridge.*

CAPEL MANOR INSTITUTE OF HORTICULTURE AND FIELD STUDIES *Hertfordshire*

The romantic trappings of a 17th-century garden – colourful knot-patterns of spring flowers, a sundial and domed arbour – belie the educational purpose of Capel Manor. Yet all the gardens here serve to illustrate various gardening practices – in this case those of the Elizabethans. Capel House, a Georgian mansion, and its 30 acre estate, provide the setting for courses run by the Institute, and the gardens around the house are glorious examples of the horticulturalist's art. The walled garden contains superb greenhouse collections, together with small units designed to advise and inspire the amateur gardener. Here, too, the development of the shrub rose is illustrated, with varieties ranging from albas, heavy with furled petals, to the sprightly blooms of the modern shrub. There are rock and water gardens, vineries and nutteries, and one of the oldest copper beeches in England, planted in 1760.
LOCATION *Just off junction 25 of the M25, 2 miles N of Enfield.*

CASTLE ASHBY *Northamptonshire*

'Thames, Thames, thou wilt never forgive me!' cried Capability Brown as he surveyed the waterways he had created at Castle Ashby, home of the Marquis of Northampton. His landscape survives in the lakes and bridges, walks and follies set out in the 1760s. Many of the trees still standing were planted then – the mature beeches, chestnuts and the great cedars of Lebanon. The Elizabethan mansion, built of pale golden limestone, is girdled by wide lawns. The

elegant orangery and formal Italian garden were designed in the 1860s by the architect Digby Wyatt, as were the terraces by the east front.
LOCATION *Off the A428, 8 miles E of Northampton.*

CASTLE DROGO *Devon*

The great massif of Castle Drogo rises 900 ft above the River Teign, its castellated granite towers standing sentry at the edge of Dartmoor. The castle and its gardens evolved between 1910 and 1930, born of a dream shared by the Drewe family and the famous architect Sir Edwin Lutyens. Above a valley of rhododendrons the path leads to the main gardens, a series of terraced beds and lawns linked by granite steps. At the highest level, a circular bastion of clipped yew encloses an arena of smooth lawn. Below is the rose parterre, its formal lines drawn out in yew. Here, serpentine paths of Mogul design wind through herbaceous borders.
LOCATION *Off the A30, 1 mile S of Chagford.*

CASTLE KENNEDY GARDENS *Dumfries and Galloway*

On a ribbon of land between two lochs the medieval fortress of Castle Kennedy stands in ruins, destroyed by fire in 1716. Later in the 18th century, Field Marshal Dalrymple – 2nd Earl of Stair and British Ambassador to France – created a garden beyond its walls, with avenues radiating outwards from a pond shrouded in water lilies. His inspiration was Versailles, his work-force the hapless troops under his command. Rows of dark ilex and twisting monkey-puzzle provide a backdrop for scarlet-flowered embothrium shrubs or variously coloured azaleas. Past the great landscaped mound called the Giant's Grave, stand huge specimens of *Rhododendron arboreum* brought from the Himalayas over 100 years ago.
LOCATION *On the A75, 3 miles E of Stranraer.*

CAWDOR CASTLE *Highland*

Legend and Shakespeare name Cawdor as the castle where Macbeth murdered Duncan, King of Scotland, in 1040 – mistakenly, for building only began in 1370. The Thanes of Cawdor have lived there for 600 years, and what peace they salvaged from their bloody history is reflected in these tranquil gardens. The 16th-century stone walls of the kitchen garden once formed part of the castle's outer defences – now they protect only fruit trees and herbs. In the 18th-century flower garden, delicate shades and scents of roses mingle with lavender, beside slender pillars of yew. The 'wild garden', an artful tangle of azaleas and rhododendrons, willows and bamboos, slopes down to Cawdor burn.

LOCATION *On the B9090, 5 miles S of Nairn.*

CHARLECOTE PARK *Warwickshire*

There is a sense of historical continuity at Charlecote Park, where medieval oak palings fence in the deer and sheep – as they did in 1583 when Shakespeare was caught poaching in the park. The association is remembered in one of the borders of the north garden, filled now with plants mentioned in his plays. Heartsease and columbine mingle there with deadly hemlock and aconite. The beautiful 16th-century gatehouse of pink brick remains unchanged since Shakespeare's day, and the adjoining forecourt garden is laid out as an Elizabethan parterre. A splendid avenue of limes escaped Capability Brown's landscaping axe in the 18th century.

LOCATION *On the B4086, 6 miles S of Warwick.*

CHESTER ZOO *Cheshire*

The magnificent array of flowers and shrubs at Chester Zoo rivals even the animals in popularity. Some 80,000 plants, propagated in the zoo's own glasshouses, fill the beds each year. Pansies and polyanthuses, tulips and daffodils, spread colour through the grounds in spring. Summer bedding proves more dazzling still, with begonias and fuchsias glowing in abundance. New plantings of roses each year add colour to an already lavish display. The jewel in the botanical crown is the tropical house, with its indoor garden.

LOCATION *On the A41, 2 miles N of the city centre.*

CHIRK CASTLE *Clwyd*

The exterior of Chirk Castle remains as it was when completed in 1310 – a rare survival of Edward I's Welsh border fortifications. It stands in beautiful parkland, with terraced lawns at the foot of great cylindrical towers. Imposing topiary, like rows of conical guardsmen, seem but another line in the castle's defences. A tapestry of ramblers adorns the walls,

roses, jasmine and climbing hydrangeas shot through with golden honeysuckles. Rhododendrons, magnolias, azaleas and hydrangeas in variety are the pride of the shrub garden, and hidden among the trees is the rare *Fraxinus spaethiana*. *Embothrium coccineum* and *Crinodendron hookerianum* glow like beacons against a dark ring of Douglas firs.

LOCATION *On the A5, half a mile from Chirk.*

CHOLMONDELEY CASTLE GARDENS *Cheshire*

Cholmondeley Castle stands on a wooded hill, overlooking the beauty of its gardens. Some of the great cedars and oaks on the slopes below are as old as the castle itself, which was built in the 19th century by the 1st Marquis of Cholmondeley. The variety and beauty of flowers and shrubs in the many gardens and walks is breathtaking. In spring, blue *Anemone apennina* undercarpet the pendulous blossoms of *Prunus longipes* down the Cherry Walk, to be replaced in autumn with fuchsia 'Mrs Popple'. Honeysuckle and lavender join fragrant forces with roses by the tennis courts, where even the boundary nets succumb to the climbing varieties.

LOCATION *Off the A49, 7 miles W of Nantwich.*

CLAPTON COURT GARDENS *Somerset*

In the heart of Somerset's cider-making country stands the largest ash tree in Great Britain – over 200 years old, with a huge girth measuring 23 ft. Round about it the lovely 10 acre gardens of Clapton Court flourish with equal luxuriance. Each

season adds its own variety to terrace and woodland, rockery and water garden. Legions of daffodils parade in spring under the flowering cherries and plums, their advance interrupted by glorious displays of magnolias or camellias. Rhododendrons and azaleas gather in glowing hoards by the woodland streams. Sweet-scented geraniums, roses and fuchsias follow in summer. The performance reaches its climax as the maples turn to autumnal red, and the sorbus trees adorn themselves with clusters of orange berries.

LOCATION *Off the B3165, 3 miles S of Crewkerne.*

CLUMBER PARK *Nottinghamshire*

Only the outline remains of the mansion around which the park developed – it was demolished in 1938. But the ambitious schemes for the park itself survive. Grebes and coots, ducks and herons flock to the vast lake – created by damming the River Poulter. The landscape bears the imprint of Capability Brown, seen in the 'rounds' of mature trees, but the most spectacular planting was the work of the designer William Sawrey Gilpin in the 19th century. From east to west across the park, an avenue of limes – the longest in Europe – stretches for almost 3 miles. The avenue is 20 yds wide with 10 yds between each tree – a total of 1,296 trees. In autumn the trees seem to leave a trail of fire across the landscape. Temples and pleasure gardens by the riverside evoke memories of the splendour of Clumber's past as the garden of one of England's great houses.

LOCATION *Off the A1, 4½ miles SE of Worksop.*

DEPARTED GRANDEUR *Nothing now remains of the Duke of Newcastle's mansion at Clumber. But the park survives, with its 3 mile long avenue of limes.*

COTSWOLD WILDLIFE PARK
Oxfordshire

At ease in an alien setting, white rhinos graze on the lawns of a 19th-century manor, and peacocks wander happily through the park. Exotic wildlife and English landscape meet in a strange but peaceful partnership at Cotswold Wildlife Park. On the site of the old greenhouse, where peaches and carnations grew, there is now a tropical house. American alligators bask in a pool under glorious displays of plumbagos and thunbergias. Hummingbirds dart between gold and scarlet hibiscus flowers. A few old apple trees in the walled kitchen garden are remnants of another age. Fruit and vegetables made way for aviaries and flower beds brimming with spring and summer colour. On the lawns around the house massive trees stand grouped, or in splendid isolation – like one great oak reputed to be 600 years old.
LOCATION *On the A361, 2 miles S of Burford.*

COUNTY DEMONSTRATION GARDEN *Cornwall*

A complete library of gardening books has been brought to life on an open site near Probus, lashed by the salt-laden winds. Cornwall County Council has established over 50 demonstration plots to explore the many potentials of small gardens in varying soil and site conditions. Roses bloom by the score, illustrating the results of different pruning and feeding methods. A section on garden design shows the labour-saving qualities of different forms of paving and other landscape materials, then there are well-stocked borders for the dedicated plantsman. Bamboos, cordyline palms and the sword-leaved New Zealand flax combine to create a 'tropical' garden. A glimpse of the many special plant collections will drive every aspiring gardener to fill his own plot at home with narcissi, lilies and garden pinks, fuchsias, miniature conifers, or some of the vast collection of shrubs which show a wide range of colour, shape and texture.
LOCATION *On the A390, 8 miles SW of St Austell.*

THE COURTS *Wiltshire*

Hidden behind screens of holly and yew, the gardens of The Courts are slow to share their secrets. Beyond each lawn or path or pond lies another, concealed from the first by shrubs or banks of flowers.

There was a woollen mill on the site, and weavers once aired their grievances at The Courts, built in the 1700s. Beyond a shady fernery are eight stone pillars – smothered now in roses – from which the cloth was hung to dry after washing. Near by is a pond of water lilies, where *Nymphaea odorata* 'Escarboucle' glows like a cluster of crimson stars against the dark leaves. White and scarlet plumbagos fill the conservatory, which opens on to neat lawns and borders. The arboretum is also a wildflower reserve, where Lent lilies, wild tulips and snake's head fritillaries shine through the long grass.
LOCATION *On the B3107, 2 miles W of Bradford-on-Avon.*

CRARAE *Strathclyde*

A special talent has been at work at Crarae, and the result is one of the loveliest woodland gardens in Britain. A sheltered gorge, with a stream flowing through it, provides the setting – and the gentle climate of Scotland's west coast is kind to the many exotic shrubs and trees. The gardens, begun early this century by the Campbells of Succoth, extend over 40 acres, with Loch Fyne seen in magical perspective, spreading away to the east. The ever-present green of conifers, many of them rare, is warmed by the fire of embrothriums flowering in summer. Snowy eucryphias melt into autumnal displays of sorbus, prunus and acers. A bewildering diversity of eucalyptus species have been established. A number of the unusual plants now so at home here were grown from seeds sent by the intrepid plant collector Reginald Farrer, at the beginning of the century. One of the greatest spectacles at Crarae is the flowering of massed rhododendrons, spreading through the woodland with such exotic, yet natural, effect.
LOCATION *On the A83, 10 miles SW of Inveraray.*

CULCREUCH CASTLE *Central*

Within 20 miles of Glasgow's industrial clamour, in the Fintry Hills, Culcreuch Castle gleams pale against a background of dark trees. In the park to the south, a tranquil loch throws back reflections of the great 15th-century fortress – once the Clan Castle of the Galbraith chiefs, and now home to the Barons of Culcreuch. Daffodils, azaleas and rhododendrons ring the spring colour changes through the

grounds. Ornamental heathers cast a pink and purple haze over the large walled garden, where roses shelter from the extremes of Scotland's weather. A lively burn makes its busy way through the pinetum behind the castle, past rare conifers brought from all over the world.
LOCATION *On the B818, 17 miles SW of Stirling.*

CULZEAN *Strathclyde*

Culzean hangs above the sea, and seems to grow naturally out of the sheer cliff. The castle was designed by Robert Adam in the late 18th century, for David, 10th Earl of Cassillis – and its sumptuous garden reflects the grandeur of the Adam style. Crenellated parapets and pavilions grace the terraces of the Fountain Court – a formal garden with an orangery, and a fountain formed like a giant shell. A few

ADAM MASTERPIECE *Culzean Castle, designed by Robert Adam, rises above terraced gardens where tender plants flourish, protected by high stone walls.*

camellias linger in the Gothic camellia house, but bloom more abundantly still in the open, keeping company with rhododendrons and magnolias. The walled garden has fine herbaceous borders and fruitful crab-apple trees. The 565 acre estate, which became Scotland's first Country Park in 1967, takes in 3 miles of coastline with exhilarating views of the Firth of Clyde.
LOCATION *On the A719, 12 miles S of Ayr.*

DARTINGTON HALL *Devon*

The stone figure of a reclining woman, sculpted by Henry Moore, remains where he placed it in 1947 – against a backdrop of chestnut trees four centuries old. 'I wanted the figure to have a quiet stillness and a sense of permanence...' he said, and so reflected the mood of the gardens them-

RESTING PLACE *Ancient chestnuts look down on shaven yew and box which shelter Henry Moore's 'Reclining woman' at Dartington Hall.*

selves. The emphasis here is on form, and the strong compositions made by trees and lawns, paths and terraces achieve that stillness which Moore described. A sense of permanence comes with the ancient trees and traces of a medieval past. Dartington Hall was built in the 14th century by John Holand, Duke of Exeter. The tiltyard where he jousted is still to be seen – framed by grass terraces and a herbaceous border of silver and blue, lightened by soft yellow verbascums and day lilies. Walks of camellias and rhododendrons spring into seasonal colour. The formal gardens merge into parkland and a wooded area known as 'Eldorado'.
LOCATION *On the A384, 1 mile NE of Totnes.*

DAWYCK BOTANIC GARDEN
Borders

Generations of owners have poured their love and knowledge of trees into the beautiful woodlands at Dawyck. The Royal Botanic Garden at Edinburgh, which has administered the arboretum since 1978, inherited from previous owners a superb legacy of mature trees. Some of the great larches near the house were reputedly planted in 1725, and a silver fir as early as 1680. The Dawyck beech (*Fagus sylvatica* 'Fastigiata') – which grows like a tall column – originated here. Dark conifers rise to heights of 100 ft or more. Rhododendrons, azaleas and a variety of flowering shrubs transform a professional arboretum into a woodland garden. Stone balustrading lines some of the numerous walks and a noisy stream.
LOCATION *On the B712, 8 miles SW of Peebles.*

DELAPRÉ ABBEY *Northamptonshire*

In Norman French, *delapré* meant 'place of the meadow', and this park, so near to the city centre, is part meadowland still. In the mid-12th century a Cluniac nunnery was founded here. Little remains now of the abbey, dissolved in 1538 by Henry VIII, beyond the rectangular form of the much-altered building, and the occasional visit of a ghostly nun. The house is now the Northamptonshire Records Office, and is approached through rolling parkland. Views from the terraced lawn before the house range over open grassland, now taken over as a golf course. Fresh-scented herbs fill the walled garden, enclosed in 18th-century stonework. Herbaceous borders and wall shrubs add wide bands of colour, broken by two sculptures in brick. Paths lead away from the house to an area of woodland, and a peaceful water garden.
LOCATION *On the A508 (London road), 1 mile S of Northampton city centre.*

DOCWRA'S MANOR *Cambridgeshire*

Erratic in shape yet level throughout, Docwra's Manor presents a formidable challenge to the garden designer. Here is a 17th-century house, surrounded by a flock of dependent farm buildings, courtyards and walls. The challenge was met by using part of the farmyard for new houses, and transforming the rest into a series of enclosed gardens. Each developed a character of its own, ranging from open lawns to areas so dense with plants that the dividing paths seem to vanish in the throng. The potential monotony of a flat site has been alleviated by planting in raised beds, stone troughs and sinks. Tree paeonies, cistus and yellow-plumed verbascums add height to the low-lying ranges of herbaceous plants. There is at Docwra an air of the exotic and unfamiliar, as wild flowers from the hills and plains of southern Europe appear among the native species. Different members of the same plant families have been shepherded together in all their variety, and species roses thrust their scented heads through the wild and artistic assembly.
LOCATION *Off the A10, 8 miles SW of Cambridge.*

DODDINGTON HALL *Lincolnshire*

The imposing east front of Doddington Hall – the main approach to the house – gives no clue to the romance of the gardens behind. The Elizabethan house of pink brick and ivory stone is flanked by two gardens, both enclosed by their original 17th-century walls. The east garden is severe in its simplicity – formal lawns and contained shrubs. The west garden is in exuberant contrast – a bright green puzzle of box-framed parterres, filled with low-growing bedding roses. From the wide borders of herbaceous plants, lace-edged with dianthus, comes the heavy scent of old-fashioned shrub roses. An avenue of Irish yews leads out to the garden, carrying the eye through to another avenue of Lombardy poplars. Four acres of wild garden submit annually to the invasion of spring flowers, rhododendrons and climbing roses. Rare herbs are grown in a garden near the house.
LOCATION *On the B1190, 5 miles W of Lincoln.*

DOROTHY CLIVE GARDEN
Staffordshire

In 1939, Colonel Harry Clive – retired army officer and justice of the peace – determined to build his wife a garden. As an invalid, Dorothy Clive had to confine her walks to circuits of the lawn – a route so monotonous that even her dog refused to follow. In the disused and overgrown gravel pit behind the house, Colonel Clive hacked out the paths which make the framework of the present woodland garden. Under the canopy of oak and beech already there, he planted rhododendrons – a wonderland of purple, lavender and deepest plum. Japanese cherries, magnolias and hundreds of Exbury azaleas, red, amber and gold, were set among the older trees. Dorothy Clive died in 1942, but the gardens were extended – first by her husband, then by the Trust he established to protect it. A landscape garden, with wide views of the Shropshire hills, has a rich array of ornamental trees. The informal beds harbour shrub roses, heathers and coloured thymes. The latest development is a garden of sloping rock and scree, with a pool where irises thrive among primulas and ruby wandflowers.
LOCATION *On the A51, 9 miles SE of Nantwich.*

DRUMLANRIG CASTLE
Dumfries and Galloway

The magnificent pink sandstone Drumlanrig Castle, home of the Duke of Buccleuch and Queensberry, stands on raised ground overlooking the Nithsdale hills. Balus-traded terraces of the same warm stone frame the formal parterres, now being restored to their early 18th-century intricacy. The restraint of these gardens near the castle gives way to informal but landscaped woodland, where Victorian ladies savoured nature's beauty from the comfort of two delightful summerhouses. The park contains some remarkable trees, including a giant sycamore. The first Douglas fir to be planted in Britain still survives here. It was sent as a seed in 1827 to the Estate Manager of Works, by his brother, the plant collector David Douglas.

LOCATION *On the A76, 3 miles N of Thornhill.*

DYRHAM PARK *Avon*

Passing first through a deer park, the drive leads to a view of Dyrham Park unchanged almost since it was landscaped at the end of the 18th century. The parterres, avenues and canals, then a century old, were swept away on the park side, but the shapes remain in the garden beyond the house. There, the outlines of the former patterns are still seen in dry weather, scorched on the grass. The 17th-century house of pale Bath stone was offset by plantations of dark cedar, and groups of oak, beech and chestnut spill down the near slopes. The view behind rolls away towards the Bristol Channel and the mountains of Wales. At right-angles to the west front is the medieval parish church, below which shrubs and rampant climbers clothe a high terrace wall. The limes and ilex trees were part of the 18th-century landscape scheme, but

the pond is all that remains of a spectacular 17th-century cascade.

LOCATION *On the A46, 8 miles N of Bath.*

EMMETTS GARDEN *Kent*

On the cool, exposed summit of Ide Hill is a 4 acre garden of fascinating trees, including a giant Wellingtonia that can be seen from Crowborough Hill, over 12 miles away. The arboretum was planted between 1893 and 1928, and its appeal lies less in its casual design than in the beauty of the trees themselves. Grassy paths wind through the glades of exotic shrubs and trees, which are sheltered from the wind by more hardy native species. There are many unusual specimens – like the fragrant *Zenobia pulverulenta*, from the southern United States, with delicate white bell-flowers. More familiar magnolias, rhododendrons, camellias, tulip trees and handkerchief trees scatter their blossom through the dark foliage, and bluebells flood the woodland floor in spring.

LOCATION *On the B2042, 3 miles SW of Sevenoaks.*

ERDDIG *Clwyd*

The owners of Erddig have been loyal to traditions of formal gardening for two and a half centuries. The fervour of late 18th-century landscapists was curtailed, expressing itself only in the undulating meadows and woods beyond the west front. Restored to their form of 1740, the gardens transform fruit growing into a decorative art. A long central path leads to a canal, and on either side are neat ranks of apple trees,

trained into pyramids. The boundary walls are lined with the horizontal branches of espalier apples and pears, and fan-trained peaches and apricots. Old varieties of narcissi grow in the borders below, between clematises and climbing hydrangeas. In the bee garden, scalloped hedges of English yew once formed sheltered niches for the hives. Examples of Victorian formality survive – like the parterre with its fountains and bedding plants in shades of silver, yellow and blue.

LOCATION *Off the A483, 1 mile S of Wrexham.*

FARNBOROUGH HALL *Warwickshire*

The Holbech family, who have lived at Farnborough since 1684, expressed a great spirit of adventure in their garden design. Although there are fine trees and a rose garden near the house, the dominant theme of the gardens is exploration. Long, curving tentacles of water – the Sourland and Rookery pools – draw the eye away from the house into the distances beyond. The most spectacular feature of this 18th-century landscape is the Grass Terrace. It follows the snaking contours of a hilly ridge, rising ever higher throughout the 800 yds of its length. Flanking one side of the path are great laurel-framed scallops, like balconies carved out of the hillside. Each is marked with a tree, a Scots pine or a graceful lime. Two small temples lure the inquisitive onwards. A tall obelisk heralds the end of the walk, with breathtaking views over the Warwickshire plains towards Edgehill – scene in 1642 of the first battle of the Civil War.

LOCATION *Off the A423, 6 miles N of Banbury.*

FINLAYSTONE GARDENS *Strathclyde*

The fiery preacher John Knox, founding member of the Church of Scotland, is said to have celebrated a 'reformed communion' here in 1556 – under a yew tree near the house. Rather than fell a tree with such treasured associations, the owners moved it 40 ft to its present site during alteration work to the house in 1900. Wide lawns slope at a gentle tangent down to the River Clyde. In spring, daffodils lie thick under oak and ash, while azaleas and rhododendrons blaze a trail of colour through the nearby woodland. Formal beds of geometric design, edged with yew, contrast with the softer outlines of shrubs and magnificent trees. The Finlaystone Burn makes

VANISHED KINGDOM *Neptune surveys a grassy slope at Dyrham where once he ruled a water garden.*

its way over steep waterfalls to the Clyde, attended by a secluded garden of water-loving plants.

LOCATION *Off the A8, 6 miles E of Greenock.*

FOLKESTONE MUNICIPAL GARDENS *Kent*

'Flowers instead of Potatoes', rejoiced the *Folkestone Express* in its headlines of June 30, 1928 – reporting the opening of the Kingsnorth Gardens. The site, owned by William, 7th Earl of Radnor, had been used for allotments before it was presented to the town in 1926. The council transformed the 3½ acre plot into a garden with distinct variations in mood and style. There are

TOWN GARDEN *Formal or informal, Folkestone's Kingsnorth Gardens are always colourful.*

trim blocks of lawn and cube-shaped topiary, with ornamental pools in the formal Italian style. Vivid herbaceous borders of scarlet and yellow relieve the cool islands of green. Thousands of roses break the bounds of their tidy beds, at odds with the stately decorum of the surrounding trees.

LOCATION *Castle Hill Avenue, Shorncliffe Road, Folkestone.*

FRITTON LAKE *Norfolk*

By the curving side of Fritton Lake, a mosaic of brilliant colour lies wedged between dark woods and the silver water. The 'Old English Gardens' add a touch of 18th-century charm to the modern attractions of this vast country park. Low box hedges line the formal beds, filled with the most startling array of colours. Tulips, roses and dahlias enhance the scene with warmest reds and yellows. At the heart of the gardens stands a boy in bronze, the

work of Kathleen Scott, widow of the famous Antarctic explorer. Paths lined with herbaceous borders lead down to a lake – formed out of the scars left by peat cutting in the 12th century. Wildfowl and watersports on the lake, and woodland walks all vie for attention, but the quiet elegance of the Old English Gardens holds its own.

LOCATION *Off the A143, 5 miles SW of Great Yarmouth.*

GLASGOW BOTANIC GARDENS *Strathclyde*

Great halls and domes of glass rise up in Arabian splendour by the banks of Glasgow's Kelvin river. The Kibble Palace, opened in 1873 and covering 23,000 sq. ft, is one of the largest glasshouses in Britain. A tour of the palace is a tour of the world, with plants representing every continent. From the Andes come the rosy bellflowers of lapageria, from Australia a unique collection of tree ferns – and the kangaroo paw. In spring, camellias from Japan gleam against the main dome, their colours bright as silk embroidery. The main range of glasshouses near by contain an even greater selection, from the familiar coffee and cocoa plants to the exotic Victoria water lily – with leaves 5 ft across and flowers that bloom for a day. The grounds offer a choice of gardens both attractive and informative, with peaceful walks by the tree-lined river.

LOCATION *Great Western Road, Glasgow.*

GLENDURGAN *Cornwall*

As the Helford river winds its way to the

sea, it touches the foot of a hidden valley – a fantasy of exotic flowers and trees. A family of Falmouth shipping agents introduced plants from all over the world, establishing gardens through west Cornwall. Glendurgan, planted in the 1820s and 1830s, was one of these. The walled garden dates from this period and now shelters tender shrubs – among them mimosa and clouds of blue ceanothus. Through the valley gardens extraordinary sights unfold – the knotty trunks of giant tulip trees, vast fan-shaped gunnera leaves, or the recumbent Chusan palm shedding its skin of bark like some mammoth serpent. A great maze of laurel, discovered on the hillside, adds another element of mystery. Rhododendrons and camellias, magnolias and hydrangeas bloom flamboyantly on the slopes, and in the grassy glades wild primroses, columbines and Lent lilies make their modest presence felt.

LOCATION *Off the B3291, 4 miles SW of Falmouth.*

GREAT COMP *Kent*

The struggling amateur gardener will take heart from a visit to Great Comp. The owners had no professional expertise when they bought the property in 1957, yet have achieved on this 7 acre site some of the style and splendour associated with larger and more famous gardens. Established trees, hedges and paths were left largely untouched as the gardens evolved around them. To north and south of the 17th-century house, wide lawns cut swathes of brilliant green through an ocean of shrubs and trees. Small paths plunge through the thickets, past setpieces of particular beauty – a temple or a tower, a ruin or an urn – flanked by climbers and herbaceous plants, flowering shrubs and majestic conifers. One of the loveliest aspects of these gardens is the rolling sea of heather to the south of the house – a tide of purple and bronze, breaking in soft waves against the edge of the lawn.

LOCATION *Off the B2016, 8 miles W of Maidstone.*

GREENBANK GARDENS *Strathclyde*

Greenbank House was built in 1763 by a Glasgow merchant. A walled garden of 2½ acres was added, to provide the quantities of fruit and vegetables required for a large household. Now this garden is run as a demonstration centre, stocked with plants readily available on the market, and advice is given on how to raise them. An inspiring selection of annuals and perennials line the paths which divide the garden – proving that herbaceous borders should never be dull. Individual sections cater for specialist interests. A 'spring garden' offers a range of bulbs, mixing well with heathers and conifers. Another illustrates the attractive informality of island beds, with long-flowering annuals like echiums, pink mallows and the fragrant claries. There are fruit and vegetable plots – a link with the past – and an area devoted to gardening for the disabled. The garden is surrounded by pleasant woodland.

LOCATION *Flenders Road, Glasgow.*

GREY'S COURT *Oxfordshire*

Alleys of blossom and scent,
The old walls breathing it back
Render an ancient content.

So wrote the contemporary poet Robert Gittings in *This Tower My Prison*, remembering that alliance of old buildings and fragrant flowers which characterises Grey's Court Gardens. The medieval fortifications of the de Grey barons lie in ruins about a 16th-century manor of brick and flint. The ancient walls provide shelter for various small gardens – one devoted to roses, another smothered in cascades of deep blue wisteria. At the foot of the main tower, a pool of water lilies makes a gleaming centrepiece for the white garden, framed by magnolias, Californian poppies and the blue-white blossoms of ceanothus. The elaborate 'Archbishop's Maze' – its structure dictated by Christian symbolism – was inspired by Archbishop Robert Runcie's enthronement address at Canterbury in 1980.

LOCATION *Off the B481, 3 miles NW of Henley.*

HALL PLACE *Kent*

Travellers on the busy Dover road near Bexley may be tempted from their route by a glimpse of the quiet lawns and colourful beds of Hall Place Gardens, the 16th and 17th-century house to which they belong is now a museum, and the gardens have been largely restored to the patterns of their Tudor past. The formal designs of the Elizabethan rose garden are blocked in with 3,000 bushes, to which new ones are added each year. An enclosed garden with bedding plants, framed by buttressed walls of yew, continues the Elizabethan theme. Impressive topiary evokes royal heraldic

traditions. The ten 'Queen's Beasts' – among them the lion and the unicorn – were cut in yew to mark the coronation of Elizabeth II in 1953. Other displays include herbs, rock and water plants and spring flowers.

LOCATION *At the A2/A223 junction, 1 mile E of Bexley.*

HAM HOUSE *Greater London*

When the diarist John Evelyn visited Ham House in 1678, he could hardly contain his enthusiasm for '… the Parterres, Flower Gardens, Orangeries, Groves, Avenues, Courts, Statues, Perspectives, Fountaines, Aviaries …' Most of these had vanished by 1976, when work was begun to restore this important 17th-century garden to its original splendour. Now all has returned, with the exception of fountains and aviaries. The whole gives an impression of embroidery worked on a background of green velvet. The knot garden is a lattice of box-edged beds, filled with silver-leaved cotton lavender, the angles marked by box pyramids. Even the 'Wilderness' of azarole thorn trees, field maples and hornbeam hedges, is an orderly interpretation of nature in the wild. At the foot of this intriguing garden flows the Thames – in John Evelyn's words, 'the Sweetest River in the World'.

LOCATION *On the A307, 1 mile S of Richmond.*

HARDWICK HALL *Derbyshire*

In 1591, Bess of Hardwick, Countess of Shrewsbury – aged 70 and four times widowed – poured the wealth accrued from her marriages into the building of Hardwick Hall. The magnificent Elizabethan house has scarcely altered, and nor have the walls of the garden courts around it. The forecourt garden, with its plain areas of lawn, is closest in character to the original 17th-century designs. Borders run beside the ornate boundary walls, where mossy saxifrages and candytufts spill round the stems of flowering shrubs. In the east garden the eye is drawn away from a deep pool and shrub rose borders to fields and a distant avenue of limes. The main garden of 7½ acres is divided into four by alleys of yew and hornbeam. Fruit trees – both old and new varieties – fill two sections and a third is laid to magnolia-shaded lawn. A nuttery and herb garden claim the fourth. The White Rose of York and other old rose varieties flower among the clematises and honeysuckle against the wall.

LOCATION *Off the A617 and M1, 6½ miles NW of Mansfield.*

HATFIELD HOUSE *Hertfordshire*

Hatfield is steeped in the memory of Tudor and Stuart monarchs, and its gardens reflect that glorious period of its history. The elegant Jacobean house was built by Robert Cecil, 1st Earl of Salisbury and Chief Minister to James I. Near by stands one remaining wing of the Tudor palace where Henry VIII once housed his children. James I – who planted the surviving mulberry in the garden – later exchanged Hatfield for property owned by Cecil. The gardens fell victim to the landscaping fever of the 18th century, but have since been gradually restored. The warm russet brickwork of the Old Palace frames a knot

VICTORIAN HARDWICK *The gardens at Hardwick Hall as they appeared in the 19th century.*

STUART SPLENDOUR *A typical old-English garden, crowded with roses and paeonies, larkspur and lupins, offsets the splendour of Hatfield House.*

garden of 15th, 16th and 17th-century plants. Steps lead down to the formal scented garden of aromatic herbs and flowers – here is every fragrance ever dreamed of in an English garden. Camellias, rhododendrons and wild flowers shelter among the trees of the Wilderness.
LOCATION *On the A1000, S of Hatfield centre.*

HELMINGHAM HALL *Suffolk*

In the years before 1660 and the restoration of Charles II to the throne – members of the Sealed Knot Society met in secret at Helmingham, plotting the return of their king. Perhaps they walked in the privacy of the moated garden beside the manor of Tudor brick. Today, this garden retains much of its Elizabethan character, with prominence given to fruit and vegetables. The formal lay-out is softened by exuberant herbaceous shapes and colours in the long, cruciform borders. Drawbridges, which are raised every night, cross the deep moat, which is well stocked with fish. Beyond is the park with its herds of red deer and Highland cattle.
LOCATION *On the B1077, 9 miles N of Ipswich.*

HERGEST CROFT *Herefordshire*

The soil at Hergest Croft is so hospitable that even oriental trees thrive as well there in the Herefordshire hills as they do in their native habitats. Three generations of one family have collected shrubs and trees from all over the temperate world to clothe the 50 acres of Hergest Croft. The botanical travels begin in the garden by the house, with views across the lawn to golden Japanese maples among the beeches and magnolias. The Azalea Garden sustains the eastern mood with specimens of Himalayan whitebeam, and Chinese and Turkish hazel. In the steep-sided valley of Park Wood, rhododendrons radiate colour under canopies of larch and oak. Climbing paths between conifers, rowans and maples provide unforgettable views of flowering trees and shrubs below.
LOCATION *Off the A44, W of Kington.*

HILLIER ARBORETUM *Hampshire*

The aspiration of the Hillier Arboretum is 'to grow the widest range of hardy woody plants that can be grown in the temperate regions'. The result is the largest collection of ornamental trees and shrubs in the world. Visitors come to study – or simply to browse through 100 acres of scented, flowered or leafy woodland. There is no barren season here – even winter brings the witch hazel boughs out in clusters of curly, lemon-peel flowers. Spring belongs to the magnolias, camellias and cherries – and the exquisite displays of azaleas and rhododendrons. July is the month for the sweet mock orange and star-flowered deutzias, while August is given to the heathers and snowy eucryphias. Autumn pieces together a bewildering patchwork of yellow leaves, scarlet berries and golden fruit.
LOCATION *Off the A31, 3 miles NE of Romsey.*

HOLEHIRD GARDENS *Cumbria*

Few gardens can rival the superb Lakeland setting of Holehird – where the distant blue and silver-green of the fells are as much a part of the gardens as the trees and lawns. Views of Lake Windermere, Coniston Old Man and Crinkle Crags – with the occasional glimpse of high Scafell – form the backdrop to a terraced garden. In the foreground is a fountain with water lilies at its base, fringed with edelweiss, Siberian wallflowers and purple asters. Flowering shrubs and evergreens fill the borders, and self-sown ferns take root in limestone crevices. Past the Mansion House – now a nursing home – is the old orchard where the Lakeland Horticultural Society has its garden. Alpines, heathers, conifers and shrubs in profusion illustrate the range of plants that will grow here – despite the vagaries of Lakeland weather.
LOCATION *Off the A592, 1½ miles N of Windermere.*

HOLKHAM HALL *Norfolk*

Holkham Park – seat of the Earls of Leicester – is like a realm of its own, with church and model farm, cottages, gardens and park. The rolling vistas were created by the combined genius of the great 18th and 19th-century landscapists – William Kent, Capability Brown, Humphry Repton, William Eames and W. A. Nesfield. Typical of the grand scale and scheme of the park is the southern approach to the house. The drive passes under a triumphal arch, rising slowly through a mile or more of grassland and fine trees to a tall stone obelisk. There, still half a mile away, is the imposing

BOXED IN *Sober tendrils of box hedging frame flamboyant roses in a formal garden at Holkham Hall.*

Palladian mansion of Holkham Hall. Great symmetrical medallions of box filigree adorn the lawns, flanking a magnificent fountain. A little Doric temple hides among the trees, and a lake snakes its way through woodland to the north.

LOCATION *Off the A149, 2 miles W of Wells.*

HOPETOUN HOUSE *Lothian*

Hopetoun House is one of the masterpieces created by the great 18th-century architect William Adam – and is regarded by many as his finest achievement in Scotland. The perfect complement to such a house – with its neoclassical façade and curving colonnades – is the simple, landscaped grandeur of its gardens. Immense carpets of lawn stretch around it and, to the west, a vast oval pond is set like a silver ornament in the acres of grass. Beyond it a trail leads through beautiful woodland to a park of red deer. An avenue of limes turns southwards towards another deer park, this time of fallow deer, the herd grazing peacefully by the ruins of a 17th-century tower. Here, too, is the spring garden, and a walled garden centre.

LOCATION *Off the A904, 1 mile W of South Queensferry.*

HORNIMAN GARDENS *Greater London*

On a high hill, overlooking south-east London, are the brightly planted gardens of the Horniman Museum, once the home of F. J. Horniman – tea merchant, politician and collector. In 1901 he gave the gardens and his museum to the London County Council. The gardens mirror his collecting zeal – seen in the Dutch Barn he brought from Holland, which is now used for gardening demonstrations, and in the wealth of beautiful trees. Nature trails point to the finest specimens – maples, chestnuts, limes, beeches, redwoods and many more. A delightful trail leads along a section of an old Victoria to Crystal Palace railway line – a wild setting of dog-rose and dogwood, comfrey and mugwort, oak, yew and walnut trees. There are further gardens of roses, water plants and flowering shrubs.

LOCATION *London Road, Forest Hill, SE23.*

HOWICK GARDENS *Northumberland*

The end of the 19th century saw a revolution in gardening styles, casting away Victorian formality in favour of the 'wild garden'. At the forefront of the movement was a forceful young Irishman, William Robinson, and it is his influence which pervades the gardens at Howick Hall. Quiet grace, fresh greenery and changing cameos of colour – these were the demands Robinson made of a garden, and Howick fulfils them all. Woodland paths and glades around the 18th-century house, former home of the Earls Grey, make natural display cases for exotic trees and shrubs. The seasonal colours come and go – beginning with daffodils, rhododendrons and azaleas. Sunny primulas and bright poppy-flowered mecanopsis grow with the abandon of flowers in the wild. Hydrangeas and agapanthus introduce the blues of high summer, and autumn lends fire to the gatherings of maple.

LOCATION *Off the B1339, 5 miles E of Alnwick.*

ICKWORTH *Suffolk*

Frederick Augustus, 4th Earl of Bristol and Bishop of Derry, frequently escaped his episcopal duties to scour the Continent for works of art. Ickworth, begun in 1795, was less a home than a museum for the treasures he found, a central rotunda with great curving corridors leading to wings on either side. The gardens follow the sweeping lines of the house – a formal setting for the bishop's masterpiece. The west wing itself is an orangery – the fruit trees replaced now with the cool greens of ivy-leaved plants. Evergreens hedged in by high walls of box sweep up to the south front. A path from the rotunda leads to a curving terraced walk, with views across the park. The 'Albana' walk follows a trail through avenues of yew and copses of oak, ash, beech and sycamore. To the north, stemming a dark tide of cedars, is a vast oval of grass – framed in roses and herbaceous plants of yellow and white, purple and blue.

LOCATION *Off the A143, 3 miles SW of Bury St Edmunds.*

JEPHSON GARDENS *Warwickshire*

Fashionable folk of the 19th century came to Leamington Spa to take the cure, and found relief not only in the saline waters, but in the soothing environment as well. The gentle River Leam glides through an elegant town of Georgian terraces and Regency crescents. By its banks are the beautiful Jephson Gardens, named after the physician Dr Henry Jephson who brought fame to the spa in the early 1800s.

Wildfowl on the garden lake seem unperturbed by arching jets of water from fountains shaped like coronets. Great chestnuts and cedars of Lebanon lend an air of unhurried serenity, a mood shared by the sublime Tree of Heaven. Under spreading trees both familiar and strange, wide bands of colour trespass on the lawns – the spectacular displays of bedding plants in pink and crimson, buttermilk and blue.

LOCATION *Off Newbold Terrace, Leamington Spa.*

KIFTSGATE COURT GARDENS *Gloucestershire*

In 1920 there was nothing but a paved formal garden before the porticoed and pillared Georgian front of Kiftsgate Court. Now, much influenced by the style of the famous Hidcote Gardens near by, Kiftsgate has its pavilion of flowers. Small gardens open out like galleries or rooms, each with its own scheme of colour. The wide border is a profusion of silver, lavender and pink – with tissue-petalled paeonies, indigoferas and the purple-red of martagon lilies. Pass under a chestnut tree, then over a bridge, and there is the yellow border. The accents here are stronger, both in shape and hue. Golden euphorbias stand out sharply against shafts of delphinium blue, while tawny lilies and acers add deeper, warmer tones. The rose border is a clamour of colour broken only by the soft white of the irrepressible climber 'Kiftsgate'.

LOCATION *Off the A46, 3 miles NE of Chipping Campden.*

KILDRUMMY CASTLE GARDENS *Grampian*

High·on a steep-sided hill, the medieval ruins of Kildrummy Castle look down on a magical scene. A little burn trips through a narrow valley where in 1902 Japanese gardeners were brought in to create a water garden of falls and pools. There is a stone bridge, a copy of a 14th-century original, which in April frames the golden spathes of *Lysichiton americanus* growing beside the water. Beyond the stream is a medieval quarry, where alpines and shrubs now grow. The gardens are screened by the pale drapery of silver birch among the dark green of conifers, with rhododendrons colouring its steep banks in spring. In autumn, the crimson and gold of acers burns above ground carpeted with gentians and colchicums.

LOCATION *On the A97, 8½ miles W of Alford.*

KILLERTON *Devon*

The rhododendrons grow deep and thick at Killerton, draped in scarlet festoons across the clump of Dolbury Hill. This volcanic mound rises behind the house, with lawns advancing up its lower slopes to meet the crown of woodland above. Paths wind through the trees, past beeches, conifers and a summer display of flame-coloured azaleas. There is a quiet harmony between garden, wood and park – an atmosphere established in 1808 by the gardener John Veitch. He founded that famous firm of nurserymen who transformed the gardens of Britain in the 19th century with their exotic imported plants. Killerton became a trial ground for redwoods, spruces, cedars and Wellingtonias, tulip trees, magnolias and a host of other species. A thatched summerhouse and rockery lie hidden among the trees. Beside the house is a terraced parterre of herbaceous plants, and beyond stretches a great expanse of parkland.

LOCATION *Off the B3185, 7 miles NE of Exeter.*

KINGSTON HOUSE *Oxfordshire*

There is a striking contrast between the two gardens of Kingston House. The Charles II manor house backs on to smooth lawns and tall Wellingtonias, with views over a ha-ha to parkland and an avenue of beech. Walls of mellow brick provide the support for climbing shrubs, with herbaceous plants swelling the borders below. The wall to the north supports a terraced walk – older than the house – with creeping rosemary underfoot. At one end is the 18th-century gazebo, built over an Elizabethan cockpit – and from the terrace grows an ancient yew, thought to be 350 years old. This walk overlooks the second garden – a lush woodland of flowering shrubs, trees and bulbs. Narrow earthen paths vanish into the wilderness of magnolias, paeonies, palms and heather. Unusual specimens abound, like *Diascia barberae* with its shell-like pink flowers.

LOCATION *On the A415, 6 miles W of Abingdon.*

LAMPORT HALL *Northamptonshire*

Lamport Hall can claim a dubious distinction – the first settlement of garden gnomes in England was established there. Only one of the original gnomes survives, consigned now to a glass case in the house.

Imported from Germany, they added the finishing touch to a magnificent rockery, built in 1848 and one of the earliest in the country. It forms a steep slope, over 20 ft high, of rocks, caves and ravines – a miniature alpine hillside. Ferns, ivies and dwarf conifers provide green background, and the local branch of the Alpine Garden Society is replanting the whole rockery with alpine plants from their own collections. The underlying structure of the gardens dates from the 17th century, with terraced walls overlooking the lawns. An Italian garden was created in 1858, with a shell fountain and box-edged beds. Near the house is a lily pond, and a rose garden of modern floribundas and hybrid teas – with additions of the old, heavy-scented *Rosa rugosa*. Wisterias and magnolias replace the fruit trees which once lined the wall of the kitchen garden.

LOCATION *On the A508, 8 miles N of Northampton.*

LEA RHODODENDRON GARDENS *Derbyshire*

Rhododendrons reached these shores over 400 years ago, and are a familiar sight in British gardens. Yet their lasting beauty protects them from that contempt which familiarity proverbially breeds. Shepherded together in their hundreds, as they are at Lea – the appeal of these flower-laden shrubs is at its strongest. The gardens were established in 1935, on the site of an old quarry. Specimen trees were introduced to provide the dappled shade in which rhododendrons thrive. From February through to August the great kaleidoscope of colour turns under a canopy of birch and maple. Every shade of pink is represented from deepest rose to salmon, every yellow, every purple and red. The hybrids borrow colour from the old species and conjure up new combinations of their own – like the Loderi 'King George', whose pink buds fade into pure white flowers with hearts of emerald-green. There is a rock garden of alpines, heathers and dwarf conifers – and a thyme lawn of cool grey-green soothes the eye baffled by so much colour.

LOCATION *Off the A6, 3 miles SE of Matlock.*

LETHERINGHAM WATER MILL *Suffolk*

Bat willows shimmer in the meadows by an old mill of brick and weatherboard, spanning the waters of the River Deben.

Letheringham Water Mill, built over 250 years ago, has 4 acres of gardens – with a beautiful woodland walk and benches by the river bank. Water borders the Stream Garden on two sides, and the air is filled with the sound of its chuckling progress. The spring invasion is led by daffodils and hellebores, supported by the pert little monkey-flower, mimulus. Day lilies and creeping jenny add splashes of brilliant yellow in summer. Flowers are given priority in these gardens, and borders around the millhouse lawns are dense with shrubs and herbaceous varieties. Blocks of intense colour are achieved by massed displays of tulips, and again in late summer when the dahlias arrive. Paeonies, lilies, salvias and plumbagos, anchusas and wallflowers fill the intervening months.

LOCATION *Off the A12, 2½ miles W of Wickham Market.*

LITTLECOTE *Wiltshire*

The Tudor manor of Littlecote is long and low, with walls of rose-pink brick. The River Kennet moves languidly through the surrounding park, and the gardens seem to take their mood of peace from the wide and rolling countryside. Open expanses of lawn, marked here and there by massive yews, only emphasise the stillness. Movement is confined to the busy profusion of borders and beds, where snapdragons jostle in crowds of crimson, yellow and pink. The south border of green and gold, purple and white follows the straight stone-edged lines of a trout stream as it crosses the lawn. In the walled garden climbing roses drape themselves over the walls, and water lilies laze on the surface of a circular pond. The remains of a Roman villa have been found in the park, and the Orpheus mosaic, now restored, can be seen at the site.

LOCATION *On the B4192, 3 miles W of Hungerford.*

LITTLE MORETON HALL *Cheshire*

Little Moreton Hall and its garden, framed by a square moat, are triumphant examples of the pattern-maker's art. The late 16th-century timber-framed house is a fretwork of black and white – quite breathtaking in its intricacy. In 1975 the neglected garden was restored to its original formality, with a knot garden of box and gravel, and the whole was hedged about with hornbeam, thorn and honeysuckle. The design was taken from *The English Gardener*,

173

MATCHED *The intricate timbering at Little Moreton Hall is matched by the symmetry of its recently restored knot garden.*

published in 1688 by Leonard Meagre – who described 'the furnishing of Gardens with divers Forms and Knots'. Old plants with evocative names – mourning widow, thrift, lemon balm and sweet cicely have been introduced in the surrounding borders. Meagre advises that a knot garden be erected 'in such a place where it may yield most delight', and, seen from the house or a grassy mound near by, this 'Garden of Pleasure' clearly does just that.

LOCATION *Off the A34, 4 miles SW of Congleton.*

LONGLEAT *Wiltshire*

It might have startled Capability Brown to see lions roaming through the landscape he devised in the 1750s. Yet neither the wild beasts nor the ingenious entertainments offered at Longleat mar the graceful lines of the park. The plantations of trees, the lake and the sweeping vistas are magnificent still – a monument to Brown and the designers who followed him. The parterres beside the Elizabethan mansion were excluded from the landscaping schemes. They remain a formal delight of rose-filled beds lined with box, or domes of yew interlaced with silver-leaved plants. Sir Jeffrey Wyatville, the 19th-century architect, designed the elegant orangery – discovered now behind a sturdy wall of yew, with a 'Secret Garden' beyond. The Azalea Drive becomes a place of annual pilgrimage for lovers of this species. One of the world's largest mazes is to be found at Longleat, and there are various horticultural events, like the regular display called 'The Fuchsia Experience'.

LOCATION *On the A362, 4 miles SW of Warminster.*

LUTON HOO *Bedfordshire*

Changing tastes in garden design have left their mark on Luton Hoo. The 3rd Earl of Bute enlisted the talents of Capability Brown in the 1760s to create a landscape for his new mansion. The River Lea was dammed to form a lake to the east. Lawns spread down from the house to meet it, and rise again on the other side to merge with fields and 'rounds' of oak, ash and beech. To the south are the terraced gardens designed early this century, introducing an air of French formality. Stone walls and balustrades, backed by yew, define a rectangular area of lawn, framed by paths and herbaceous borders. Semicircular steps lead down to the magnificent rose parterre. Eight box-edged beds blaze with colour all summer long – watched over by a leaden Cupid, perched above a pool of golden water lilies. A hidden rockery garden is both wild and intimate, with pools and islands and an arched stone bridge. Helianthemums (rock roses) gleam there like fireflies among dwarf conifers and acers.

LOCATION *Off the A1081, 1½ miles S of Luton.*

LYDNEY PARK GARDENS
Gloucestershire

There are ruins of a Roman temple in Lydney Park, and evidence of earlier settlements still. Romans and ancient Britons deemed this a magical place, and it remains so today. Most of the planting dates from the 1950s, yet has a quality as deep-rooted and old as the god Pan, whose statue guards the entrance to the gardens. Spring and early summer are the best seasons at Lydney. Magnolia blooms are among the first to appear, flushed with pink or white and unadorned. Along the deer-park fence, Japanese cherries build up in clouds of blossom above the banks of daffodils. Beyond the park is the main woodland garden, where small lakes lie strung together by a stream. Paths twist through the glades of rhododendrons for which the gardens are famous. Most spectacular are the tall big-leaved varieties – among them *Rhododendron falconeri*, with its pale honeycomb-coloured flowers suspended in clusters among foot-long leaves of jade.

LOCATION *On the A48, half a mile W of Lydney.*

MALLENY HOUSE *Lothian*

There have been no doves now at Malleny for many years, but the curious dovecote with its saddle-back roof remains as an unusual feature of this garden. The present Malleny House was built in the early 18th century, with additions made in the 1800s. Evidence of an earlier house and garden is seen in the four majestic yews standing like great monuments of the megalithic age, yet only planted in 1603. There is no elaborate scheme to the gardens – rather they reflect the personal tastes and preferences of the last owner, with an emphasis on rhododendrons and shrub roses. Since the National Trust for Scotland took over Malleny in 1968, the collection of roses has been extended and now rivals any to be found in the east of Scotland.

LOCATION *Off the A70, in Balerno.*

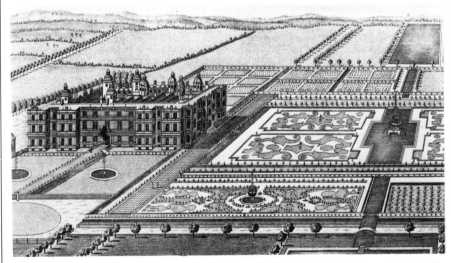

LUCKY ESCAPE *The parterre at Longleat survived the improving hand of Capability Brown in the 1750s.*

MANDERSTON *Borders*

The 18th-century mansion was enlarged and embellished at the turn of the century by Sir James Miller, 'one of the most wealthy Commoners in the country', according to the magazine *Vanity Fair* in 1890. Sir James spared no expense in refurbishing the house and garden. Three terraces were built to the east, with croquet and tennis lawns framed by stone walls and ballustrades, backed by rhododendrons and enormous trees. The fourth terrace, to the south, is laid out in formal beds filled with hostas and roses, and low topiary. Beyond the lakes and woods are the distant Cheviot Hills. In the mid-1950s, a garden of rare azaleas and rhododendrons was carved out of the woodland, and peat beds near by now hold 180 dwarf species. To the north is a delightful formal garden of fountains, statues, prettily shaped beds of precisely placed bedding plants and herbaceous borders, with stone lions guarding a pergola shrouded in roses.
LOCATION *On the A6105, 2 miles E of Duns.*

MANNINGTON HALL and GARDENS *Norfolk*

Mannington Hall and its gardens leave an impression of warmth and colour – of towers and battlements in flint and terracotta reflected in a moat, and roses everywhere. Built in the late 15th century, the manor is owned by a branch of the Walpole family, to which belonged both Lord Nelson and Sir Robert Walpole, England's first Prime Minister. The park around the house extends to 20 acres, with a wood of chestnuts and poplars – and a man-made lake where blue and yellow irises bloom in summer at the water's edge. The modern rose garden is awash with floribundas and hybrid teas, and climbers wreathe the walls in colours from flame through to pink and snowy white. Roses creep into the walled garden, as a backdrop for herbaceous borders of blue and pink, yellow and orange, and into the lovely scented garden. The chapel garden, around a church of Saxon origin, glows with maples in autumn and daffodils in spring.
LOCATION *Off the B1149, 2 miles N of Saxthorpe.*

MANOR FARM *Oxfordshire*

The museum at Cogges recreates the atmosphere and life-style of an Edwardian farm, with demonstrations of equipment and techniques used at the turn of the century. An important part of this living exhibition is the walled kitchen garden, filled with the plants and laid out in a manner favoured by the Edwardians. The garden adjoins the farmhouse of pale Cotswold stone – parts of which were built in the 13th century. The rhubarb and the globe artichokes form neat ranks in the formal, rectangular beds – making dramatic, leafy displays among the other vegetables. Decorative touches have been added to soften the functional note. The vegetable plots are fringed with lavender and dianthus, while the apple trees are trained into orderly, espaliered shapes. Flowers line the perimeter walls, and an arch of climbing roses lends an air of graceful abandon to an essentially practical garden.
LOCATION *Off the B4022, 1 mile E of Witney.*

MARGAM COUNTRY PARK *West Glamorgan*

Margam Country Park has grown up out of the ruins of a great country estate, which was itself founded upon the dissolution of a medieval monastery. Lawns and trees now invade the remains of the abbey, where the chapter house can still be seen. One of the survivors of the secular period that followed is the 18th-century orangery, built to house 100 citrus trees. Legend insists that these trees were salvaged from a wreck on the coast near by – the golden cargo being a gift intended for royalty. Oranges still thrive in part of the building, and the rest is used for exhibitions. Near the orangery is a giant maze, planted in 1982 with green and golden conifers. The gardens around the 19th-century Margam Castle are being restored, and the 830 acres of park, with lake and woodland, offer peaceful walks among wildfowl and deer.
LOCATION *On the A48, 5 miles SE of Port Talbot.*

MARWOOD HILL *Devon*

Eucalyptus trees may seem unusual in a Devon valley, but they thrive at Marwood Hill, which also offers further surprises. In the 1960s, a stream at the valley bottom was dammed to form three small lakes. Primulas, irises and arum lilies now throng together by the water among the willows and different varieties of dogwood. In summer, white plumes of pampas grass spring up by the waterside. Below the modern house, tucked into the hillside, are beds of rhododendrons. The scarred slope near by, once a quarry site, is studded in May with pink lewisias, followed by clusters of purple ramondas. West of the house are the more formal rose beds, and the dense plantations of rare and exotic trees. Camellias in amazing variety fill a greenhouse in an old walled garden, and another is devoted to a remarkable collection of Australasian plants.
LOCATION *Off the B3230, 4 miles N of Barnstaple.*

MELLERSTAIN *Borders*

In 1909, at a period when British garden designers were abandoning formality in favour of the 'wild garden', Mellerstain returned to the old values of neat parterres and studied vistas. From the mansion, ballustraded steps lead down to two squares of lawn – great quilted coverlets of green with designs appliquéd in box. The geometric beds are filled with old roses, fragrant and densely petalled – the Damasks, Gallicas, Centifolias, Bourbons and Hybrid Musks. More steps descend to a vast avenue of smooth grass. Clipped hedges on either side guide the eye past forests of mature trees, to a lake where swans and Canada geese spend tranquil days. Drawn like a veil of blue across the horizon is the distant line of the Cheviot Hills.
LOCATION *On the A6089, 7 miles NW of Kelso.*

MILTON'S COTTAGE *Buckinghamshire*

In 1665, when the Great Plague was sweeping through London, John Milton escaped to the Buckinghamshire countryside to finish his epic poem *Paradise Lost*. The Tudor cottage, with its tall brick chimneys and huddle of steep roofs, is kept as it was when he lived there. The garden is a convivial bustle of familiar plants – exemplifying the 'cottage' style. Snapdragons, hollyhocks and golden rods cluster together with lavender and rosemary, apples and pears. The mulberry tree was taken as a cutting – 35 years ago – from one grown in the gardens of Christ's College, Cambridge, when Milton was a student there. He was already blind when he came to Chalfont St Giles, but perhaps through the profusion of scents which coloured the air, roses made the most vivid impression – remembered in *Paradise Lost* when Satan discovered Eve:

*Veiled in a cloud of fragrance, where she
        stood,
Half spied, so thick the roses blushing
        round
About her glowed . . .*

LOCATION *Off the A413, in Chalfont St Giles.*

MORTON MANOR *Isle of Wight*

Centuries of gardening expertise have left
Morton Manor with a legacy of walled
terraces and a formal rose garden. A manor
was established here in the 13th century,
but the present house was rebuilt in 1680.
The ancient box hedge surrounding a
sunken Elizabethan garden predates the
house, and a collection of mature conifers
adds an air of venerable age. Rhododendrons, azaleas and camellias add their
festive colours to a garden of flowering
shrubs and splendid trees. An ornamental
pond offers a haven to varieties of water-
fowl, chattering in the shade of giant
gunnera leaves. Goldfish dart among the
water lilies in a pool of their own.

LOCATION *Off the A3055, 1 mile SW of
Brading.*

MOTTISFONT ABBEY *Hampshire*

A monastic settlement was established at
Mottisfont in 1201, beside a clear spring
which rises to the west of the present
Georgian house, which stands on the site
of the abbey. At the foot of wide lawns the
River Test hurries by, teeming with trout.
The lawns are overlooked by cedar, chestnut and beech – many of which were
planted when the garden was landscaped
in the 18th century. An extraordinary
London plane towers 100 ft above the
river, where two trees have grown into one
– with branches spreading over an area of
1,500 sq. yds. Scarcely less spectacular is
the walled rose garden. It contains all the
historic varieties collected over a period of
40 years by Graham Thomas, Gardens
Adviser to the National Trust. Irish yews
frame a central fountain, around which a
portrait gallery unfolds – with glowing
examples of virtually every old European
rose still in cultivation.

LOCATION *Off the A3057, 4½ miles NW of
Romsey.*

MUNCASTER CASTLE *Cumbria*

The Romans once built a fort here, taking
advantage of the magnificent site overlooking Eskdale, Scafell and the Cumbrian

ranges. The present castle, built of red
sandstone, was begun in the 13th century.
A terrace was built in the 18th century,
pursuing the distant River Esk for a quarter
of a mile as if binding the views of the
valley to the gardens themselves. The extensive gardens, surrounded by 77 acres of
woodland, are famous for their rhododendrons. Notable plant collectors scoured the
forests of China and the Himalayas between the two World Wars, and many new
species were sent back as seeds to Muncas-
ter. Magnolias, camellias and colourful
maples make their seasonal contributions
to the woodland scene. There are countless fine specimens to fascinate the lover of
trees, particularly the collection of nothofagus, or 'false beech', from South America.

LOCATION *On the A595, 1 mile E of Raven-
glass.*

OXBURGH HALL *Norfolk*

Oxburgh Hall – with its soaring, turreted
gatehouse of Tudor brick – retains the
character of a 15th-century fortified manor,
despite Victorian alterations. A broad and
shallow moat is drawn around four sides,
and from the battlements the views stretch
away over level fields and woodland. Ten
acres of lawn skirt the manor, with flower
borders and climbers making their assault
on the walls. Laid out below the walls in
pink gravel, squared grass plots and clipped box edging is an ingenious parterre.
Cotton lavender and blue rue gleam silver
among the arabesques of bright bedding
plants, interspaced with rounded tussocks
of yew. The parterre dates from 1845,
based on a French design of over a century
earlier. The herbaceous border, lining a
wall near by, holds fragrant day lilies,
lupins, poppies and deep blue campanulas
and delphiniums. A kitchen garden offers
formal arrays of quinces, mulberries and
medlars within walls of Gothic-style Victorian brick.

LOCATION *Off the A134, 7 miles SW of
Swaffham.*

PECKOVER HOUSE *Cambridgeshire*

Peckover House presents a Georgian
façade, elegant but unadorned, to the River
Nene, in Wisbech. Behind the house is a
luxurious garden, hidden from the casual
gaze of passers-by. Carefully tended over a
century or more, this large town garden
has curving paths and spotless lawns, with
trees and shrubs planted to measured and
formal effect. 'Wilderness Walk' provides a

contained woodland of hollies, laurels,
yew and box. A less formal combination
lies to the west of the house, where
flowering shrubs mingle with hostas, al-
chemillas and vincas. A small pool, edged
with starry sedums, hydrangeas and lilies,
invites a pause. Past topiary peacocks, a
path leads to a delicate summerhouse of
white and green. Twin borders are divided
into sections by hedges and slender, metal
pillars. In each the succession of colours
flare and die and flare again – as the
seasons bring yellow to doronicums, day
lilies and euphorbias, white to the roses
and blue to perovskias and agapanthus.

LOCATION *North Brink, Wisbech.*

PENCARROW *Cornwall*

Pencarrow is approached down a mile-
long, wooded drive, past an ancient British
encampment. It is primarily a tree-lover's
garden, laid out in the early 19th century
by Sir William Molesworth, Bt. By 1854 he
had planted nearly every known conifer
that would grow in the British climate.
Many of these still stand, notably an avenue
of Chilean monkey-puzzles, and a Japanese
tiger-tail spruce of enormous girth. The
house was built about 1776, and the climbing roses and wisterias about its walls are
cut low to reveal the fine Georgian exterior. A sunken Italian garden, with curving lawns and central fountain, lies just
behind the house. Near by is a great
rockery of grey Bodmin granite. Camellias,
azaleas and rhododendrons swamp the
rockery and drive in spring, bringing warm
colour to the dark backdrop of conifers. A
palm house and bog garden add further
variety, and trails lead through the trees to
a small lake.

LOCATION *Off the A389, 4 miles NW of
Bodmin.*

PENRHYN CASTLE *Gwynedd*

Away to the north lie Anglesey and Puffin
Island, to the east is the outline of Great
Ormes Head with the Irish Sea beyond.
The 19th-century castle – built of grey
Mona Marble in the Norman style – is stark
and imposing like the views it commands.
Green waves of grass wash up to the walls,
broken by copses of beeches, oaks and
Japanese maples. Queen Victoria recorded
her visit in 1859 by planting a Californian
Big Tree, which still stands. An unexpected
contrast to the grand scale of lawns and
trees is the secluded walled garden. Snow-
drops and wild cyclamen grow by the path

SAVED *After years of neglect, Penshurst Place was restored in the 19th century.*

leading to its gate. The highest of three terraces is graced by a formal parterre, lily ponds and an attractive loggia. In August, white-flowering eucryphias line the central walk. The middle terrace harbours shrubs that flower through the seasons – from winter viburnum to the hydrangeas, honeysuckles and cornus of summer. Japanese bamboo, New Zealand pampas grass and giant-leaved gunnera introduce a wild note to the lowest level of the garden.
LOCATION *Off the A5, 1 mile E of Bangor.*

PENSHURST PLACE *Kent*

The great Elizabethan poet Sir Philip Sidney was born at Penshurst Place in 1554, and the spirit of his age pervades both house and gardens. A series of enclosed gardens unfolds as an extension of the house, following the rectangular lines of its courtyards and walls. The style of the gardens, and much of the content, is medieval still. An Italian parterre, though added in the 19th century, is Tudor in inspiration. Four panels of scarlet roses, edged with box, stand round an oval pond. Here, and throughout the gardens, great slabs of yew have been chiselled into steps and walls with the skill of a master mason. Behind these perfect hedges other gardens lie hidden – of nuts, of roses, one of magnolias and another of grey-leaved plants. They are linked by changing borders of paeonies and lilacs, or apple trees with herbaceous flowers between. There are pools of water lilies and water hyacinths, with goldfish gleaming in the dark waters.
LOCATION *On the B2176, 6 miles SW of Tonbridge.*

PETWORTH PARK *West Sussex*

Petworth Park and Pleasure Ground are among the landscape masterpieces forged by Capability Brown in the 18th century. His sensitivity to colour and form, shadow and light is evident in the swirling hills, their contours underlined in chestnut, beech and oak. From the west front of the house, acres of open parkland sweep down to a serpentine lake. Deer roam the park, and the prevailing mood of idyll and romance was caught in the 1820s by William Turner in his paintings *A Stag Drinking* and *Fighting Bucks*, which hang in the house. Petworth House is partly medieval, but the bulk of the palatial mansion dates from the late 17th century. The Pleasure Ground near by, though transformed by Brown, retains the shape of the formal garden established over 100 years earlier. Brown added the curving paths and temples, and many of the flowering shrubs and fine trees.
LOCATION *In Petworth, West Sussex.*

THE PINES *Kent*

St Margaret's Bay, with its curve of shingle beach and tall chalk cliffs rising behind the village, has beauty enough. But one of the residents, Mr Frederick Cleary, decided to add a garden to its pleasures, and The Pines is the result of his considerable labours. Opened in 1971, the garden was created out of an area of wasteland: an additional gift of land increased the site to the present 6 acres. A waterfall and lake were constructed, surrounded by lawns – with a rockery, bog garden and unusual ornaments. A bronze statue catches Sir

Winston Churchill in frozen stride, and a robust ship's figurehead – in the shape of Britannia – stands in the shadow of trees. From the lake, an avenue of elms stretches away to the southern boundary, with formal beds of tulips making blocks of colour between.
LOCATION *Beach Road, St Margaret's Bay.*

PLAS NEWYDD *Gwynedd*

The lawns around Plas Newydd – home of the Marquis of Anglesey – sweep down to the Menai Strait and the warm waters of the Gulf Stream. Exotic trees and shrubs thrive in the damp, frost-free climate. Humphry Repton's landscape, created at the turn of the 18th century, has been clothed with conifers and deciduous trees – providing light shelter for banks of azaleas and rhododendrons. The collection of camellias is superb, and the tumultuous hedges of viburnum are among the best in Britain. Hydrangeas abound, in company with white-flowered eucryphias or the flame-flowered Chilean fire bush. Near the house is a formal garden of roses and summer flowers. An area of woodland by the shore has been cleared to form a wild garden of rhododendrons.
LOCATION *On the A4080, 1½ miles SW of Llanfairpwllgwyngyll.*

POLESDEN LACEY *Surrey*

Early this century, Polesden Lacey provided the elegant setting in which kings and politicians were entertained by the renowned society hostess the Hon. Mrs

CHARM IN STONE *A gargoyle peers over a carved head in the walled garden at Polesden Lacey – just two of the estate's charming stone residents.*

Ronald Greville. By a lawn near the house are the blue spruces, planted in the 1920s by the kings of England, Spain and Egypt. Such exalted company demanded luxurious surroundings: outdoors these were provided by a procession of walled gardens. Each is devoted to a different floral theme – of roses, irises or lavender. Noble statuary adorns the courts and lawns – medieval Venetian wellheads, a Roman sarcophagus and 18th-century terracotta statuettes from France. The sunken garden is fragrant with thyme, and the bank above is edged with young cedars of Lebanon. Shades of silver and blue shroud the neighbouring rock garden, where lilac and hydrangeas grow beneath a silver-leaved weeping pear. A terraced walk, 480 yds long, is named after the playwright and wit, Richard Brinsley Sheridan, who lived in an earlier house on the site in the 1800s.

LOCATION *Off the A246, 3½ miles SW of Leatherhead.*

POLLOK PARK *Strathclyde*

Glasgow is a city rich in gardens and parks, and Pollok is one of the finest. It was laid out in the 18th century, around the severely classical mansion. The village of Pollok Town was demolished to ensure an unimpeded view over White Cart Water and the fields beyond, and its inhabitants were moved to a nearby town. The present gardens owe most to improvements made in the late 19th and early 20th centuries. Formal terraces, gazebos and parterres were constructed near the house, and enthusiastic planting transformed the park, giving rise to the present woodland garden of exotic Japanese maples, magnolias, prunus and azaleas. Sir John Stirling Maxwell, 10th Baronet of Pollok, collected over 1,000 species of rhododendron, flooding the park with colour. The woods rustle with the tread of deer and fox, or echo with the wild cry of kestrels.

LOCATION *Haggs Road, Glasgow.*

PORT LYMPNE ZOO PARK and GARDENS *Kent*

Protection is the theme of Port Lympne – preservation of the endangered species of wildlife, now at home in the park, and restoration of the unique house and its gardens. The house was built before the First World War, with the curving gables and tall chimneys of the Dutch colonial style. The gardens echo a much earlier Dutch influence, the formal and meticu-

lous patterns of the 17th century. Wide parterres flank the house, broken into geometric shapes by pools, borders and beds. A vast chessboard of flowers, hedged in yew, occupies one end of the south parterre. A similar plot, but laid out in stripes, takes up the other. Behind the house, a flight of 125 steps cleaves its way through rising terraces, each fortified with ramparts of yew, to an octagonal garden at the top. More grassed terraces drop away from the house, supporting a vineyard and fig trees.

LOCATION *Off the A20, 3 miles W of Hythe.*

PRIORWOOD ORCHARD *Borders*

Walking through the orchards at Priorwood is to see the history of Britain, revealed in the development of its fruit. Near by is Melrose Abbey, founded in 1136, and the land here was worked by the industrious monks until the 16th century. There are old damson and cherry trees, pears and gages – but the history lesson really begins with the apple walk. Britons knew nothing but bitter wild apples and tiny crab apples until the Romans introduced them to the delights of the apple now known as 'Pomme d'Api'. The walk follows the developments through the Middle Ages – with the Old Pearmain of 1200, or the Royal Russet known since the 16th century – ending with modern commercial apples like Golden Delicious.

LOCATION *In Melrose, Borders.*

RABY CASTLE *Co. Durham*

Raby Castle stands aloof from its garden, bounded on three sides by a dry moat. The waters of a lake creep up to high stone ramparts on the southern side. All around is the open park, landscaped in the 18th century, with red and fallow deer glimpsed beneath the trees. To the north of this mighty square-turreted castle is a complex of walled gardens. Two massive yew hedges form a double backbone on which the gardens seem to rest. They are believed to be as old as the castle itself, a relic of the 14th century when yew was grown to provide wood for bows. The white Ischia fig, brought from Italy in about 1789, seems an infant by comparison. The gardens are made up of sloping lawns and herbaceous borders, with shrubs and espaliered fruit trees lining the walls. Roses and heathers provide ribbons of colour.

LOCATION *On the A688, 1 mile N of Staindrop.*

RIEVAULX TERRACE *North Yorkshire*

Rievaulx Terrace is the full realisation of the romantic landscape, that vision pursued by so many landowners in the 18th century. The focal point for such a landscape – conventionally provided by a lake or folly – was already here, in the lofty ruins of a medieval abbey. A curving terrace, half a mile long, was cut into the precipice above Rievaulx Abbey. Great channels were cleared through the dense woodland which shrouded the slopes, affording magnificent views of the ruins below and on to the River Rye, snaking its way down the valley. Two temples, the interiors lavishly decorated, grace the ends of the terrace. Evidence suggests that this landscape was part of an ambitious scheme, never completed. Thomas Duncombe III, who planned it in the 1750s, seems to have intended it to link up with another on his estate at Duncombe Park, 3 miles away across the valley.

LOCATION *Off the B1257, 4 miles NW of Helmsley.*

ROCKINGHAM CASTLE *Leicestershire*

The Norman castle, built of honey-coloured stone, gazes over miles of the Welland Valley – peaceful now after centuries of turbulence. Rockingham appeared as 'Arnescote' in the BBC television series *By The Sword Divided*, and fictitious scenes of the Civil War paralleled real events here in the 17th century. Walls destroyed by the Roundheads in 1645 were used to level the west terrace, and the rose garden – behind its circular hedge of yew – follows the outlines of the ruined keep. There is a rich and still formality here – in the grassy terraces of the 16th century, or in the religious symbolism of the Edwardian Cross Garden, where lawns are divided by cruciform paths, edged with roses and lavender. Yew hedges planted 400 years ago have been shaped like two lumbering rows of elephants, adding a whimsical note. Charles Dickens once watched a ghost glide down this Elephant Walk, then into the wooded ravine known as the Wild Garden.

LOCATION *On the A6003, 2 miles N of Corby.*

THE ROYAL BOTANIC GARDEN EDINBURGH *Lothian*

The Royal Botanic Garden is hemmed in by Edinburgh streets, yet no sight or sound of the city seems to penetrate the calm.

Wandering through a landscape of pools and woodland, it is easy to forget the motive of botanical research underlying much of the planting. The remarkable collection of 400 rhododendrons is spread through Copse, Peat and Woodland gardens. A mass of the smaller species is found near alpines and herbaceous perennials, clinging with heath-like tenacity to stony outcrops of the mountainous rock garden. Magnificent plant houses contain ferns, aquatic plants, palms, orchids, cycads and commercial plants of the tropics. Fascinating research collections include the ginger family. These pungent relatives are brought together in one of the plant houses, and range from the decorative *Hedychium* to the spicy *Zingiber officinale* – source of the heat in many a fiery curry. LOCATION *Arboretum Road, Edinburgh.*

RYDAL MOUNT *Cumbria*

William Wordsworth's poetry is vibrant with his love of nature, a love which found practical expression in his gardening. He and his family lived at Rydal Mount from 1813 to 1850, and the garden today is almost as he left it. It stands at the base of Nab Scar, with wild panoramas of fells and lakes to the south. Wordsworth believed that a garden should have a 'lawn, and trees carefully planted so as not to obscure the view'. He followed these precepts at Rydal, creating a sloping lawn to the west, bounded by flowering shrubs. Above it he built three terraces, the first with a summerhouse at its end – where Queen Adelaide sat and contemplated Rydal Water when she visited in 1840. Beyond it, another terrace reaches out to the fell, and of this Wordsworth wrote:

A Poet's hand first shaped it; and the steps
Of that same Bard – repeated to and fro...
Forbade the weeds to creep o'er its grey
            line.

LOCATION *Off the A591, 1½ miles NW of Ambleside.*

ST AIDAN'S COLLEGE *Co. Durham*

St Aidan's has achieved a rare and striking alliance between the austerity of modern architecture and the soft exuberance of shrubs and trees. Built in 1964 the college dominates a hill to the south of the city, with enviable views of Durham Cathedral. Plantations of sycamores, beeches and oaks are grouped around the college complex, blending it gradually into the curve of the

GARDENER POET *William Wordsworth landscaped the garden when he moved to Rydal Mount.*

hill. The heart of the garden is the inner courtyard and its polygonal pool. Spearwort and bogbean, water lilies and creamy irises have taken root, creating an aquatic wilderness in this structured landscape. Terraces spread out like angular ripples, adorned with beds of roses. Beyond a young cedar of Lebanon, a path is lined with laburnum, trailing banners of gold in spring and early summer. One of the loveliest performances is given in spring when 12,000 crocuses come in waves of yellow, purple and white. LOCATION *Windmill Hill, Durham.*

ST FAGANS *South Glamorgan*

St Fagans Castle takes in many aspects of Welsh culture and history, from crafts and cottage industries to the grandeur of the nobleman's life. The Welsh Folk Museum in the grounds illustrates traditional skills, while the house and gardens bear witness to aristocratic pleasures of the past. The many-gabled exterior of the house proclaims its Elizabethan origin, but the ruins of a 13th-century curtain wall – now framing part of the garden – tell of an earlier castle on the site. The gardens show a Victorian formality, within a 17th-century framework. The north front overlooks regular beds and curving topiary. A mulberry grove, herb and knot gardens are found within the original walls, and a rose garden occupies what was once the village green. To the south-west, terraces drop away to a series of 17th-century fish ponds. LOCATION *Off the A48, 4½ miles W of Cardiff city centre.*

SEWERBY HALL *Humberside*

The North Sea beats at the cliffs below Sewerby Hall – a Georgian mansion of white stucco and yellow stone. Tall trees offer protection from the sea winds – chestnuts, walnuts, various oaks and a parade of soaring monkey-puzzles. The scheme of the gardens is largely Victorian, with a raised terrace and formal beds near the house. Beyond the lawns, in the encircling woodland, the glades are dredged white with snowdrops every spring. Layer upon layer of colour follows – blue, yellow and red – as violets, daffodils, anemones, campions and others flower among the ferns. A walled garden adheres to the formal convention of box-edged beds, combined with the lavish displays of a cottage-style garden. A handsome Georgian greenhouse enhances the traditional air of the Old English Garden. A high-walled rose garden continues the antique theme. LOCATION *Off the B1255, 2 miles NE of Bridlington.*

SHELDON MANOR *Wiltshire*

Roses are the theme in the gardens of Sheldon Manor – old-fashioned varieties, with subtle colours and delicate scents, weave a garland round the medieval manor house. They appear among the snake-bark maples and sorbus of the elm tree garden – named in honour of the great 250-year-old tree laid low by Dutch elm disease – and again in the Judas tree garden. In the orchard, climbing roses

tangle with clematises among the old cider-apple trees. The 13th-century porch of the manor opens on to a forecourt with three ancient yews, 60 ft high – and ducks roost in their hollow cores. Beyond are terraces leading down to a water garden. There a stone swimming-pool is framed by a 'cloister' of pleached hornbeams.
LOCATION *Off the A420, 1½ miles W of Chippenham.*

SLEDMERE HOUSE *Humberside*

Sledmere House and its park are remarkable monuments to Sir Christopher Sykes, the zealous squire who, according to an inscription on the village well, 'caused what was once a bleak and barren tract of country to become now one of the most productive and best cultivated districts in the county…' In 1776, when he inherited the house, Sir Christopher employed Capability Brown to tame 2,000 acres of the wild and inhospitable Yorkshire Wolds. In his distinctive style, Brown created a landscape of parkland and trees which can still be seen today. The gardens near the house are intimate in mood, compared with the majesty of the park – despite the group of lofty, 250-year-old chestnut trees. In the Italian garden a fountain plays among stone statues, and walls hide beneath wisterias and climbing roses, intertwined with scented honeysuckles. Passing through woodland shade, a path emerges to a blaze of colour in roses and flowering shrubs, outside the kitchen garden.
LOCATION *On the B1252, 8 miles NW of Great Driffield.*

SOMERLEYTON HALL *Suffolk*

The creator of Somerleyton's Victorian splendour – the entrepreneur and railway contractor, Sir Morton Peto – went bankrupt before he had time to enjoy it. And he sold the estate to the ancestor of the present owner, Lord Somerleyton. The original Jacobean manor all but vanished under the elaborate 19th-century additions of brick and ornate stonework. The gardens echo the sumptuous style of the house, with paths snaking through 12 acres of velvet lawns, splendid topiary and a remarkable collection of statuary. A sunken garden, with banks of rhododendrons and massed roses, is framed by an Italianate loggia – a covered walk of graceful arches and pierced stone. The maze was planted in 1846, and leads the visitor through a convoluted passage of yew, 400 yds long,

to a raised pagoda at its centre. The magnificent clock-tower dominating the stable block was the model for the tower which carries Big Ben at the Houses of Parliament.
LOCATION *Off the B1074, 5 miles NW of Lowestoft.*

SPETCHLEY PARK
Hereford and Worcester

There is so much to discover at Spetchley Park, for the plantsman and landscape enthusiast alike. The Georgian mansion is flanked by wide lawns, reaching down to a lake. A succession of gardens lies to the east, each different in content and mood. Olive trees and pomegranates share the shelter of the former melon yard with tender flowering shrubs. The exterior walls of the large kitchen garden provide a framework for crowded borders, and the air vibrates with scent and colour. Roses, paeonies, camellias, viburnum and berberis jostle for space with numerous other species. Four yew-framed plots make up the unusual Fountain Garden – a wonderland of trees and shrubs within 36 beds, divided by paths. A deer park lies beyond the ha-ha to the south of the house where herds of red and fallow deer graze among fine old oaks.
LOCATION *On the A422, 3 miles E of Worcester.*

SPINNERS *Hampshire*

Gardening enthusiasts who visit Spinners have the added delight of knowing they may buy examples of much they admire. An area of 3 acres has been carved largely out of oak woodland rooted in unpromising acid soil and set high above the Lymington river. Priority is given to plants with extended seasons, and to those interesting both in flower and foliage – like *Rhododendron yakushimanum* from Japan, with dark spear-headed leaves thrusting through knots of pale pink apple-blossom blooms. A path descends into a dell of ferns and primulas, with rodgersias and the china-blue flowers of meconopsis. Hydrangeas and camellias are represented in luxurious variety. The herbaceous selection is unusual, with hostas and other shade plants a particular speciality. In the small arboretum the mottled bark of eucalyptus trees and acers adds novel pattern and colour.
LOCATION *Off the A337, 1½ miles N of Lymington.*

STANDEN *West Sussex*

Successful compromise is the keynote of Standen's garden. A wealthy London solicitor, James Beale, bought the site in 1890 and the garden was laid out in the artificial 'gardenesque' style, of compressed landscape and artfully placed specimen plants. The architect Philip Webb, friend and colleague of William Morris, designed the house – and imposed on this scheme a formal arrangement of steps, terraces and summerhouse. Mrs Beale then introduced a flood of exotic shrubs and trees. Elements of all these preferences have been retained, resulting in a garden of abundant growth with an undertone of restraint and serenity. Steep grassy slopes overlook the Medway Valley, and the small quarry which provided stone for the house has succumbed to an invasion of ferns. Primulas, anemones and narcissi abound among the magnolias, the camellias and acers. The delicate white flowers of ladies' tresses orchid take over the upper lawns in August.
LOCATION *Off the B2110, 1½ miles S of East Grinstead.*

STAPELEY WATER GARDENS
Cheshire

In a landscape of lawns and trees, the largest water garden centre in Europe unravels the mysteries of aquatic horticulture. Many of the exhibits incorporated into the 35 acre site are for sale, ranging from spectacular floodlit fountains to a wide spectrum of moisture-loving plants. Those aristocrats of pond life – the water lilies – are displayed in 50 different variations, from the purest white of 'Albatross' to the deep fire-red of 'Conqueror'. A galaxy of small ponds shimmers in the grass, brimming over with rushes and reeds, and countless flowering species. Cascades and waterfalls mimic their natural counterparts, with names like Teesdale Waterfall, Swaledale Streamlet or Allendale Cascade. Ornamental fish are exhibited in tanks and pools – the pride of the collection being great Koi carp, some valued at £4,000 each.
LOCATION *On the A51, 3 miles SE of Nantwich.*

SUTTON MANOR *Hampshire*

The Queen Anne house stands in 56 acres of parkland, surrounded by the gentle slopes of the Hampshire Downs. It was extended early this century, to accommodate the glittering social gatherings of the Edwardian era, and in the 1930s became the home of the film magnate J. Arthur Rank. The handsome gardens now reflect the interests of the present owners – the charitable Sutman Trust. As a patron of the arts, the trust has established a superb collection of 20th-century sculpture, gathered on smooth lawns before the house. The extensive herb garden points to the trust's sponsorship of research into herbal remedies. High brick walls enclose a fragrant multitude of 180 different herb species, arranged with the quiet formality of an earlier age. A nursery centre sells examples of the many shrubs and trees seen throughout the gardens.

LOCATION *Off the A34, 7 miles N of Winchester.*

SUTTON PARK *North Yorkshire*

Three linked terraces were built at Sutton Park in the 1960s, below the south front of the Georgian house. This formal addition seems to have drawn the adjoining park – landscaped in the 18th century – into clear and dramatic focus. The terraces are mainly laid to lawn, with steps and retaining walls in brick and stone. The elegant simplicity of their design is embroidered with borders and beds. The planting of the upper terrace is airy yet rich, with delightful gradations of form and colour. The middle terrace forms a parterre of beds filled with unusual and colourful plants. A lily canal breaks the smooth turf of the lower terrace, and beyond it are the pastures and copses of the park. A beautiful woodland lies to the east, threaded by paths and a long central ride.

LOCATION *On the B1363, 8 miles N of York.*

THORP PERROW *North Yorkshire*

Walking the avenues of Thorp Perrow arboretum is like moving through a gallery of ever-changing worlds. Trees of the same genus have been grouped together in glades or strung along the paths – over 1,000 varieties crowding into this 60 acre site. The enchantment begins at once, in the 'silver glade' by the entrance lodge, where a variety of species with pale and shimmering foliage weave their spell. Gold is the theme of the laburnum walk, while the cherry avenue in spring seems submerged in powdered snow, flushed with pink. The arboretum holds some very old and rare specimens, combined with superb massed plantings – like the Asiatic

and American conifers, introduced in the 19th century. Spring and summer displays are reinforced by droves of wild flowers, and the 'autumn bays' form coves of copper and red in the vast sea of green.

LOCATION *Off the B6268, 2½ miles S of Bedale.*

TOROSAY CASTLE *Isle of Mull*

Overlooking Duart Bay, with views ranging across the Firth of Lorne, Torosay Castle stands in 19th-century Scottish baronial splendour. The terraced gardens face towards the sea, warmed by the Gulf Stream. Italian influences dictated the arrangement of formal lawns and stone ornaments, framed by elegant balustrading. A collection of 19 Venetian statues, dating from the 18th century, has a special charm. They line a gravelled walk in poses of simple, life-like grace, leading the way to a walled garden which predates the castle. In 1981, an exotic note was introduced with the addition of a stylised Japanese garden of ornamental shrubs, but the sheltered water garden dates from the earlier period.

LOCATION *Off the A849, 1½ miles SE of Craignure.*

TRENGWAINTON *Cornwall*

Among the superb gardens of the Cornish mainland, Trengwainton's collection of exotic and tender plants is unsurpassed. Species normally associated in Britain with greenhouses are found here out of doors, basking in the warmth and shelter of walled gardens. From 1925 onwards,

shrubs and trees have been gathered from all over the world. Many of the glorious rhododendron species were raised from seeds brought from Assam and Burma in the late 1920s by the famous collector, Frank Kingdon-Ward. The woodland garden presents changing cameos of foreign lands, in flowering shrubs and spectacular foliage plants. A stream follows the long drive, where primulas and lysichitons brighten the damp gloom. Strange trees loom into view – like the Australian *Dicksonia antarctica* with its great fern-fronded leaves.

LOCATION *On the B3312, 2 miles NW of Penzance.*

TREWITHEN *Cornwall*

Hybrids propagated at Trewithen appear in many gardens, at home and abroad, but lovely ambassadors like *Rhododendron* 'Trewithen Orange', or *Ceanothus* 'Trewithen Blue' only hint at the treasures to be found at their source. Since the early 1900s, a woodland garden has been developed around the framework of an 18th-century landscape. The architect of this famous garden, George Johnstone, introduced rare trees and shrubs from Australasia, America and particularly from Asia. Magnolias were his special interest, seen here in great variety, creating avalanches of heavy blossom in powder-white, pink – and even yellow, when *Magnolia cordata* begins to flower. The wide south lawn cuts a long swathe through banks of exotic vegetation, past rare specimens like the tree *Rehderodendron macrocarpum* –

THE GUARDIANS *Stone birds guard the walled garden – the only formal area in Trewithen's 28 acres.*

one of only two mature specimens growing in Britain. Camellias are among the most beautiful and abundant species established here. A walled garden (the original herb and rose garden) makes a modest and formal contrast to the exuberance of the rest.

LOCATION *Off the A390, 1½ miles E of Probus.*

TYNINGHAME GARDENS *Lothian*

The Earls of Haddington have been tending this land for the last 300 years – and each generation contributed to the gardens. The 18th-century wilderness garden has almost vanished under recent plantings of cherries, azaleas and maples. Camellias and paeonies fill the spaces between, and in spring wild primroses monopolise the woodland floor. A formal parterre of roses and raised beds by the house is a simplified interpretation of Victorian bedding schemes. The walled garden of 18th-century brick is a peaceful alliance of old and new – with box parterres and statues backed by high yew hedges, and a central avenue of mown grass. A beautiful tunnel of arching apple trees runs along the outside of the southern wall. A dreaming world of roses and clematises is discovered in the secret garden, based on a romantic French design of the 18th century.

LOCATION *On the A198, 2 miles E of East Linton.*

WALLINGTON GARDENS
Northumberland

For 164 years, until 1941, Wallington was the home of the Trevelyan family – which numbers among its distinguished members the great historian, George Macaulay Trevelyan. The house was built in 1688, and lakes, woodland and serpentine paths were laid out in the early 18th century, following the 'natural' style favoured at the time. A series of large ponds survives from this period – as does the formal gravel terrace by the south front, where rosemary and grey-leaved fuchsias mingle with roses and honeysuckles. The woods flanking the house to east and west invite exploration, but the masterpiece of Wallington's outdoor kingdom is the walled garden and conservatory. Curving steps of stone lead down from a raised walk into a secluded area of roses and Moroccan broom, fountain, pool and water garden. Throughout each spring and summer, tides of clemat-

LAKE VIEW *West Wycombe Park in 1787 – fronted by smooth lawns and framed by stately trees.*

ises, crown imperials and madonna lilies flood the garden.

LOCATION *On the B6343, 12 miles W of Morpeth.*

WATERPERRY GARDENS *Oxfordshire*

Waterperry took on an educational role in 1932, when the redoubtable horticulturalist Miss Beatrix Havergal set out to teach the skills of her profession. The present centre continues her policy with day courses, but is mainly geared to production. The estate, which borders the placid River Thame, is attached to an 18th-century manor house, with a tiny Saxon church near by. The walled garden is dedicated to glasshouses and trained fruit trees, shrub propagation, herbs and trailing clouds of wisteria. The herbaceous section is an education in itself, distributed through the garden in borders and island beds. Alpines thrive in the rock garden and alpine nursery, and examples of the many species displayed are available in the garden shop.

LOCATION *Off the A40, 8 miles E of Oxford.*

WEST DEAN GARDENS *West Sussex*

West Dean lies among the folds of the South Downs, tucked into the valley of the River Lavant – a 'winter bourne' which dries up when water levels in the chalk are low. The vast mansion – now a college of arts and crafts – was begun in 1804, and built entirely of flint, in the Gothic style. The 35 acre gardens are informal, with open lawns, herbaceous borders and an exceptional collection of trees. Particularly beautiful are the flowering species – the

blue-spangled foxglove trees, the tulip trees and handkerchief trees. In the Wild Garden are two soaring trees of heaven. Roses, clematises and honeysuckles surge over a colonnaded pergola, 300 ft long, which leads from the sunken garden to the gazebo – paved with an extraordinary floor made of flint and horses' molars.

LOCATION *On the A286, 6 miles N of Chichester.*

WEST WYCOMBE PARK
Buckinghamshire

After a visit to West Wycombe in 1773, Benjamin Franklin wrote '... the gardens are a paradise'. The distinguished American statesman and inventor was a frequent guest of its owner, the politician Sir Francis Dashwood. From 1735 onwards, Sir Francis created a classical landscape, in the rococo style which preceded Capability Brown. Here the vistas were straight, focused uncompromisingly on architectural features. An irregular lake with small islands completed the scheme. Sir Francis travelled extensively among the ruins of ancient Greece and Rome, and their influence is seen in the classical temples around the park. The Temple of the Winds, based on the Tower of the Winds in Athens, is one of the first attempts in England to reproduce an ancient monument. The landscape was altered and softened with additional planting later in the century, but the pure lines of the early plans survive. A lovely, stepped cascade, where sleeping nymphs lie at rest, leads down from the lake.

LOCATION *Off the A40, 3 miles W of High Wycombe.*

WILTON HOUSE *Wiltshire*

Monumental cedars of Lebanon tower above the smooth and level lawns around Wilton House. Their impact is so dramatic that even the massive home of the Earl of Pembroke seems to shrink before them. Some are thought to have been planted in the 17th century, soon after the species was introduced to Britain. The River Nadder flows through 20 acres of lawns, and spanning its tranquil waters is the Palladian Bridge for which these gardens are famous. Completed in 1737, it was built of stone, with graceful arches and pillars supporting a sloping roof. This was the greatest accomplishment in the master-piece of 18th-century landscaping which replaced an earlier, formal garden. An element of formality was reintroduced in 1971, when the forecourt was transformed into a garden of pleached limes and shrubs, with a fountain shrouded in a translucent spray of water.
LOCATION *In Wilton.*

WREST PARK *Bedfordshire*

The restoration of Charles II in 1660 heralded a new era of French-inspired design. The influence was still apparent in 1706, when the 12th Earl of Kent embarked upon the gardens at Wrest Park. They remain one of the few surviving examples in Britain of French formality on a grand scale. Extending as a vast woodland over the flat landscape, the gardens are divided by a broad central vista, with a canal stretched like gleaming silver along its length. An elegant, domed pavilion closes the view. Intersecting rides break through the massed trees, adorned with urns and statues. Capability Brown added curving paths and an encircling stream in the 1750s, but left the overall design intact. A pattern of scrolled parterres was formed in the 1830s, when a new house replaced the old. In an old, enclosed garden an ancient wisteria smothers 100 ft of the wall in clouds of indigo each May.
LOCATION *On the A6, 10 miles N of Luton.*

YOUNGER BOTANIC GARDEN
Strathclyde

Between 1870 and 1883, over 6 million trees were planted at Benmore, drawing a dark veil of green over the bare-sided valley. Many still survive, forming the back-bone of this wild and beautiful outpost of The Royal Botanic Garden at Edinburgh. Some of the trees are older still, like the Scots pines planted in 1820 and stretching southwards from Benmore House to the Golden Gates – a 19th-century web of gilded iron. The Formal Garden stands in extraordinary juxtaposition to the free arrangement of the rest. Here the natural dwarf conifers and cultivars fill the borders, interspersed with flowering shrubs. Conifers of all kinds thrive at Benmore, from the gigantic Wellingtonias of California to the Caucasian firs – the collection is one of the finest in the country. Rhododendrons and azaleas are another speciality.
LOCATION *Off the A815, 7 miles NW of Dunoon.*

All the gardens described in this book are open to the public, but opening times vary from place to place and season to season, so it is advisable to check in advance before planning a visit. Details of opening times are obtainable from the following organisations:

GARDENERS' SUNDAY ORGANISATION,
Bridge House, 139 Kingston Road,
Leatherhead, Surrey.
Tel. Leatherhead (0372) 377955

NATIONAL GARDENS SCHEME,
57 Lower Belgrave Street,
London SW1W 0LR.
Tel. 01 730 0359

SCOTLAND'S GARDENS SCHEME,
31 Castle Terrace,
Edinburgh EH1 2EL.
Tel. 031 229 1870

THE NATIONAL TRUST,
36 Queen Anne's Gate,
London SW1H 9AS.
Tel. 01 222 9251

THE NATIONAL TRUST FOR SCOTLAND,
5 Charlotte Square,
Edinburgh EH2 4DU.
Tel. 031 226 5922

ACKNOWLEDGMENTS

Front cover, Stourhead, Stourton, Wiltshire; page 3, Luton Hoo, Bedfordshire; pages 4–5, Barnsley House, Gloucestershire; pages 6–7, Bodnant Garden, Talycafn, North Wales.

The illustrations in this book were provided by the following photographers and agencies. Work commissioned by Reader's Digest is shown in italics.

Except where otherwise stated, credits read from left to right down the page.

Front cover Andy Williams Photo Library. Back cover Adam Woolfitt/Susan Griggs Agency. 3 Roger Scruton. 4–5 George Wright. 6–7 Andy Williams Photo Library. 8 Robin Fletcher/Bob Gibbons. 9 Harry Smith Collection. 10 Mary Evans Picture Library. 11 John Bethell. 13 Edward Leigh/The National Trust. 14 John Bethell. 15 both Sefton Photo Library. 17 Pamla Toler/Impact. 18 top Mary Evans Picture Library; bottom Kenneth Scowen. 18–19 Eric Crichton. 20 Eric Crichton/Bruce Coleman Ltd. 21 top John Bethell; bottom Mansell Collection. 22–23 Harry Smith Collection. 23 Mansell Collection. 24 centre National Portrait Gallery. 24–25 John Bethell. 26 Ray Duffurn/Fotobank. 27 Richard Jemmett. 28–29 British Tourist Authority. 30–31 Andy Williams Photo Library. 32 Andy Williams Photo Library. 33 Tania Midgley. 34 Tania Midgley. 35 Roger Scruton. 36 Roger Scruton. 37 Harry Smith Collection. 38 Harry Smith Collection. 39 Andy Williams Photo Library. 40–41 Derek Widdicombe. 42 Michael Warren. 43 Airviews. 44 British Tourist Authority. 45 left British Tourist Authority. 46 Eric Crichton. 47 Airviews. 48 top Derek Forss; bottom Mansell Collection. 49 J. Allan Cash. 50–51 Adam Woolfitt/Susan Griggs Agency. 52 top The National Trust; bottom Richard Jemmett. 53 Robin Fletcher/

Bob Gibbons. 54 Tony Lord. 54–55 Richard Jemmett. 56 The Mansell Collection. 57 Cressida Pemberton-Pigott. 58 Roger Scruton. 59 Robin Fletcher/Bob Gibbons. 60 Derek Forss. 61 Lucinda Lambton. 62 Mansell Collection. 62–63 Andy Williams. 64 Michael Warren. 65 John Bethell. 66 Michael Warren. 67 top Roger Scruton; bottom Mary Evans Picture Library. 68 Harry Smith Collection. 69 British Tourist Authority. 70 The Mansell Collection. 71 Colour Library International. 72 Airviews Ltd. 73 British Tourist Authority. 74–75 Jerry Harpur. 76–77 Eric Crichton. 78–79 John Bethell. 80 Fotobank. 82 Andy Williams. 83 Pat Morris/Ardea. 84 Mansell Collection. 84–85 Richard Bryant. 86 top Richard Bryant; bottom Mary Evans Picture Library. 86–87 John Bethell. 88 John Bethell. 89 Cressida Pemberton-Pigott. 90 Fotobank. 91 Colour Library International. 92 International Scene. 93 Tania Midgley. 94 Janet and Colin Bord. 95 left Airviews Ltd; right Mansell Collection. 96 John Bethell. 97 left Mary Evans Picture Library; right Pamla Toler/Impact. 100 left National Portrait Gallery; top right Mansell Collection; bottom Pat Brindley. 101 Richard Bryant. 102 A–Z Collection. 103 Photobank. 104 Iris Hardwick. 105 The National Trust. 106–7 British Tourist Authority. 109 British Tourist Authority. 110 Adam Woolfitt/Susan Griggs Agency. 111 Hazel le Rougetel/Biofotos. 112 Pamla Toler/Impact. 113 Pamla Toler/Impact. 114 Robert Harding Associates. 115 Michael Freeman/Bruce Coleman Ltd. 116 George Wright. 117 Michael Boys. 118–19 S. & O. Mathews. 120 Bob Gibbons. 121 Harry Smith Collection. 122 Adam Woolfitt/Susan Griggs Agency. 123 Adam Woolfitt/Susan Griggs Agency. 124 Richard Bryant. 125 Andy Williams. 126–7 George Wright. 128 top BBC Hulton Picture Library. 129 Michael Warren. 130–1 Geoff Dore/Northern Picture Library. 132 John Bethell. 132–3 Keith Morris. 134 top Keith Morris; bottom National Portrait Gallery. 135 John Bethell. 136 Ardea, London. 138 Mary Evans

Picture Library. 138–9 Andy Williams. 140 Royal Horticultural Society. 141 Pamla Toler/Impact. 142 Heather Angel. 143 The National Trust. 144 Iris Hardwick. 144–5 The National Trust. 146 A–Z Collection. 147 Tania Midgley. 148–9 Andy Williams. 151 Andy Williams. 152 John Bethell. 153 John Bethell. 154 Richard Jemmett. 155 Richard Bryant. 157 Andy Williams. 158 Robert Harding Associates. 158–9 Andy Williams. 160 Ian Yeomans/Susan Griggs Agency. 161 Iris Hardwick. 162 S. & O. Mathews. 163 Eric Crichton. 164 Tony Lord. 165 Mary Evans Picture Library. 166 Tony Lord. 167 Harry Smith Collection. 168 John Bethell. 169 Peter Baker/Photobank. 170 Mary Evans Picture Library. 171 top Fotobank; bottom British Tourist Authority. 174 top Sefton Photo Library; bottom Mary Evans Picture Library. 177 top Mary Evans Picture Library; bottom Ardea, London. 179 Mary Evans Picture Library. 181 Tania Midgley. 182 Mary Evans Picture Library.

The publishers also acknowledge their indebtedness to the following publications which were consulted for reference: The Country House Guide, Robin Fedden and Rosemary Joekes, Jonathan Cape; The Encyclopaedia of Garden Plants and Flowers, Reader's Digest; The Englishman's Garden, Alvide Lees-Milne and Rosemary Verey, Allen Lane; The Englishwoman's Garden, Alvide Lees-Milne and Rosemary Verey, Chatto and Windus; The Gardening Year, Reader's Digest; Great Gardens of Britain, Peter Coats, Spring Books; Guide to Creative Gardening, Reader's Digest; The History of Gardening, Christopher Thacker, Croom Helm; The National Trust Guide, Robin Fedden and Rosemary Joekes, Jonathan Cape; Royal Horticultural Society Dictionary of Gardening, Oxford; The Shell Guide to Gardens, Arthur Hellyer, Heinemann.

Typesetting TRADESPOOLS LTD, FROME; Printing AMBASSADOR PRESS LTD, ST ALBANS; Separations MANDARINS OFFSET LTD, HONG KONG; Paper TOWNSEND HOOK & CO LTD, SNODLAND; Binding HAZEL WATSON & VINEY LTD, AYLESBURY.

—CONTENTS—

A–Z GUIDE TO THE
GREAT GARDENS OF BRITAIN
8—161

EXPLORING BRITAIN
GREAT GARDENS

5043

PUBLISHED BY THE READER'S DIGEST ASSOCIATION LIMITED
LONDON NEW YORK MONTREAL SYDNEY CAPE TOWN

A Key to The Great Gardens

Each of the 101 main entries in the book is located on the map with a black square. The 136 gazetteer entries are marked with black dots.